MASTERS

OF THE

ITALIC

LETTER

MASTERS OF THE ITALIC LETTER

Twenty-Two Exemplars from the Sixteenth Century

by Kathryn A. Atkins

with a foreword by James M. Wells,
Curator Emeritus of The Newberry Library, Chicago

ALLEN LANE
THE PENGUIN PRESS

ALLEN LANE
THE PENGUIN PRESS

Published by the Penguin Group
27 Wrights Lane, London W8 5TZ, England
Penguin Books Australia Ltd, Ringwood, Victoria, Australia
Penguin Books Canada Ltd, 2801 John Street, Markham, Ontario, Canada L3R 1B4
Penguin Books (NZ) Ltd, 182–190 Wairau Road, Auckland 10, New Zealand

Penguin Books Ltd, Registered Offices: Harmondsworth, Middlesex, England

First published in the USA by David R. Godine, Publisher, Inc. 1988
First published in Great Britain by Allen Lane The Penguin Press 1988

Foreword copyright © 1988 by James M. Wells
Text copyright © 1988 by Kathryn A. Atkins

All rights reserved. Without limiting the rights under copyright reserved above, no part of this publication may be reproduced, stored in or introduced into a retrieval system, or transmitted, in any form or by any means (electronic, mechanical, photocopying, recording or otherwise), without the prior written permission of both the copyright owner and the above publisher of this book

Printed in the United States of America

A CIP catalogue record for this book is available from the British Library

ISBN 07139-9021-X

Dedicated to

VERENA H. PARENT

JAMES W. PARENT

RAYMOND C., JOHN,

PATTY & BETSY

ACKNOWLEDGMENTS

A book of manuscripts involves the expertise and cooperation of so many individuals and institutions that it is difficult to justify authorship for one person. To this end I submit the names of people who shared in the responsibility for the substance and graphics of the research. I thank them in the best way I know: by promising to share research with others as unselfishly as they have shared with me and to encourage with humor and patience those who embark upon impossible tasks.

To the staffs of libraries in the United States and Europe who facilitated access to the manuscripts, patiently explained procedure, and graciously granted permissions.

> The Newberry Library, Chicago: James M. Wells, John Aubrey, Tony Amodeo, Emily Miller, and Mick L. Jackson.
> Victoria and Albert Museum, London: Rowan Watson and Irene Whalley.
> Oxford University Press, Oxford: Anthony Mulgan and S. A. Milford.
> The Houghton Library, Harvard University: Eleanor Garvey, Rodney G. Dennis, and Nancy Finlay.
> Bodleian Library, Oxford: Dr. Alvinia de la Mara, Cornelia Starts, C. G. Cordeaux, Joanna Dodsworth, and W. G. Hodges.
> The Fitzwilliam Museum, Cambridge: Damaris Naylor and Paul Woudhuysen.
> Pembroke College, Cambridge: W. T. Hutton and P. A. Judd.
> The Vatican Library, Rome: Msgr. José Ruywschart and Leonard E. Boyle, O.P.
> Universiteits-Bibliotheek, Amsterdam: Carla M. Faas.
> Archivio di Stato, Venice: Dott. Maria Francesca Tiepolo.
> Kunstbibliothek, Berlin: Dr. Gretel Wagner.
> The Morgan Library, New York: Evelyn Semler and Wilhem Smet.
> British Library, London: J. P. Hudson and Janet M. Backhouse.
> The Redwood Library, Newport: Special thanks to Judy Hilliard for allowing the use of The Newport Room during periods of concentration.

To the translators who challenged their language skills with archaic passages and strained their eyes deciphering illegible manuscripts.

Italian & Latin
Dom Julian Stead and Dom Geoffrey Chase, O.S.B., Portsmouth Abbey, Rhode Island.
Professor Anthony Oldcorn, Brown University, Rhode Island.
Maria Ines Bonatti, Brown University, Rhode Island.
Professor Marvin Kendrick, University of Hartford, Connecticut.
Barbara Oranger Hawes and Linuccia Corazza DeAngelis, Bureau of International Visitors, Rhode Island.

Spanish
James Teixeira, Middletown High School, Rhode Island.
Douglas Fenner, Portsmouth Abbey, Rhode Island.

German
Professor Alexander Nesbitt, Third & Elm Press, Rhode Island.
Sabina Tuck de Werth, Rhode Island.

French
Dr. Miltiades B. Hatzopoulos, The National Hellenic Research Foundation, Greece.
Madame Suzanne Aubois, The Swinburne School, Rhode Island.

To special individuals who made extraordinary contributions.

James M. Wells, Curator Emeritus, The Newberry Library.
For encouraging the project when it was a mere list of names and for sacrificing the personal time to write the foreword.

Professor Howard Glasser, Southeastern Massachusetts University.
For designing the final format, generously granting the use of his library, tirelessly offering advice and encouragement, and teaching me book-design. A special thanks to Gertrude Glasser and her companions, Eric and Sara, for creating a comfortable environment for me to work in.

Dr. A. S. Osley, London.
For editing all the background material, translating numerous passages in Latin, Italian, German, French, and Spanish and offering helpful suggestions on the translations of others, and for giving astute, frank insights and criticism.

Professor Alexander Nesbitt, Third & Elm Press.
For editing the entire manuscript and patiently answering a daily barrage of questions.

Esther Fisher Benson, Newport.
For graciously sharing information about the late John Howard Benson and the Berry Hill Press and giving me numerous volumes of the *Journal for the Society of Italic Handwriting* for reference.

Kathy Parker, Newport.
For paste-up of thousands of letters in *Letter Study*, editing my page layouts, and resolutely keeping all the letters right-side-up and with the proper scribe.

Lee O. Gardner, Newport County Agricultural Agent.
For sharing ornithological advice on Moro's passages on hawking.

Stephen Harvard, Vice President, Stinehour Press.
For editing the Cataneo edition description and writing selected Cataneo references.

Michael Gullick, London.
For sharing binding and edition description advice for all the Newberry Library copybooks in the study.

Sister Loyola Mary, Marylhurst College.
For introducing me to the world of letter-forms.

Dr. Gunnlaugur SE Briem, Iceland.
For waiting at bus stations, making perceptive observations, and facilitating introductions.

Dr. Peter London, Southeastern Massachusetts University.
For listening and advising when the book was only an idea.

Professor Arnold Bank, Carnegie-Mellon University.
For testing the integrity of the study, offering suggestions for broadening its scope, and giving permission to use his library. A special thanks to Rose Bank, whose vibrant spirit brought encouragement.

Berthold Wolpe, London.
For editing the background information on Jean de Beauchesne, for spending two wonderful afternoons suggesting design changes and running up to his studio for answers to my endless stream of questions. A special thanks to Mrs. Wolpe for supplying nourishment and happy conversation.

Nicholas Biddulph, Central School of Art and Design, London.
For sharing his comparative letter studies and introducing me to the wealth of information in the lettering library at the Central School.

To all those friends who played a special role in the progress of the book, are not mentioned by name, but know they are remembered—I nod and smile. Their contributions are of a unique personal nature and would be difficult or inappropriate to describe in this format. They believed in me when I became discouraged, laughed with me when I took myself too seriously.

CONTENTS

19	Primary Sources	62	Giovanni Francesco Cresci
20	Sigismondo Fanti	66	Francesco Moro
22	Ludovico Vincentino degli Arrighi	70	Augustino da Siena
26	Giovannantonio Tagliente	74	Jacques de la Rue
30	Giovanbattista Palatino	78	Clément Perret
34	Gerard Mercator	82	Francesco Lucas
38	Bennardino Cataneo	86	Johann Neudörffer the Younger
42	Vespasiano Amphiareo	90	Andres Brun
46	Juan de Yciar	94	Jodocus Hondius
50	Caspar Neff	98	Jean de Beauchesne
52	Urban Wyss	103	Letter Study
56	Wolffgang Fugger		
58	Ferdinando Ruano	179	Bibliography

FOREWORD

Italic writing, named for the type face which imitated it, reached its zenith in the sixteenth century, and has recurrently declined and been revived ever since. Devised by Renaissance humanists, who wished to revive the glories of classical antiquity, it was based on two sources: the capital letters of the Roman Empire and the lower case of the Carolingian era, beginning in France in the eighth century, which survived in Italy in a purer form than elsewhere in Europe. B. L. Ullman, whose *The Origin and Development of Humanistic Script* of 1960 is the best monograph on the subject, gives credit to Petrarch and Coluccio Salutati for creating in the fourteenth century a formal book hand which was legible, strong, rapid, and economic (their cursive correspondence hands were another matter). This was the precursor of humanistic script, invented, according to Ullman, around 1400 by Poggio Bracciolini, a Florentine notary and scribe who eventually became a papal secretary. Niccolo Niccoli, who was not a professional scribe and whose manuscripts are consequently hard to identify, is credited with inventing the less formal, more cursive script that developed into Aldus's italic type.

There are differences of opinion about the causes and effects of the invention of printing from movable type in the mid-fifteenth century. Was printing necessitated by the steady increase of literacy of the era, or did it help to bring about that increase? What was the effect of the emergence of a new literate middle class? Of a growing mercantile class, which depended upon correspondence as well as double-entry bookkeeping to keep its affairs in order? Among printing's many achievements, and not the least of them, was the ability to provide abundant and comparatively cheap books to teach theology, medicine, law, rhetoric, as well as more mundane subjects such as reading, arithmetic, and writing. Writing-books, which required competent engravers to provide the essential models of the hands being taught, were slow to appear; none was published during the fifteenth century.

Writing masters were expected, during the sixteenth century, to be able to teach a wide variety of hands, varying not only by country but even by city; humanistic texts required one kind of script, liturgical works another. Commercial and legal documents were in yet other scripts, according to their place of origin. A professional writing master was expected to be skilled in a variety of these.

The earliest book teaching the italic hand appears to be Sigismondo Fanti's *Theorica et practica de modo scribendi*, published in Venice in 1514. It is not illustrated; apparently there was no engraver skilled enough to cut the blocks showing the script. Blanks were left, to be filled in by hand, or perhaps for the pasting-in of intaglio examples, but no copy is known in which the blanks have been filled.

The first book to show, as well as to explain, italic writing is Ludovico degli Arrighi's *La Operina*, issued in Rome in 1522 and devoted entirely to the chancery hand. It was followed the next year by the same author's *Il Modo de temperare le penne* . . . , which added examples of various other scripts in use, probably in order to broaden the market. The wood blocks, cut by various engravers including Ugo da Carpi and Eustachio Celebrino (both of whom published writing-books of their own), are *tours de force*, reproducing with remarkable fidelity Arrighi's strong, clear hand. That Arrighi should have begun with the chancery hand is logical. He had been employed during the reign of Leo X (1513–1521) in the papal chancery, where the hand was taught and used for the writing of briefs, letters which had to be executed quickly and legibly. The books were highly successful, going through a number of editions and being widely imitated by Arrighi's successors. He was also a type designer, and his italic fonts are the basis for most modern italics.

Arrighi's immediate successor, Giovannantonio Tagliente, published his first book, *Lo presente libro* . . ., in Venice in 1524. Since Venice was a great mercantile center, Tagliente presented numerous commercial scripts, as well as italic, together with others for the use of engravers, embroiderers, and other artisans. His hands were more highly decorated, more exuberant than those of Arrighi. Giovanbattista Palatino, whose *Libro nuovo d'imparare a scrivere* appeared in Rome in 1540, and whose works continued to appear as late as 1587, is credited with designing inscriptions on Roman monuments as well as providing the lettering for two maps of Rome; he also provided a wide variety of scripts and alphabets.

Later Italian books include those of Vespasiano Amphiareo (*Uno novo modo d'insegnar a scrivere* . . ., Venice, 1548), whose *bastarda* combined looped ascenders and descenders from the mercantile hands with chancery letter forms; a page from one of his manuscript books is reproduced here. Ferdinando Ruano (*Sette alphabeti* . . ., Rome, 1554), a scribe in the Vatican Library, shows various book and display hands as well as chancery. Giovanni Francesco Cresci (*Essemplare di piu sorti lettere*, Rome, 1560) another Vatican scribe, was among the most prolific of the sixteenth-century scribes; his books went through numerous editions. Cresci stressed speed and attacked his predecessors for their clumsiness. His letter forms are decorated with prominent, somewhat exaggerated club-like serifs. His 1570 book, *Il perfetto scrittore*, is the first Italian writing-book printed from copper plates, a technique that made possible a greater contrast between thick and thin strokes than that provided by bad wood blocks.

The italic hand quickly spread throughout Europe. The first writing-book published outside Italy was that of Gerardus Mercator (*Literarum latinarum . . . scribendarum ratio*, Antwerp, 1540), who was best known as a cartographer. Italic was especially useful on maps, since it was legible even when written small. Other Low Country books included Clément Perret's *Exercitatio alphabetica nova et utilissima* . . . (Brussels, 1569). Juan de Yciar's *Arte subtilissima* . . . (Saragossa, 1548) was the first Spanish manual, followed by Francesco Lucas's *Arte de escrivir* (Toledo, 1571) and Andres Brun's *Arte . . . para aprender de escrivir perfectamente* (Saragossa, 1583). The Spanish books are notable for the strength of the hands displayed as well as for the excellence of their engravers.

The Germans and German-speaking Swiss were next. Caspar Neff, a schoolmaster and arithmetician, first published his *Thesaurium artis scriptoriae* . . . in Cologne in 1549, the same year that Urban Wyss, a schoolmaster and printer, issued his *Libellus valde doctus* in Zurich. Wolffgang Fugger, publisher and printer, launched his *Ein nutzlich und wolgegrundt formular* in Nürnberg in 1553—the first book from a great center of calligraphy and illustrated books. Johann Neudörffer the Younger, a member of a well-known family of writing masters and printers, published his *Kurtze ordnung* . . . there in 1567.

The first French printed writing manual was Jacques de la Rue's *Exemplaires de plusiers sortes de lettres* (Paris, 1565). Credit for the first English book goes to Jean de Beauchesne, a Huguenot writing master who fled to England after the Saint Bartholomew's Day massacre, and John Baildon, an English printer; their *A booke containing diverse sortes of hands* . . . was published in London in 1570. Beauchesne later became writing master to the Princess Elizabeth, daughter of James I, later Queen of Bohemia.

Printed writing-books, good as they were—and many were triumphs of the engraver's art—give only an imitation of actual writing. The engraver could not catch the contrast between thin and thick strokes, the color, the rhythm of the actual hand; sometimes he regularized it and actually improved it. For that reason, if one is to judge accurately a scribe's ability, one must see his real work, not a printed copy. Many of the authors of the printed books reproduced here were not only teachers but highly skilled professional scribes. But not all scribes, no matter how proficient, published printed manuals.

Manuscript writing books and exemplars, being unique, are usually not available for the student to see and to study. Pages from five of them, all excellent examples of these deluxe works, all presumably written for wealthy and influential patrons or as samples of the best work of their authors, are shown in the present volume. Three of these works are by men who published printed books: Amphiareo, Neudörffer, and Beauchesne. The others, Cataneo and Moro, as far as we know, did not. All are splendid in their execution, showing the italic hand in actual use and at its best.

Ms. Atkins has provided students of the sixteenth-century italic hand with a highly useful and inspiring tool. She has examined and studied dozens of printed and written books before choosing the twenty-two here shown. Considered as a whole, they give an excellent overview of the variety, skill, and professionalism of their scribes, as well as of the development of the cursive script in its most glorious age. The translations bring to life the substance as well as the form of the texts; the bibliographies and notes provide students in search of further knowledge with sources where they can find it. The reproductions, in actual size and often enlarged, provide an inspiration as well as a challenge to their users.

James M. Wells
Custodian Emeritus
The John M. Wing Foundation on the History of Printing
The Newberry Library, Chicago

Dear Reader, As I look out my studio window a flock of Canadian geese is flying overhead and the Portuguese farmers are harvesting the cow corn. It is already the fall of 1984; I have spent five years on this research project. I feel disbelief at the passing of time; however, I learned long ago that creative endeavors have a life and rhythm of their own and that it is our task merely to accept them and work accordingly.

Despite my protestations, this compilation of italic exemplars of twenty-two scribes and over 2,500 letters has become a book. Five years ago it presented itself as a research project for teaching calligraphy to adults in continuing studies and to college students in graphic design.[1] I wanted to teach from primary sources and found it frustrating hunting for historic exemplars in a multitude of journals and books. My belief in the use of primary sources came from personal inclination as well as early teacher training.[2] It seemed unnatural for me to restrict the students' learning to my own exemplars or to others of the twentieth century when the hands had developed during another time.

The specific direction of the project was greatly influenced by the rich tradition of lettering here in southern New England. From 1705, when The John Stevens Shop was founded, this area has continually attracted craftsmen who make their living by writing, drawing, and carving letters and who share a basic belief in historic letter forms. They are friends and colleagues: Alexander Nesbitt, Ilse Buchert Nesbitt, John E. Benson, John Hegnauer, Howard Glasser, Raphael Boguslav, and Brooke Roberts.[3] They are diverse in their artistic methods and personal philosophies but they share a common bond. Each of them works in a straightforward manner, meeting the everyday needs of the community, and each adheres to a high standard of excellence. Craftsmanship is more than something they strive toward; it is a way of life.

Because of my training and environment it was very natural for me to teach calligraphy from primary sources. Along with exercise sheets, I taught from exemplars in *Renaissance Handwriting, A Book of Scripts, Three Italian Classics, Lettering,*[4] and various manuscript photographs from The Houghton Library and The Morgan Library. Since I had access to more copybook facsimiles of specific scribes, the study started to develop around copybooks rather than random manuscripts. It was this choice that was later to determine the starting date for this study at 1514 rather than a half-century earlier, when the italic hand was actually evolving.

The selection of the italic hand as the basis for this study was an acceptance of what was already going on in the classroom. It was the hand I routinely taught to beginners. It was adaptable to the requirements of everyday living in the twentieth century. It was relatively easy to write and read, and it was a suitable hand for the student who was interested in only an introductory level in calligraphy. The italic hand was to have been a starting point for a larger study that was to include simple roman, textura, and uncial. Needless to say, I have reconsidered the scope of the study. It is for others to delve further.

The list of twenty-two scribes evolved from Arrighi, Tagliente, and Palatino. It never occurred to me that my Study would exceed more than eight scribes. Alexander Nesbitt encouraged me to study the German scribes, namely, Neudörffer the Elder,[5] Wyss, and Fugger, and sketched out a preliminary list of fifteen scribes from other countries.

These conversations with Alexander Nesbitt catapulted the entire project from a teaching exercise to research at The Newberry Library. It was at The Newberry Library in 1979 that I finalized a list of twenty scribes. There was no way to reduce the scope of the project after seeing the extensive collection of Renaissance copybooks. Under the able assistance of Tony Amodeo in Special Collections an entire cart of sixteenth-century copybooks was brought to my table.[6] During the course of three days I chose about fifty exemplars to be photographed; title pages were not included. The exemplars were chosen for a particular visual quality as well as for a broad geographical representation. The visual quality was of the hand at its peak of evolution in the copybooks. No effort was made to choose specific types of italic over others; therefore the cursiva, formata, and other variants are shown together. This visual criterion led me to eliminate scribes like Hercolani and Hamon even though their timeframe was suitable. Cresci was the only exception; he was included because of his historical importance.

The beginning and ending dates were set during that visit. The little book of Jean de Beauchesne written for Queen Elizabeth I was on the first cart.[7] I could not resist its diminutive beauty. With this selection, the date of 1612 became the absolute limit for the period under study. Had it not been for this lovely book and the fact that it was a manuscript, the study would have ended with Andres Brun in 1583. Sigismondo Fanti's *Theorica et Pratica* (1514) also became essential. It predated Arrighi and Tagliente, and included a description of the italic hand but showed only blank spaces where the exemplars were to have been.

There is no question that the scope and beauty of the collection at The Newberry made it difficult to limit the study. Later it became impossible to restrict the study to twenty scribes. The research was as frustrating as it was exciting because of my extreme language limitations. My three years of high-school Latin was of little help with original German, Italian, or French. Something as simple as looking through card-files became a colossal endeavor. There were always the added complications of scribe's name being spelled in a variety of ways as well as the scribes being

PREFACE

known by various names.

Because of my personal curiosity in the subject matter of the exemplars, I turned to the Dominican monks at Portsmouth Abbey for translations. Later twelve people assisted in the translation work, but it all started with one Dominican monk, Dom Julian Stead. The translations were and still are a source of great delight and continual surprise. They run the gamut from instruction on geometric letter-form construction[8] and spiritual advice on saving one's immortal soul[9] to a treatise on giving a bird raging hunger[10] and a bill charging a client for a shipment of silk.[11] The exemplars were picked for their visual quality, the translations merely followed.

By the time the original set of photographs arrived from The Newberry Library, I had already started a comparative letter study of italic minuscule letters with my students at the Swinburne School in Newport. I decided to enlarge the letters rather than show them in original size so the beginners could see the constructions. The individual letters were enlarged to about a half-inch in body height. I required that the exemplar pages be photographed exactly to size, with all page edges showing. When these Newberry photographs were enlarged it was difficult to limit the number of letters; it was ridiculous to confine each scribe to one of each letter when there were as many variations as there were letters. The decision to include italic majuscules was made by the exemplars. To exclude them was impossible; to include them created a rather interesting design problem with their vast height-range and flourishes.

By this time I knew the study had become research for a book and I returned in earnest to The Newberry for photographs of the title pages, for background information on each scribe, and for a second look at each copybook so I could describe the edition. A. S. Osley's book *Scribes and Sources* had recently been published; it offered a wealth of information.

When all the photographs had been compiled, over 2,000 letters had been sorted and pasted, and research cards were stacked, I went to Howard Glasser, a designer and professor of graphic design and calligraphy, to seek assistance in designing the text and photographs into a book. The following year I spent designing the rough draft of the dummy, preparing background material, and finding suitable translators for the remaining exemplars.[12]

When I met David Godine in the winter of 1983 and signed a contract, the book entered its final phase. It was his express wish that the scope of the study be expanded to include original, signed manuscripts from each of the scribes. With this directive the study went beyond the collection of The Newberry to include manuscripts from many libraries abroad. As a result, a Tagliente from Archivio di Stato,[13] a Palatino from the Bodleian,[14] a Perret and Mercator from Pembroke College,[15] an Arrighi from Universiteits-Bibliotheek,[16] a Cresci and Ruano from the Vatican,[17] and an Amphiareo from The Houghton[18] were added. During this phase the list of scribes reached its final complement of twenty-two with the inclusion of the Cataneo from The Houghton Library[19] and a Moro from The Victoria and Albert.[20] While I waited for the remaining photographs to arrive from Europe I was in correspondence with Dr. A. S. Osley in London, who kindly reviewed background material and made numerous changes and additions to the translations.[21]

Now that publication time is drawing near, I look back on the many developmental stages of this project and am amazed at the way everything has fallen into place. The project has a look of finality, but it really marks a beginning. Letters and exemplars have been compiled but they have not been analyzed. There is also much information yet to be found. It is my hope that discoveries I was unable to make in research will be made in dialogue with readers. Many specific questions remain unanswered. Who were Cataneo and Moro? Was there ever a copy of Fanti's *Theorica et Pratica* with examples of the italic alphabet? Are there any signed manuscripts by Wyss, Yciar, Lucas, or Brun? Does anyone have any information on Jacques de la Rue or Johann Neudörffer the Younger? Do any copybook woodblocks still exist? The list of questions is endless. Answers may not exist, but there is a chance that they do. They may be stored in a private research file, in the vault of a library, or in the memory of a scholar. If they are, the information will undoubtedly be shared with the general community of scribes and scholars.

A remarkable body of Renaissance manuscript research has been compiled over the years by the scholarship and dedication of various individuals such as Peter Jessen, Jan Tschichold, James Wardrop, A. S. Osley, Berthold Wolpe, Alexander Nesbitt, Arnold Bank, and Alfred Fairbank. Unfortunately, very little is easily accessible to the calligraphy student. If we are to upgrade the quality of writing and lettering both here and abroad we must take more initiative to ensure that primary sources are available for teaching and study.

With rare exception, the exemplars I have compiled have been published before. I have combined a sampling under one cover. When Arnold Bank, in his wonderfully frank manner, quipped about my initial research, "Here comes another one inventing the wheel," there was truth in the statement. He had been doing comparative letter studies thirty years ago with his students at the Art Students League in New York. In 1955 he published a comprehensive list of writing-masters' copybooks.[22] James Wardrop spent his life compiling and studying a body of Renaissance manuscripts so extensive as to make this Study a mere footnote.[23] A. S. Osley's contribution to copybook translation, description, and anal-

ysis is a singular achievement by a scholar living in our time.

Why are there not more copybook facsimiles on the market today? The "how-to" books are commendable and indicative of honest initiative on the part of teachers, but they are only part of the answer to teaching letter forms. All the historic hands evolved from the practical needs of society during a specific time; because of the natural spontaneity of their development they have an integrity that twentieth-century renderings simply cannot have. Superb examples of most of these hands are stored in libraries, just waiting to be researched and published. Rare-manuscript libraries are very generous in granting permission to publish manuscripts in their collections either free of charge or for a nominal fee, and only ask that they be properly acknowledged. Their staffs are uniformly helpful and knowledgeable. They do a commendable job of identifying and cataloguing manuscripts, but they are perennially understaffed and meagerly endowed. They are always amenable to the efforts of conscientious researchers. Somewhere in the calligraphic movement there must be lettering artists willing to volunteer their efforts to this task.

I have a dream about a time when the collections of all manuscript libraries will be catalogued in an efficient database. The sheer enormity of the task is staggering, but it has been done to a certain extent in medicine and the sciences; why not then in the arts? I am not suggesting that manuscripts be studied on a computer; I am suggesting that the computer be used as a card file. So much wasted time and energy could be saved. I have spent untold hours learning new procedures for each library, searching through files, filling out forms, and waiting for manuscripts to be retrieved from vaults. If the manuscripts were on a database, needless trips would be averted and fragile manuscripts would be spared unnecessary handling. This would leave time for important research and analysis. I realize that my proposal is probably politically naive and exorbitantly expensive, but it is worth dreaming. After all, why are we preserving manuscripts if not to learn and share?

Learning and sharing are what this book is really about. I hardly look upon it as a definitive work on the italic hand. I look upon it as one approach to my own teaching and learning needs. I have benefited immeasurably. The study is as exciting to me now as it was years ago. If my efforts benefit anyone else I will be pleased.

Kay Atkins
Middletown, Rhode Island

1. For the past ten years I have been teaching calligraphy at various schools: The Swinburne School, Newport, Rhode Island, Southeastern Massachusetts University, North Dartmouth, Massachusetts, and Brown University, Providence, Rhode Island.
2. In 1963 I received a B.S. in Education at Marylhurst College, Oregon, and in 1983 a Masters in Art Education from Southeastern Massachusetts University. It was at Marylhurst College that I was introduced to calligraphy by Sister Loloya Mary and Lloyd Reynolds.
3. Alexander Nesbitt, writing master, typographer; Ilse Buchert Nesbitt, bookmaker, printmaker, typographer; John Benson, stonecutter; John Hegnauer, letter carver; Howard Glasser, designer, professor of graphic design, calligrapher; Raphael Boguslav, designer/calligrapher; and Brooke Roberts, stonecutter.
4. See the bibliography.
5. Johann Neudörffer the Younger's book was chosen instead of Johann Neudörffer the Elder's because it was a ms., because he was the lesser known of the two, and because the exemplars were in perfect condition for photography. My intention was to include the Elder's *Fundament* (1519) but unfortunately it had no italic examples.
6. The majority of the Renaissance copybooks at The Newberry Library are housed in the John M. Wing Foundation. It was through the kind permission of James Wells, Curator Emeritus, that I was allowed to study them. Without his assistance the project would not have been possible.
7. Jean de Beauchesne's book to Queen Elizabeth I was chosen over Beauchesne and Baildon's *A Booke containing divers sortes of handes*, because it was a manuscript and had not been published before. Individual letters from the latter are featured in the *Letter Study*.
8. Ferdinando Ruano, *Sette alphabeti di varie lettere*, 1554.
9. Johann Neudörffer the Younger, *Kurtze Fürweisung*, 1578.
10. Francesco Moro, *Arte Della Strozaria e farsi perfetto stroziero*, c. 1560–70.
11. Vespasiano Amphiareo, *Letter to Lucas*, N.D.
12. See the acknowledgments.
13. Consiglio de X, Misti, filza 5, carta 127, Holograph and letter to the Doge and Council of Venice, 1491.
14. MS.Canon.Ital.196, *Writing Book*, N.D.
15. MS. Pembroke 113, Ortelius: *Album Amicorum*, 1596.
16. MS.11.A.19, signature XV D 6, *Ethica* for Vittoria Colonna, 1517.
17. Ruano, Vat.Lat.317,258v, *Expositio Rationis Dominicae*, 1554. Vat.Lat.3841,80v, *Epistolae*, 1551.
    Cresci, Vat.Lat.6185,135, *Letter of Gianfrancesco Cresci to Cardinal Guglielmo Sirleto*, 1572.
18. MS.Typ.166. *MS Writing Book*, c.1548.
19. MS.Typ.R46, *Writing Book in Italian*, 1545.
20. Moro, *Arte Della Strozaria* . . .
21. Dr. A. S. Osley corrected background material and translations. His scholarly attention to detail is gratefully acknowledged.
22. Arnold Bank's list of writing masters and their copybooks was issued in September 1955 in conjunction with the Inter-Nationaal Congres voor Boekdrukkunst en Humanisme. The lecture was entitled "Calligraphy and Its Influence in the Time of Plantin."
23. The James Wardrop Collection is housed in the Duke Humphrey Library at the Bodleian, Oxford University.

# PRIMARY SOURCES

Primary Sources is a compilation of sixteenth-century italic exemplars from American and European libraries for the study of the italic hand. Copybooks of twenty-two writing masters form the basis for the study. They are arranged in chronological order according to first edition date to show comparisons in the italic letter between 1514 and 1612.

Every attempt has been made to reproduce each page in its present condition. Most exemplars are reproduced actual size with full margins, page edges, and whatever irregularities five hundred years have given it. The enlargements form a dramatic departure from the traditional page formats from which they have been selected. The title pages are shown, but in reduced form, and the scribes' signatures are enlarged considerably.

Each exemplar has been chosen to show majuscule and minuscule italic alphabets and texts. All the exemplars and title pages have been translated from the original languages into English. On pages where there is an alphabet but no text, translations from the same scribe have been added, demonstrating the scribe's attitude toward writing, his method of forming individual italic letters, or his general observations about the italic hand. The result is a varied series of translations, including biblical quotations and the literature of the ancients as well as simulated bills of lading, poetry, and encouraging letters to the reader.

The title pages offer a wealth of information. Not only are the usual items included, namely, title, author, printer, place and date of publication, but also table of contents, purpose, date, duration of privilege, and a subtle sales pitch.

Care has been taken to show each exemplar not just as a single page, but as part of the copybook. To this end, title pages are always shown, and library editions are described. There are brief explanations of everything from page sizes and bindings to border decorations and placement of writing instruction. Where information is available, the woodcutter or engraver, the printer, the person to whom the book is dedicated, and the audience for whom the book is written are identified.

Since the emphasis of this study is on the exemplars, information on the scribes is brief. An attempt is made to list the various professional activities for which the scribe is remembered and to identify birth and death dates and places, when available. Readers interested in thorough biographical information on the scribes are encouraged to read *Scribes and Sources* and *Luminario*, by the distinguished scholar A. S. Osley.

SIGISMVNDI FANTIS

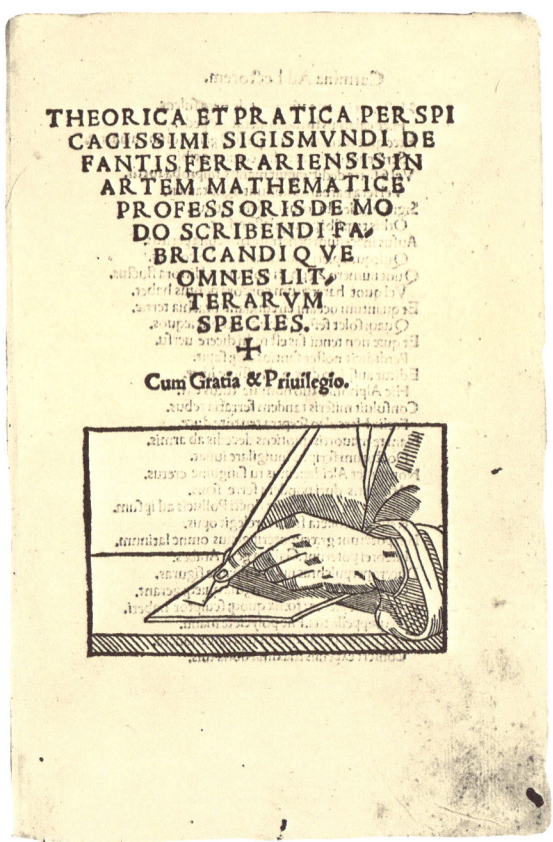

SIGISMONDO FANTI

1514, VENICE   **Theorica et Pratica**
Theory and Practice

AUTHOR

Origins: d. Ferrara

Activity: Arithmetician, astrologer, architect

BOOK

Printer: Joannes Rubeus of Vercelli

Technique: Text typeset, illustration in woodcut

Size: 5½″ × 8⅛″

Audience: Chancery scribes, secretaries, merchants, artists, and children.

Dedication: Alfonso d'Este, Duke of Ferrara

Edition Description: Reproduced with the kind permission of The Newberry Library, Chicago, Illinois, Wing ZW 14.F212, 2 fly leaves, 76 pages printed in black. The cover and spine are black leather with decorative blind-stamping. The spine bears Fanti's name, the title, and the Newberry shelf-mark stamped in gold. Illustrations include arm positions for writing, quill-cutting, the instruments of writing, and a full-page geometrically constructed Roman *A*. One-half-inch to one-inch borders decorate two section headings. Instruction for Rotunda, Textura, Roman capitals, and Italic are given in type throughout the book. There are usually two one-inch letters illustrated on each page. Only the italic alphabet is described but not shown.

PRIMVS.

EXEMPLVM. II.

Questi sono li tracti che uano in la cancellaria littera: uidelicet.

EXEMPLVM. III.

Questæ sono le maiusculæ le quale se adoperano a la lra cancellaria si in capo uerso come per dentro a qlla.

EXEMPLVM. IIII.

Questa e una forma canzellarescha la quale da multi e existimata abenche in questi medesimi Volumi uariamo & de piu uariæ fortæ canzellarcschæ secundo li costumi de læ regionæ acerrimæ d edicamo. acioche læ mentæ siano in parte satiffactæ: come de uolume in uo

---

1   Theory and practice of how to write and construct all kinds of letters by the exceedingly perspicacious Sigismondo Fanti of Ferrara, professor of the art of mathematics.
Translation by Dom Julian Stead.

Signature enlarged from 1.

2   These are the strokes used in chancery writing: Namely, these are the capital letters used in chancery lettering both at the beginning of a line and in the midst of it. This is a style of the chancery hand which is held in high regard by many people: but in these same books we show variations of it and deal carefully with different kinds of chancery script according to the custom of the localities in which they are practiced, so that [the reader's] mind is to some extent satisfied as [you will clearly see] from book to book.
Translation by Dom Julian Stead and A. S. Osley.

Ludouico Vicentino

LUDOVICO VINCENTINO DEGLI ARRIGHI

c. 1522/24, ROME **La Operina**
The Little Work

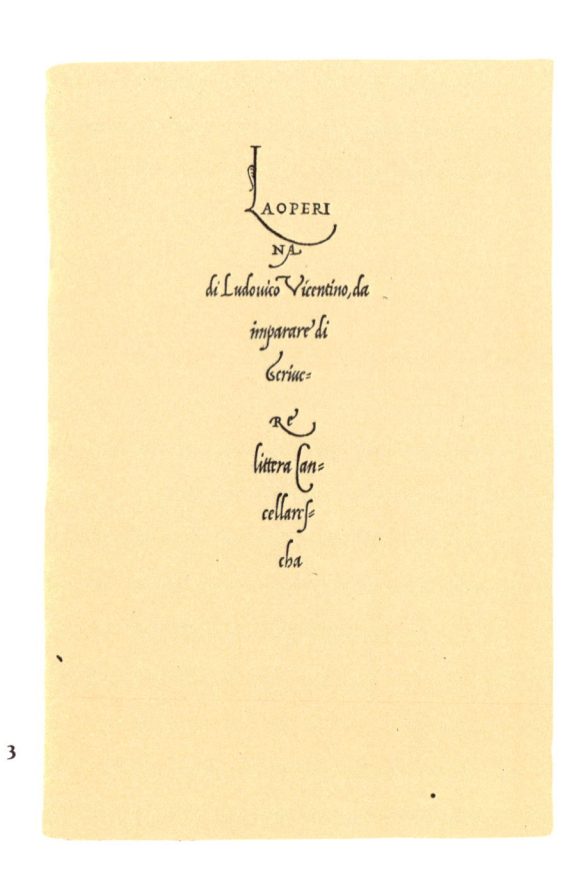

AUTHOR

Origins: b. near Vicenza c. 1490; d. Rome, 1527.

Activity: Copier of briefs in the Papal chancery, book copyist, typeface designer, publisher/printer of luxury books, map letterer

Age at edition date: late 20s

BOOK

Woodcutter: Ugo da Carpi, cartouche by Eustachio Celebrino

Technique: Woodcut

Size: 5¼" × 7¾"

Audience: "Anyone who wishes to learn."

Edition Description: Reproduced with the kind permission of The Newberry Library, Chicago, Illinois, Wing ZW 535.L9611, 3 fly leaves. Two editions are bound together: *La Operina*, 16 leaves (featured in these pages), and *Il modo de temperare le Penne*, 16 leaves. The cover is brown leather with a blind-stamped border and a human profile in the center. There are impressions of what were once clasps. The spine, of the same leather, is in very delicate condition. The only illustration in *La Operina* is a reverse tailpiece on the last page which reads "*Cvm Gratia & Privilegio.*" The book is written entirely in the italic hand in a centered format. The text includes a letter to the reader, writing instruction, exemplars with quotations and alphabets, and exemplars with alphabets only. Many pages are signed by Arrighi.

3 The Little Work of Ludovico Vicentino for learning to write the Chancery letter.
   Translation by A. S. Osley.

Signature enlarged from 3.

Good capitals are not difficult to make when with the small letters you have acquired a firm hand, and most of all I should tell you the two beginning strokes of the small are the same as those for the large: as you continue to write you will recognize the similarity. Nothing else needs to be said save that you should now learn to make the capitals, as drawn for your especial example. (*Not shown.*)

   Translation from John Howard Benson's *The First Writing Book: An English Translation and Facsimile Text of Arrighi's Operina, The First Manual Of The Chancery Hand*, 21. New Haven and London: Yale University Press, 1954. All Arrighi texts by John Howard Benson were translated by his friends: Reverend Henry K. Pierce, Erich A. O'D. Taylor, and Vincent Esposito. They are reproduced with the kind permission of Esther Fisher Benson.

4   With the guidance of God, Supreme and Immortal: Such is the human condition: One man finishes his course tonight, and another is born tomorrow. Only virtue tames and changes dread death. Ludovico Vicentino wrote this in the Parione quarter of Rome in the year 1522.
    Translation by A. S. Osley.

To the kind Reader:
Besought, indeed compelled by many friends, most gracious Reader, that having regard for public use and profit not only in this age, but also for posterity, I would give some examples of the writing and regular formation of the characters and particulars of the letters (which today are called Chancery) willingly I have undertaken this task: and since it was impossible to offer enough examples of my own hand to satisfy all,
I have set myself to study this new invention of letters and to put them into print, and they are as close to handwriting as my ability can achieve. If they do not exactly answer in every respect, I beg you to excuse me, since the press cannot entirely represent the living hand.
I hope nonetheless that by following my instruction you will obtain your desire. Long life, and Health.

   Translation from John Howard Benson's *The First Writing Book: An English Translation and Facsimile Text of Arrighi's Operina, The First Manual Of The Chancery Hand*, 3. New Haven and London: Yale University Press, 1954. (*Not shown.*)

5   MS.11.A.19, signature, XV D 6. *Ethica* for Vittoria Colonna, October 1517. Reproduced with the kind permission of the Universiteits-Bibliotheek, Amsterdam.

tant recte' quidem iudicare' non possunt: nisi fortu
ito. Magis autem ad ea comprehendenda fortasse'
fuerint apti. Cum igitur nostri maiores ea quæ'
ad facultatem ferendarum legum pertinent sine'
perscrutatione' reliquerint: nos ipsos illa fortasse'
præstat considerare' et omnino de' republica per
tractare' oportet: ut quoad fieri potest ea philoso
phia perficiatur quæ' circa res humanas uersatur.
Primum itaq₃ siquid recte' sit a maioribus dictu₃
id enitamur recensere'. Deinde' ex congregatis reb⁹
publicis considerare' quænam ciuitates et rerum pu
blicarum singulas euertunt atq₃ conseruant. Et quâ
ob causas aliæ' recte' gubernantur: aliæ' contra. his
enim perspectis magis fortasse' perceperimus quæ'
nam sit Respublica optima et quomodo unaqueq₃
disposita quibusue' legibus utens ac moribus bene'
fuerit constituta. Dicamus igitur hinc initio sum
pto.

Ludouicus Vicentinus Scribebat Romæ' Anno
Salutis. M.D.XVII. Mense' octob.

GIOVANNANTONIO TAGLIENTE

1524, VENICE **Lo presente libro**
The present book

AUTHOR
Origins: b. Venice c. 1468; no trace after 1527.
Activity: Writing master in the service of the Venetian Republic, publisher/printer of various educational books, typeface designer
Age at edition date: mid-50s

BOOK
Woodcutter: Eustachio Celebrino
Printer: Giovannantonio Tagliente & Hieronymo Tagliente
Technique: Woodcut and type
Size: 6" × 8"
Audience: State chancery employees, "Anyone who wishes to learn," and children of noble families.
Dedication: Hieronymo Dedo, Grand Secretary of the Venetian Republic.
Edition Description: Reproduced with the kind permission of The Newberry Library, Chicago, Illinois, Wing ZW 535.T1267, 1 fly leaf, 44 pages printed in black. The beige paper cover is printed with horizontal braid and floral motifs in black and light blue. The spine is in delicate condition. The title page is damaged with ink. Writing instruction is set in type on the last twenty-five pages. The final page is an illustration of the instruments of writing. A few pages are reverse. Instruction for the italic hand is in a centered format in the first portion of the book. The Rotunda alphabet is identical to that of Fanti. One unusual page shows a Rotunda *D* and *S* four inches in height. Page formats include alphabets, texts and alphabets, and writing instruction and alphabets. All borders are made with ruled lines.

6   The present book teaches the true art of excellent writing of divers various sorts of letters which are made by geometrical principles, and with the present work everyone will be able to learn them in a few days, by my teaching, rules, and examples, as you will see here in the following. Work of Tagliente, newly composed with favor in the year of our salvation MDXXIIII.

Translation by Barbara Oranger Hawes.

Signature enlarged from 6.

> Eglie manifesto Egregio lettore, che le lettere Cancellaresche sono de varie sorti, si come poi veder nelle scritte tabelle, le quali io scritto con mesura e arte, Et per satisfatione de cui apitisse una sorte, et cui un altra, Io to scritto questa altra variatione de lettere la qual volendo imparare osserua la regula del sottoscritto Alphabeto:
>
> A a. b. c. d. e e. ff. g. h. i. k. l. m. n. o. p ſ.
> ſſ &
> . o. q. r. s ſ. t. u. x. y. z. &.
>
> Le lettere cancellaresche sopranominate se fanno tonde longe large tratizzate e non tratizate ET per che io to scritto questa variacione de lettera la qual imparerai secundo li nostri precetti et opera
>
> A a a. b. c. d. e e. f. g. h. i. k. l. m. n. o. p. q. r. s ſ. t. u. x. y. z. &.

7 And I will show, distinguished reader, that the chancery letters are of various types, as you can see in the examples I have written for you with care and artistry. And for the satisfaction of anyone who has the chance to use another variation, I have written another alphabet. If you wish to learn it, observe the formation of the letters below.

The cancellarescha letters above may be round, long, wide, drawn, and not drawn. I have, therefore, written this variation which you will learn according to our rules and examples.
   Translation by Barbara Oranger Hawes.

8 *Consiglio di X*, Misti, filza 5, carta 127, holograph and letter to the Doge and Council of Venice, 1491. Reproduced with the kind permission of the Archivio de Stato, Venezia, Italy.

Ill.mo & Excellentissimo Principi Suoq. pio & glorioso consilio Humiliter & devote exponit p. parte sua fid[eli]s
servitoris & subditi Johanis Antonij de taiet[is] Cuius originarij Cum sit ch[e] a persuasio[ne] de multi virtuosi Zentilhom[eni]
& Citadini El se sia riducto in questa inclita cita p[er] propallare & insignare El vero Secreto & l'amaistrame[n]to d[e]
scrivere ogni varieta de litere: ch[e] p[er] homo del mo[n]do scrivere si possi: come ha[bi]a[m]o p[er] tuta italia & etia[m] in questa
p[er] experientia d[e] dimostrato cu[m] brevita e spexa poca: Et deliberato vivere et morire ne la patria sua: Et s[otto] lom-
bra dela sublimita v[ost]ra, e dimostrare tale secreto: Ali scriptori & secretarij de la v[ost]ra Signoria et ad ogni al[tro]
ch[e] di tale virtu overo scie[n]tia se delectara: Riverenteme[n]te supplica di gra[tia] ch[e] ala v[ost]ra Ill.ma Sig[no]ria p[iaza]
provederli di qualch[e] conveniete Sallario: si ch[e] mediante quello el dicto possa vivere cu[m] la sua famiglia
sumb[r]a di v[ost]ra sublimita: Offeredosi lui de Insegnare et amaistrare el Scrivere cancellaresco con le
rason: a tuti li Zoveni dedicati ala cancellaria de v[ost]ra ex.tia sine aliqua inpensa ulterius ad ogni altra
p[er]sona che vora imparare a scrivere solu[m] p[er] ducati duo p[er] ogni sorte de litera che'l vora: Si Antiqua cancell[aresca]
mercadantesca Moderna overo bastarda & Cuius celssitudini & gr[ati]e humiliter Se comedat &

GIOVANBATTISTA PALATINO

1540, ROME **Libro nuovo d'imparare a scrivere**
A New Book for Teaching Handwriting

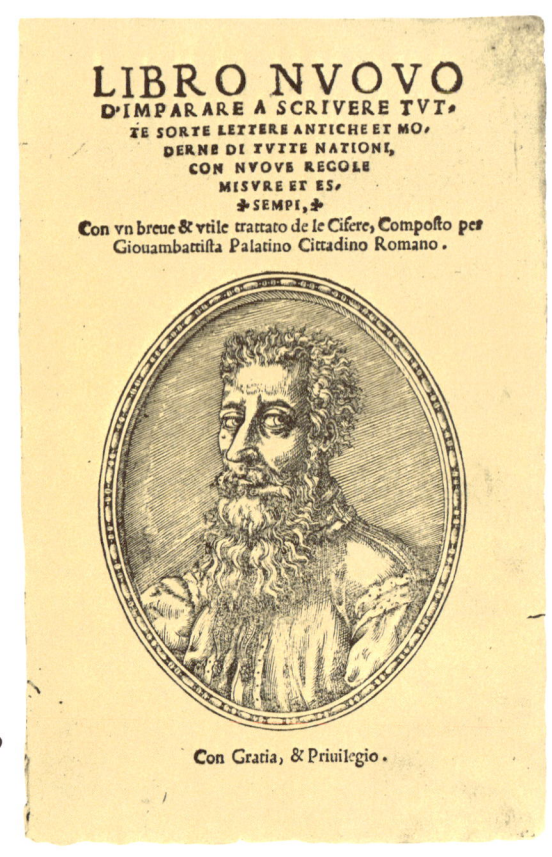

AUTHOR
Origins: b. Rossano in Calabria, c. 1515; d. Naples, post 1574.
Activity: Public notary, graphic designer, map letterer
Age at edition date: c. 25

BOOK
Printer: Baldassare di Francesco Cartolari
Technique: Woodcut and type
Size: 5¼" × 8¼"
Audience: Diplomatic secretaries, "Anyone who wants to learn."
Dedication: Cardinal de Lenoncorte
Edition Description: Reproduced with the kind permission of The Newberry Library, Chicago, Illinois, Wing ZW 535.P173, 1 fly leaf, 52 pages printed in black. The cover and spine are vellum over pasteboard. Portions of closure straps are still intact. *Libro de orni sorte lettere* is written in brown ink on the cover in the Rotunda style. Illustrations include a portrait of Palatino on the title page, the instruments of writing, and a candle with a butterfly sitting on the flame on the last page. Most of the exemplars are framed by borders of ruled lines. A few alphabets are written on cartouches. Instruction in the italic hand follows a centered format or a flush-left format. At least seventeen pages are signed by Palatino.

10

> Essempio per fermar la Mano.
>
> Aa a b c d e' f g h i k l m n o p q r ß
> t u x x y z & c̃
>
> Lutio che la sua dextra errante coce,
> Horatio sol contra Thoscana tutta,
> Che ne foco, ne ferro a virtu noce.
>
> Johannes Baptista Palatinus Scribeba
> Roma, apud Peregrinum
> Anno
> MDXXXX

9 New Book for learning to write all sorts of letters ancient and modern of all nations, with new rules, measurements and examples with a short, practical treatise on the Ciphers, composed by Giovanbattista Palatino, Roman Citizen. With favor and privilege.
Translation by Dom Julian Stead.

Signature enlarged from 10.

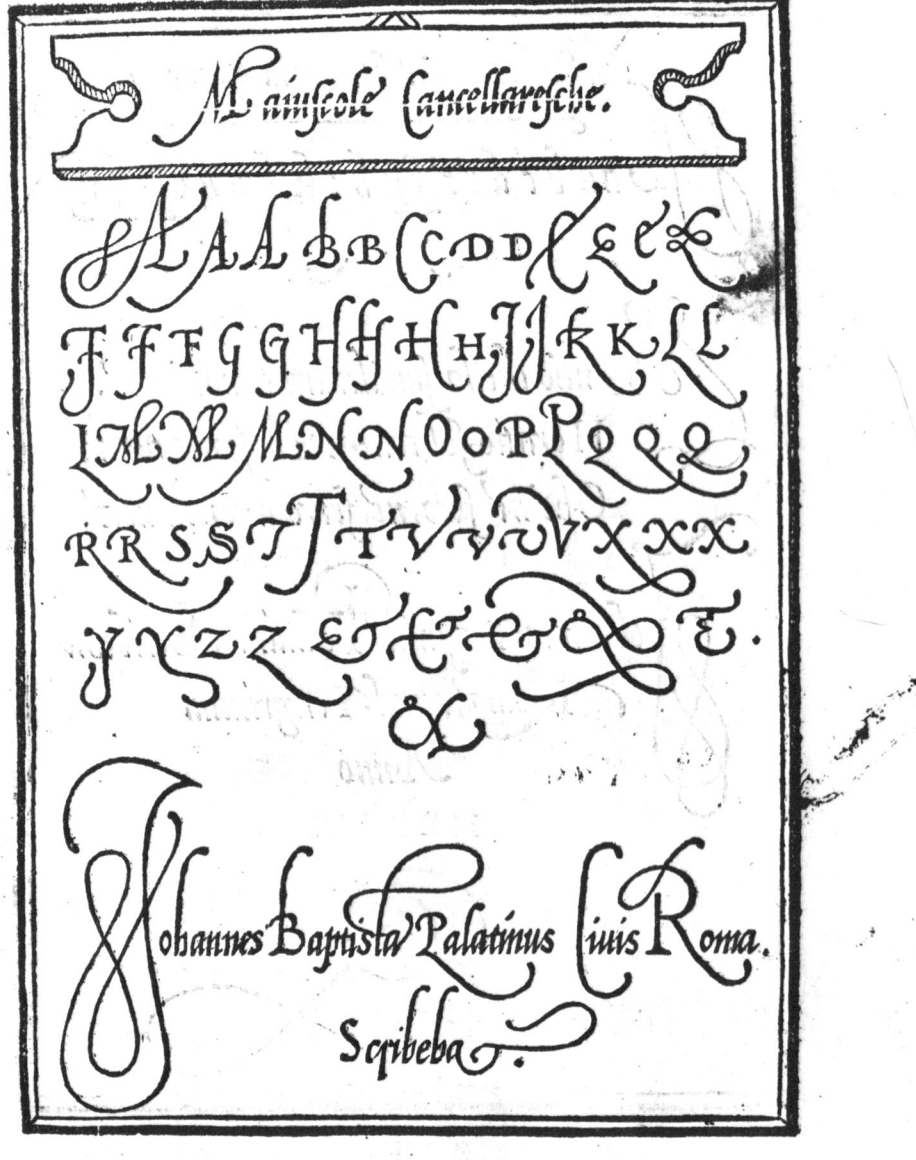

The Method and Rule which should be followed by everyone who is beginning to learn writing.

To write evenly and with a steady hand, I would judge it well to use the method mentioned by Quintilian and practiced by me with more than one whom I have taught, and certainly I have found it most useful, for those who have employed it have developed in a very few days a fine, steady and sure hand; the said method is this:

First, one should have a tablet of hard wood or of copper, and upon it should be cut or engraved all the letters of the Alphabet, done accurately, with their beginnings and all somewhat enlarged, and then have a stylus of tin the size of a small goose quill, and not hollow but solid, so that it is heavy, and, when once it has been used, the hand will be light and swift. Upon this stylus you will form the "plowshare" as is done with the quill but there is no need to split it. And let the beginner himself practice by going repeatedly over the incised letters with the point of the stylus, commencing where each letter begins, and then following as one would writing with a quill. And let him practice in this way so long that he knows by himself how to proceed surely.

Text from *Instruments of Writing*, translated from the writing book of Giovanbattista Palatino, Rome, 1533, by the Reverend Henry K. Pierce. Newport: Berry Hill Press, 1948. Reproduced with the kind permission of Esther Fisher Benson. (*Not shown.*)

11   MS. Canon. Ital. 196, *Writing Book*, N.D.
Reproduced with the kind permission of the Bodleian Library, Oxford, England.

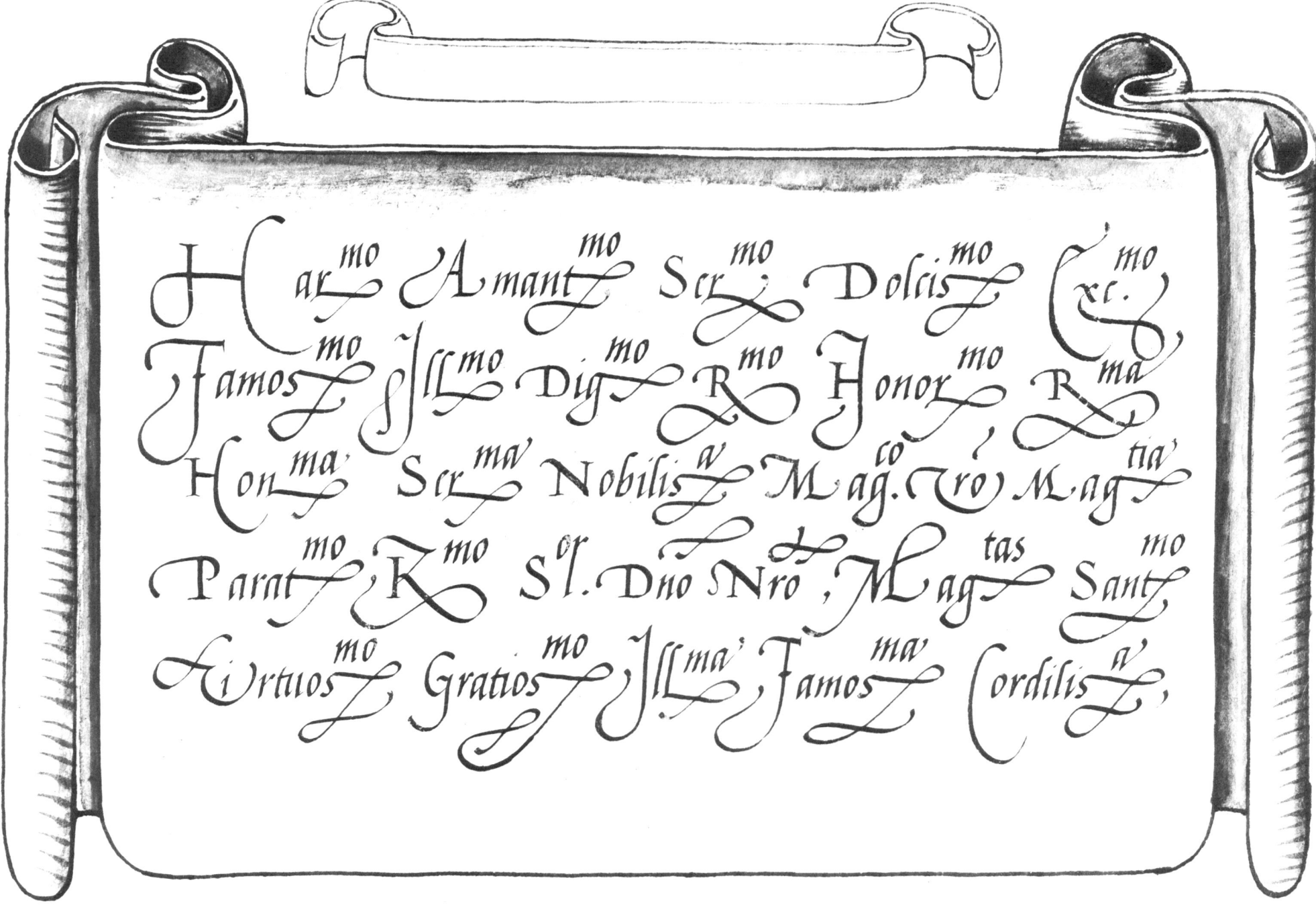

Gerardus Mercator

GERARD MERCATOR

1549, ANTWERP (FIRST EDITION, 1540)   **Literarum latinarum . . . scribendarum ratio**
How to Write Latin Letters

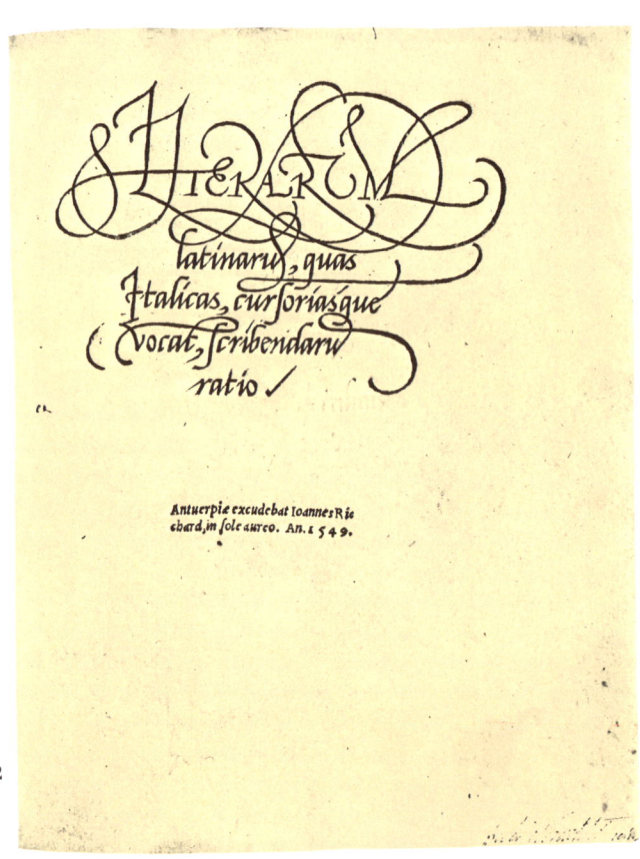

AUTHOR

Origins: b. Rupelmonde in Flanders, 1512; d. Duisburg, 1594.

Activity: Scientific instrument maker, cartographer, engraver, geographer

Age at edition date: 37

BOOK

Printer: Johannes Richard and Gerard Mercator

Woodcutter: Gerard Mercator

Technique: Woodcut and type

Size: 5¹⁵⁄₁₆" × 7⁹⁄₁₆"

Audience: Map, globe, and instrument makers.

Edition Description: Reproduced with the kind permission of The Newberry Library, Chicago, Illinois, Wing ZW 5465.M537, 4 fly leaves, 27 pages printed in black. The cover is black leather with thin gold lines around the edges. There is ornate gold stamping on the spine with the words, *Mercato Litterae Latinae*. Illustrations include instructions for quill-cutting, and arm positions for writing. Two pages are set in type, the remainder are written in the italic hand with a few type insertions. Writing instruction follows a centered format. The entire text is given to the instruction of the formation of the italic hand. Three final pages feature alphabets only.

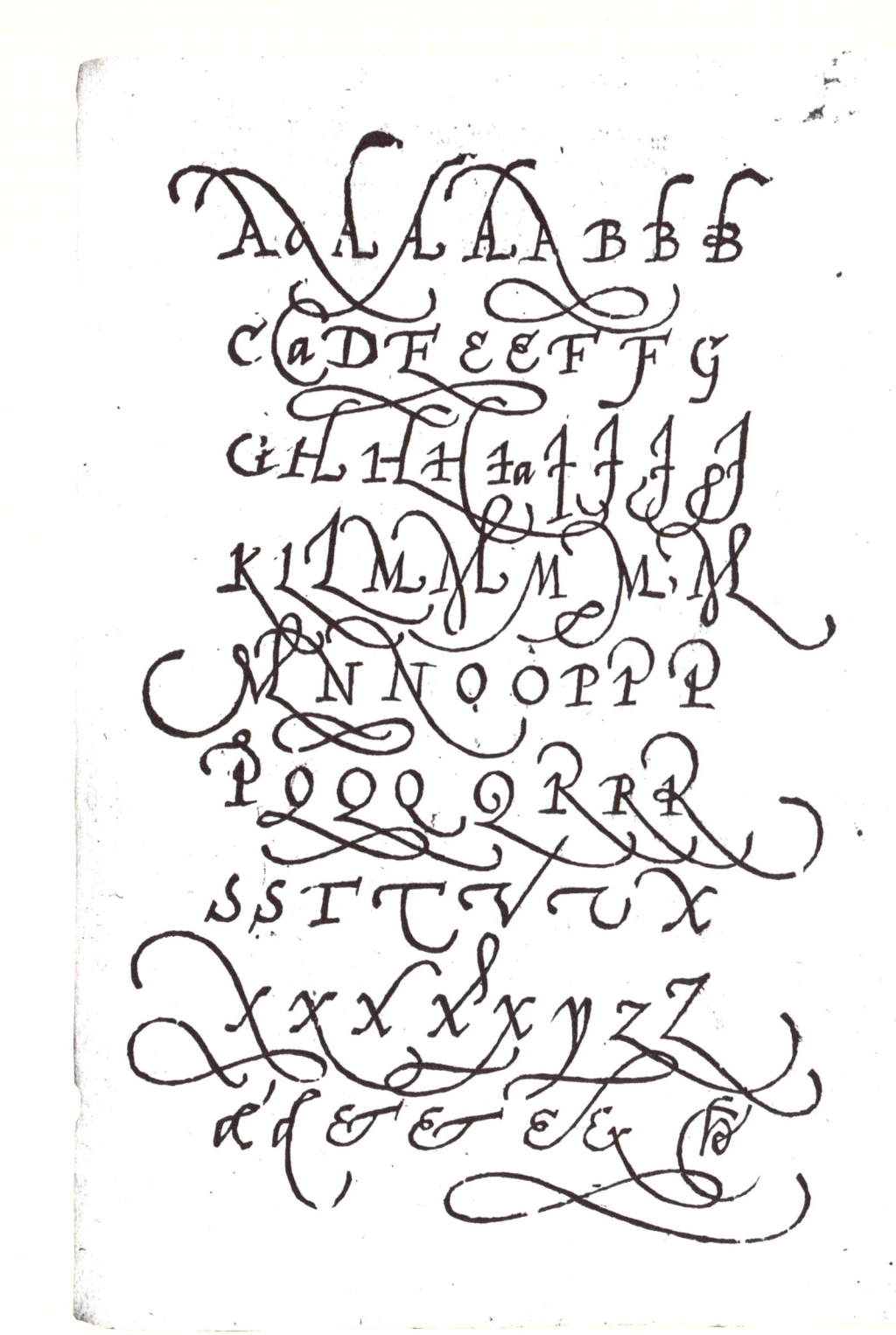

12 How to write the Latin letters which they call italic or cursive.
Translation by Barbara Oranger Hawes.

Signature enlarged from 13.

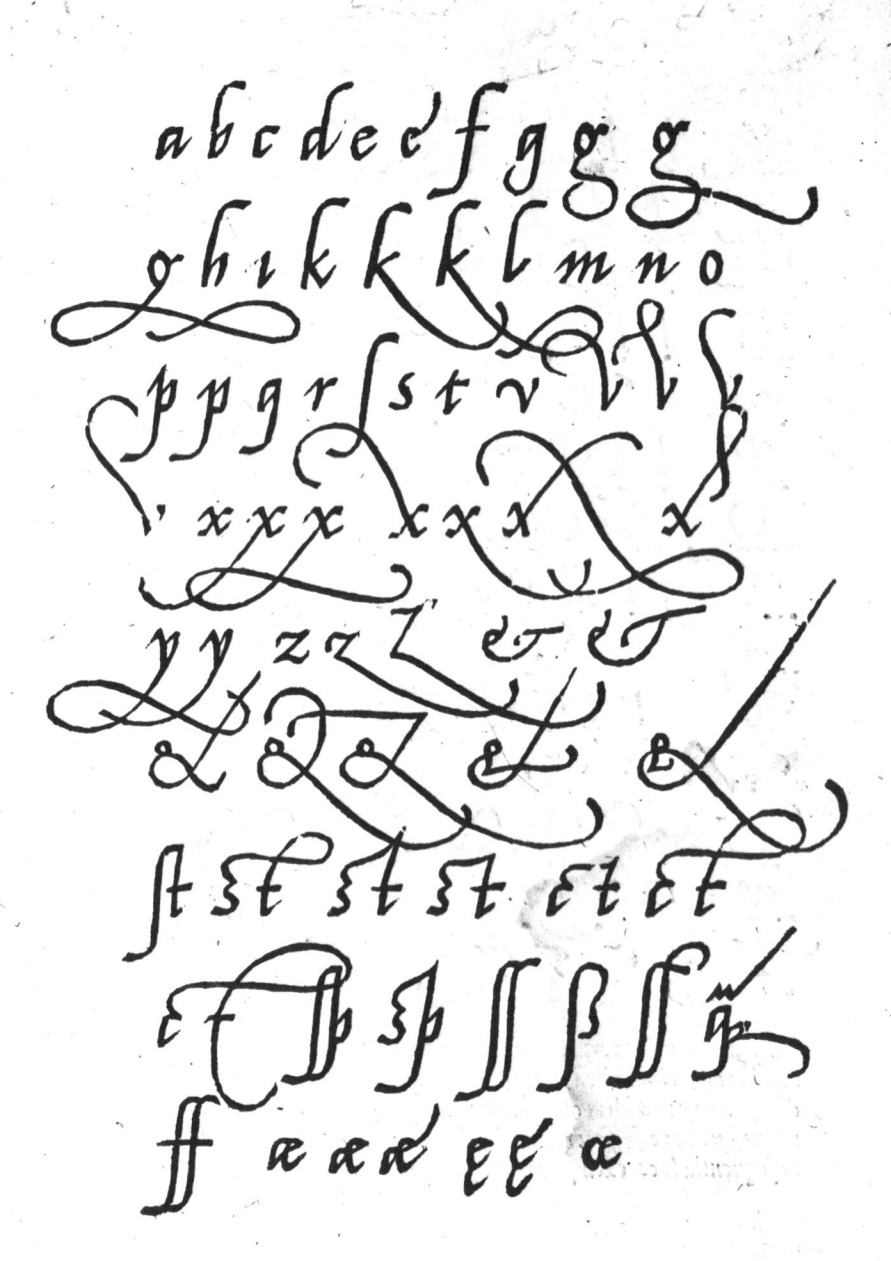

How to write Latin letters which they call italic or cursive.

>Translation from A. S. Osley's *Scribes and Sources*, 197. London: Faber & Faber; Boston: David R. Godine, 1980. Reproduced with the kind permission of A. S. Osley. (*Not shown.*)

And now let me give you a few general rules.

a is constructed from *c* and *ı* in this order: ccaa.

b from *l* and *ı*, thus: llb or from *l* and *ı* thus: llb but the former method is more reliable.

c was explained at the beginning of this chapter.

d is formed from a closed *c* thus: *c* and *l* in this order: ccd, but the pen is moved diagonally from *c* to the top of the next element, as follows: ccd so that the down-stroke to the beak of *c* may be made with greater certainty.

e is formed from *ı* but with a slight change. For the hair-line should not spring straight from the down-stroke, but from a short thick line of the following shape ˘ which is added like a foot to the medium curved down-stroke in this fashion: ιι. Then the pen is brought slightly round to the original start of the line, and a very short curve is made along the upper parallel thus: ιι. Then, in the same direction, shape the head of the letter as in *c* but dropping down a little, like this: ce. Finally, close it with a fine line to the left, which must, however, not fall to the centre of your first line, thus: c eee.

13   MS. Pembroke 113, Ortelius: *Album Amicorum*, 1596 (1575 page date). Reproduced with the kind permission of the Masters and Fellows of Pembroke College, Cambridge.

Suprema mundi optima.
Doctissimo viro D. Abrahamo Ortelio
Geographo Regio, longe amiciss: & di
lectissmo Gerardus Mercator in
symbolum perpetuę amicitię scripsit.
           Duisburgi 5. Kal. Octob.
                1575.

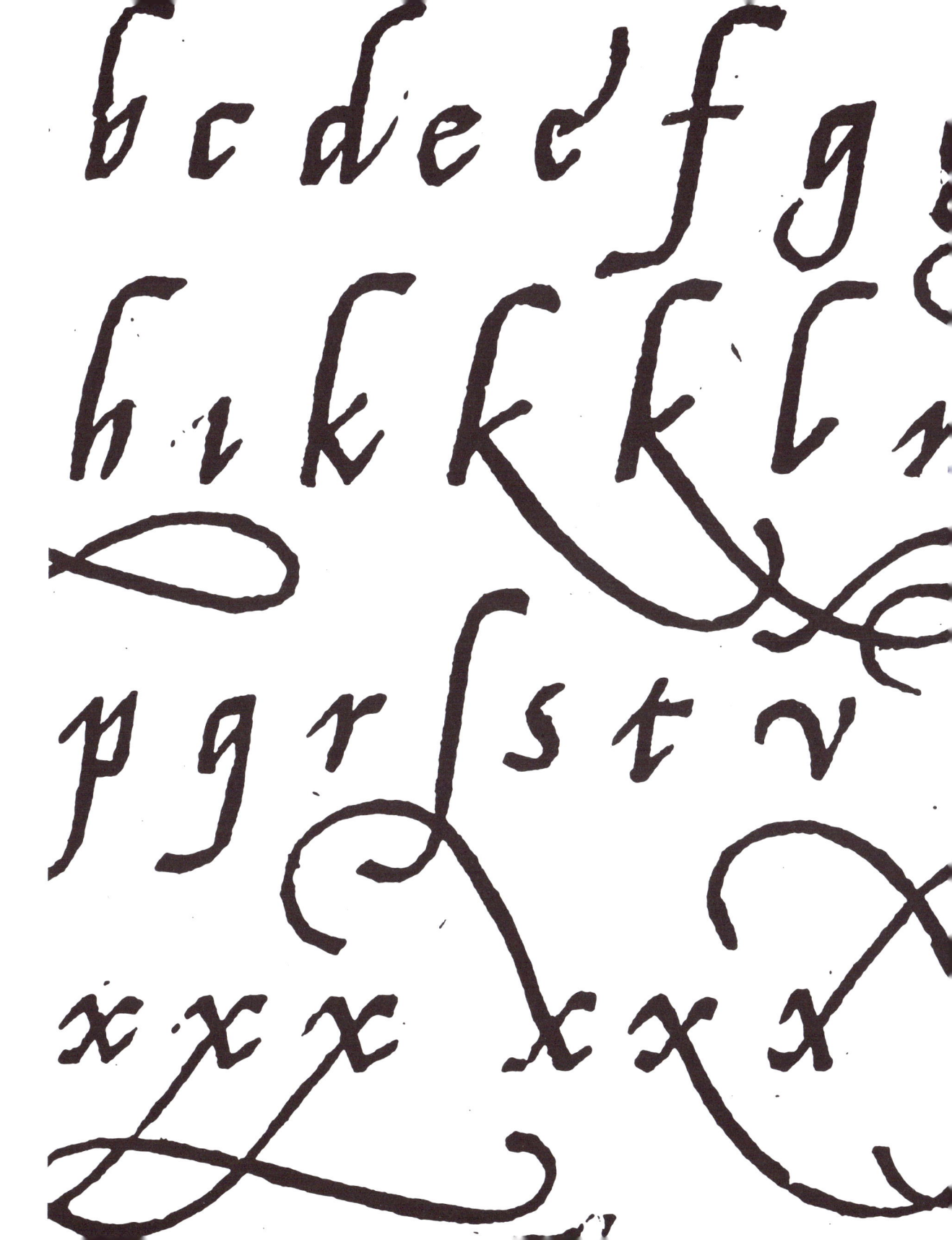

b c d e f g
h i k k k k l
p q r s t v
x x x x x x

Bennardino Cataneo

BENNARDINO CATANEO

FEBRUARY 1545, SIENA

Writing Book in Italian
(untitled)

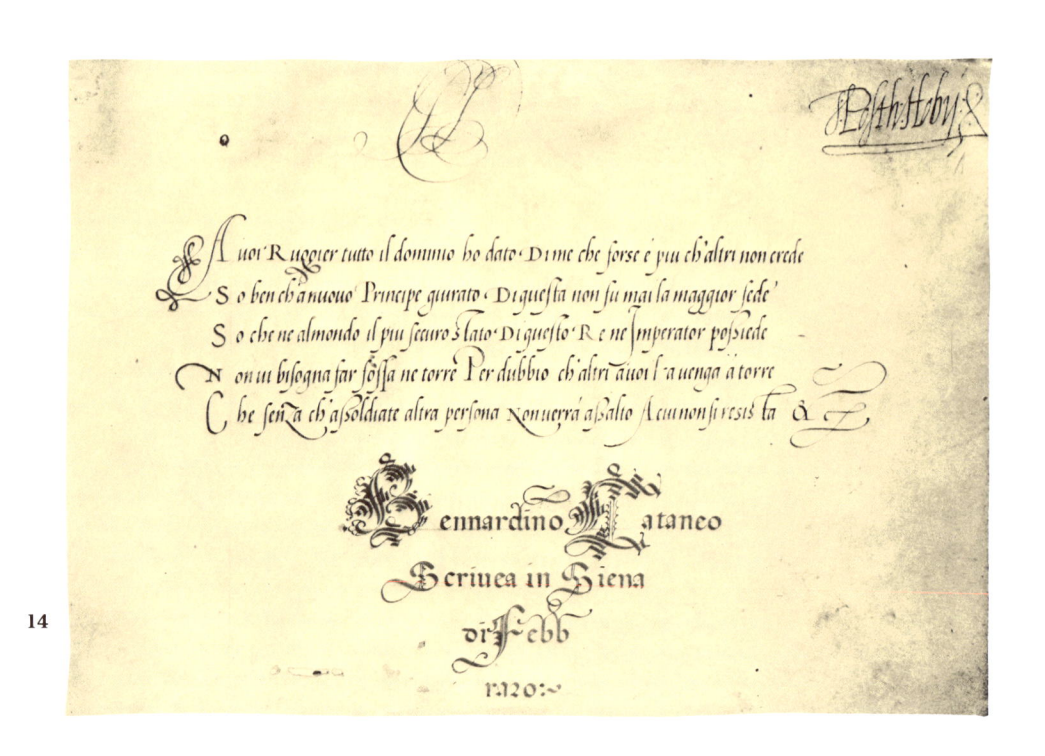

AUTHOR
Activity: Writing master at the University of Siena, c. 1544–1560

BOOK
Technique: Manuscript
Size: 7¼" × 5⅛"
Audience: Edward Raleigh.

Description: Reproduced with the kind permission of The Houghton Library, Harvard University, Cambridge, Massachusetts, M S.Type 246, 2 fly leaves, 20 leaves in Italian on vellum written on one side in brown with gold accents. The original binding is brown morocco leather with gold stamping on the front and back. The words on the cover read *Odoar/Do Ra/lygh*. There is no writing instruction. Three pages are signed by Cataneo in different styles. Each page follows a similar format with a quatrain from Ariosto's *Orlando Furioso*. Each line begins with a flourished italic capital in gold. On one page the quatrain is followed by a lower-case italic alphabet; on three others it is followed by an upper-case italic alphabet. There are no borders and no illustrations. Two distinct chancery scripts are presented: a *corsiva*, with full swashes on the projecting strokes, and a *formata* (such as that described by Palatino) with serifed projectors. Ownership marks and notes appear on the manuscript for (among others) Sir Thomas Posthumous Hoby, 1556–1640, and Stephen Penny, 1779.

15

Chi mette il pie nell'Amorosa pania Cerchi ritrarlo, e non u'inueschi l'ale
Che insomma, Amor non è se non insania A giuditio de saui unuersale
Et se ben come Orlando ogniun non smania Suo furor mostra à qualch'altro segnale
Et quale é di pazzia segno piu espresso Che per cercar'altrui perder se stesso
Varij oli effetti son ma la pazzia È tutt'una però che li fa uscire, Gli è come &

Human.^{mo} Illmo Laud.^a Mag.^{co} N.^{ro} Ones.^{ma} P.^{ma} Quint.^o Reuer.^{mo}

14 Ruggier has given his dominions to us
    Listen not to the skeptic
    I know I have given oath to a new Prince
    My faith was never stronger
    I know that in the whole world
    No king no Emperor a safer State has
    Erect neither tower or hollows make
    —Conquered it will never be—
    Without hired soldiers
    We'll resist the enemy assaults . . .
        Translation by Maria Ines Bonatti.

Signature enlarged from 14.

15 Whoever finds his feet in amorous fetters
    Had best withdraw them
    And clip not his wings
    For love is a flattering illness.
    As the universal judgment of sane people shows
    Though no one could pine as Orlando
    In everyone a windy passion blows.
    What is the single sign of madness
    Seeking another and getting lost
    Various the effects, teeming the madness
    Which harbors them.
    It is so . . .
        Translation by Maria Ines Bonatti.

Se la mia uita dall'aspro tormento Si puo tanto schermire e da gli affanni
Ch'io uegga per uirtù de gl'ultimi anni Donna de bei uostr'occhi il lume spento
E i capei d'oro fin farsi d'argento E lassar le ghirlande, e i uerdi panni
E l uiso scolorir che nei miei danni A lamentar mi san pauroso, e lento
Pur mi dara baldanza Amore Ch'io ui de miei martiri scouriro Quai &

16

A aa A bb cc dd ee ff g g h h i k ll mm nn o pp qq rr ſs ſi ßt tt uu v x y x z &

Se la mia vita dall'aspro torment[o]

Ch'io vegga per virtù degli ultimi [anni]

E i capei d'oro fin farsi d'argento

E'l viso scolorir che nei miei danni

Pur mi darà baldanza Amore [...]

16 If my harsh embittered life
   Could be relieved of its torments
   And I might see in my last days
   Lady, thy lustrous eyes spent
   Thy gold hair silver
   Thy face, thy garlands, thy green clothes fade . . .
   My heart aches and my tongue is dry
   Yet Love will awaken courage in me
   And I'll discover which of my torments . . .
   Translation by Maria Ines Bonatti.

Fr Vespasianus Amphvareus Ferrarese

VESPASIANO AMPHIAREO

c. 1548, probably FERRARA

MS Writing Book
(untitled)

AUTHOR

Origins: b. Ferrara c. 1501; d. probably Venice c. 1563.

Activity: Franciscan monk, public writing master in Venice

Age at time of the MS: c. 47

BOOK

Technique: Manuscript

Size: 8⅜" × 5⅝"

Description: Reproduced with the kind permission of The Houghton Library, Harvard University, Cambridge, Massachusetts, MS.Typ 166, Gift of Mr. & Mrs. Philip Hofer. Signed ms., 1 fly leaf, 38 vellum pages, written in brown, red, and blue on both sides. Nineteenth-century blue marbled boards cover the ms. The spine is brown leather with gold tooling. The pages follow in alphabetical sequence with red or brown ornamented Fraktur capitals of one to two inches in the upper left corner of each page. Page headings are in red Rotunda with blue Versal or Fraktur capitals. Three pages are signed, eleven are italic. No title page is evident. Each page has a similar format including lines of quarter-inch text followed by an alphabet. The final pages contain seventeenth-century examples of the lettering of Alessandro Fomelli Il Sorbi and Giulio Cesare Tellani.

Lettera Cancellaresca Del frate

Facilmente si comprendono gli intimi precordij delli huo
mini confabulando seco delli quottidiani ragionamenti
dalli loro monimenti & d'altre mille sopravenienti occasio
ni. Onde gli sapientissimi et esperimentissimi Philosophi
insegnorono alla posteritate' questi documenti, per il che obli
gatissimi sempre dobbiamo essere alle memorie loro

Diuerte amalo Et fac bonum, inquire pace.

Signature enlarged from 18.

17 Cancellarescha

The delight of the country
Full of scented blossoms,
The cool, fresh stream,
These I view from afar, as I cry,
Sensing their sweet breath.
Now I have lingered long
Under your grateful shade,
Your sheltering bough, my Crown,
By your favor bound to surrender
My just Grief,
That I may the more
Devote to you, and You find pleasure in,
My unwearying Service.

May the Name of the Lord be blessed.
Praise the Lord—All Peoples
Translation by Marvin Kendrick.

A a b c d e f g h y l m n o p q r ſ s t u x y

Quintiliano ester e compagni di roma demo dare questo di xx d'ottobre due
cinquecento cinquantacinque d'oro in oro quali sono p la valuta di tanti
ermesini hauuti questo di sopra detto Equali dinari sono da pagari
p tutto ottobre prossimo che viene Come appare allibro. D. arj 6
Et piu demo dare questo di sopradetto ducati cinquanta d'oro in oro.

A A a. B b b. C c D d d. E e F f f g g g.
H h y J K L M m N n O o P p Q q q
R r ſ s f T T t f V x y z
Fr Vespasianus Amphyareus Ferrarese or. mnor

18 Quintiliano Ester and Company of Rome must give this 20th day of October 555 gold duros in gold which are for the value of so many pieces of silk which they had this above mentioned day. Which monies are to be paid for the whole of the month of August as appears in the book. D.arj 6. And furthermore they must give this above mentioned day 50 gold ducats in gold.

Translation by Tony Oldcorn.

19   MS. Typ 13, *Address to Lucas*, N.D.
Reproduced with the kind permission of The Houghton Library, Harvard University, Cambridge, Massachusetts.

Friar Vespasiano. These few prayers have been collected for all the Sundays of the year and the 1st Sunday in Lent, which are said at the Masses, and written by me in various styles with the best diligence I am capable of. I give them to you for your dear son, so that by reading them he may thank the Supreme God, and may your Lordship accept them with the same love I offer them, begging your Lordship whenever you see fit to employ me as you would one of your most trusted servants.
I kiss your hand and I recommend myself.
Lovingly, Friar Vespasiano.
   Translation by Tony Oldcorn.

Juan de yciar

JUAN DE YCIAR

1550, SARAGOSSA (FIRST EDITION: 1548)

Arte subtilissima por la qual se insena a escrevir perfectamente
The Very Subtle Art by Which One is Taught to Write Perfectly

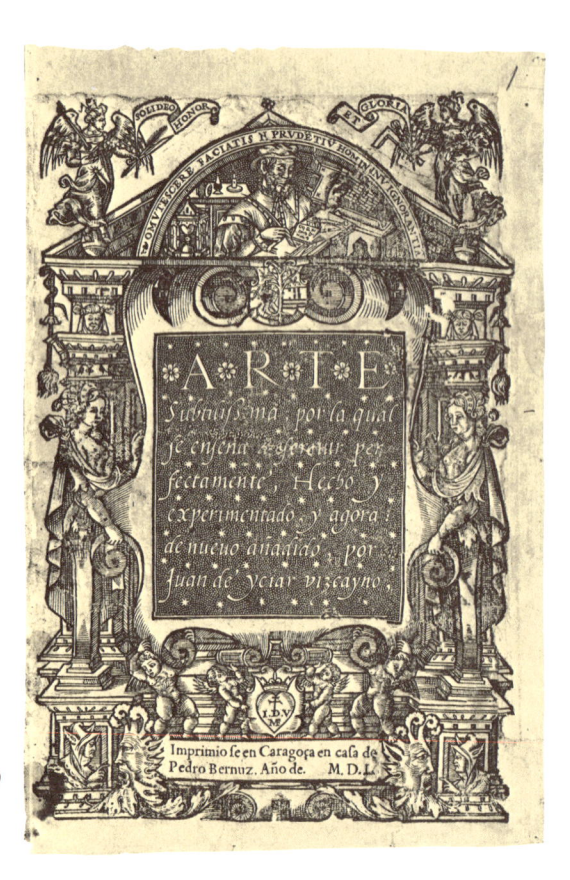

AUTHOR
Origins: b. Durango in Viscaya 1522/23; d. Logrono, post 1573
Activity: Copyist of choir and service books, teacher, tutor to Prince Carlos of Spain, priest, author of an arithmetic book
Age at edition date: 27

BOOK
Woodcutter: Jean de Vingles
Printer: Pedro Bernuz
Technique: Woodcut and type
Size: 5⅛" × 7⅝"
Audience: "For those who desire to learn."
Dedication: Philip II, Spain

Edition Description: Reproduced with the kind permission of The Newberry Library, Chicago, Illinois, Wing ZW 540.I64, 2 fly leaves, 86 pages printed in black. The cover is goat parchment over boards with gold-tooled decoration and the words, *Juan Iciar, Ano.MDL*. The spine has two black leather inserts that read, *Iciar, Arte de Escribi, Saragoza, 1550*. Illustrations include a portrait of Yciar, and the stamp of Pedro Bernuz's printing house. The book is lavishly decorated. Numerous pages are reverse. Border decorations include: ruled lines, scrolls, and half-inch to three-quarter-inch block borders. Writing instruction is set in type at the beginning and the end of the book and in writing throughout the exemplars. Individual letters are shown in various sizes ranging from an eighth of an inch to an inch and a half. Most pages are signed by either Yciar or de Vingles, and many are dated.

20 The Very Subtle Art by which one is taught to write perfectly. Devised and tested and now newly expanded by Juan de Yciar of Biscay. Printed in Saragossa at the printing house of Pedro Bernuz in the year 1550.
  Translation by James Teixeira.

Signature enlarged and reversed from 20.

21 Hand for Writing Briefs
I was favored by receipt of your Grace's letter of the ninth of last month, although when I understood from it and from what has been previously written to me that you, most Reverend, have not found yourself in the state of health for which we all wish, I was and am more greatly pained than I could say. May it please God to keep your Grace and grant you complete health.
Juan de Yciar wrote it in Saragossa in the year 1547. I.D.V.
  Translation by James Teixeira.

22 Not possessing anything certain of this world or of its things, we build costly houses even with hell at our gates. We follow Satan and fail to keep the kind God. We offend these continuously with the riches you give us.
Juan de Yciar wrote this. 1550. I.D.V.
Translation by James Teixeira.

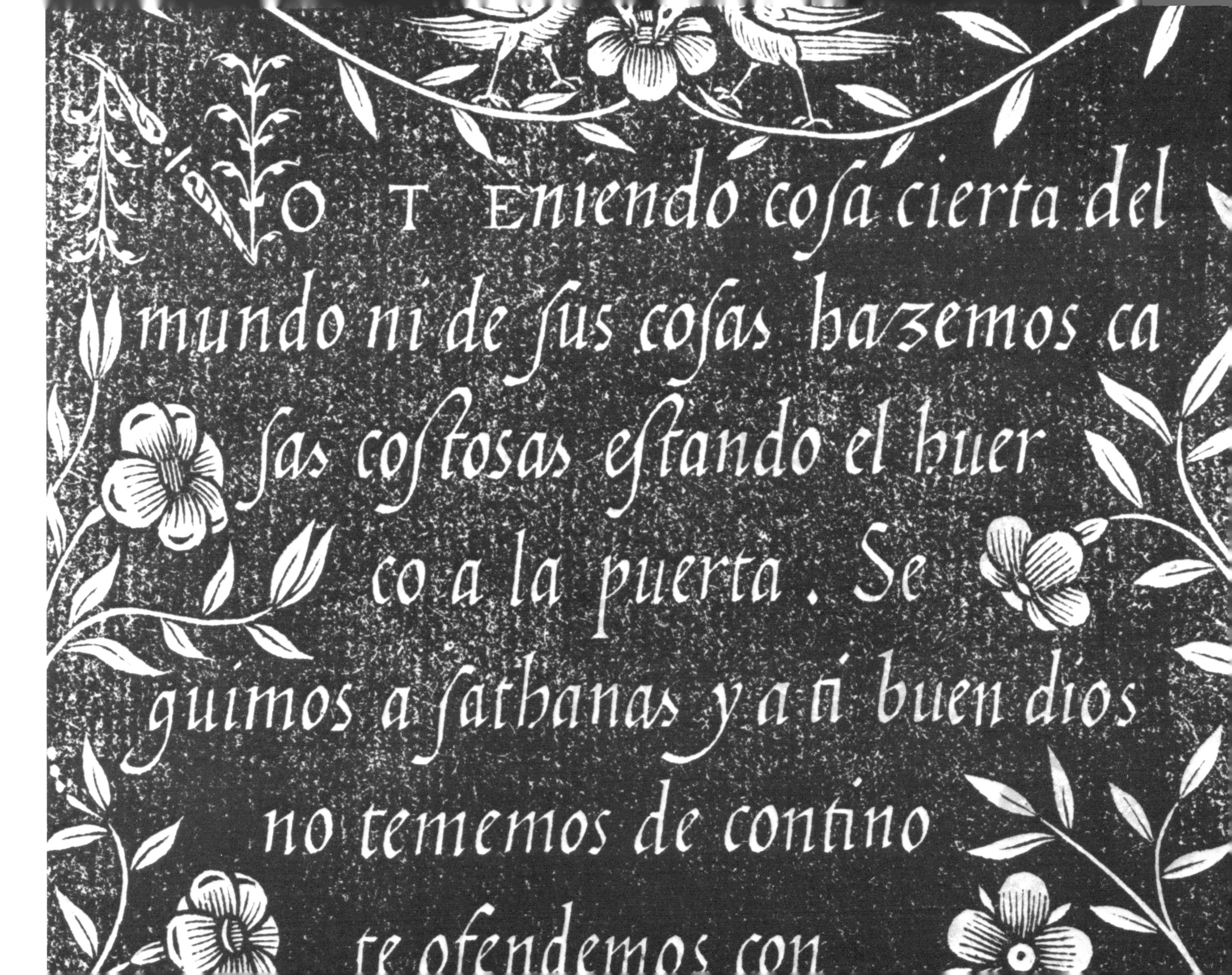

NO Teniendo cosa cierta del mundo ni de sus cosas hazemos casas costosas estando el huerco a la puerta. Seguimos a sathanas y a ti buen dios no tememos de contino te ofendemos con

Caspar Neffenn

CASPAR NEFF

1571, COLOGNE (FIRST EDITION, 1549) **Thesaurarium artis scriptoriae**
Treasury of the Art of Writing

AUTHOR

Activity: Schoolmaster, teacher of mathematics

BOOK

Printer: Cut and printed at the expense of Caspar Vopel

Technique: Woodcut

Size: 7 11/16" × 12 1/8"

Audience: Chancellery employees and scribes.

Edition Description: Reproduced with the kind permission of The Newberry Library, Chicago, Illinois, Wing ZW f547.N3, 3 fly leaves, 24 pages printed on one side in black. Two editions are bound together, both dated 1571: *Thesaurarium artis scriptoriae* (title page featured here), 8 pages, and *Ein Kostliche Schatzkamer der schreibkunst* (exemplar page featured here), 17 pages. The cover is limp vellum with the words *Neff, Coelin, 1571* written in black capitals on the spine. There is no writing instruction in *Thesaurarium artis scriptoriae*. All the pages follow a similar format. There are two complete exemplars on each page, with an unusually wide space between them. One page shows the stroking order of the lower case Textura alphabet, but most pages have either four to eight lines, an alphabet, embellished initial capitals, and a title depicting the style of writing or merely a title and a text with no alphabet. Jan Tschichold's *Shatzkamer der Schreibkunst* features photographs of Neff's first edition of 1549. It is in the collection of the University Library in Basel. The pages are half the size of the 1571 edition and feature one exemplar per page instead of two.

Page reduced.

23 A valuable storehouse of the art of writing and a treasury for the chancellery and other scribes. A very elegant and ingenious little book of various fine, pleasing scripts put together on the correct principles, many of which have never been seen before. Now newly issued by the highly experienced Caspar Neff, German schoolmaster in the commendable city of Cologne, written by his hand, and cut in the printing house of Caspar Vopel, and printed for the first time through the grace and liberality of the Roman Imperial Majesty. Scripts in various languages. In this treasury are contained German, Latin, Italian, French, English, and Flemish. Now newly printed in Cologne by Thomas von Wierdt. MDLXXI
Translation by Alexander Nesbitt.

Signature enlarged from 23.

These characters are used in the ROMAN chancery. Flee avarice, that queen of shameless vices, whom all crimes serve with shameless devotion. This avarice forsooth has a fondness for money, a thing which no sage has desired: steeped as it were in evil poisons, it enervates the man's body and mind and is diminished neither by plenty nor by want. This is a mark of excellent wisdom, that a person should possess self-knowledge, nor out of the love he has for himself, be deceived about himself, and repute himself to be a good man when he is not. For a man has the power to direct his every action, if he understands himself. (*Not shown.*)
Translation by Dom Geoffrey Chase.

Vrbanus Vuys

URBAN WYSS

1549, ZÜRICH **Libellus valde doctor**
A Very Learned Little Book

AUTHOR
Origins: d. before 23 August 1561
Activity: Schoolmaster, woodcutter, printer
BOOK
Woodcutter: Urban Wyss
Technique: Woodcut and type
Size: 9⅛" × 6³⁄₁₆"
Audience: Boys in the Fraumünster and the Grossmünster schools.
Dedication: Johann Fries
Edition Description: Reproduced with the kind permission of The Newberry Library, Chicago, Illinois, Wing ZW 538.W98a, 3 fly leaves, 54 pages printed in black. The title page is printed in red and black. The paper-patterned board cover is black stripped with a green and gold background. The spine is green leather and reads *Wiss 1549*. Illustrations include a scribe writing at a desk, a demonstration of quill-cutting, arm positions for writing, and a schoolroom with a teacher and students. There are at least fifteen different varieties of block borders which decorate the exemplars. Page formats include alphabets, quotations demonstrating styles of writing, and quotations with alphabets below them.

24 A learned, elegant and practical little book, containing many different kinds of models for writing letters.

Likewise brief and lucid instruction, whereby boys are readily guided to a true and correctly written expression of the Latin tongue. Striking and notable maxims have been extracted from Cicero from which rules not only for speaking well but for living a good life have been derived. An alphabet has been appended to each of the maxims. These alphabets offer the boys various ways of writing both Latin and Greek. All this has been written for the benefit and use of young students, cut and printed by Urban Wyss of Zürich in the year 1514. (*Not shown.*)
  Translation by A. S. Osley, recommendations by Dom Julian Stead.

Signature enlarged from 24. (*Not shown.*)

ℛ a b c d e e f g g g h i k k k l m n n
o o p p q r ſſ ſſ t v v x x x y y z z
ℯ ℯ & & & & & ſt ſt ſt
ſſ ſt st st e t ch ſp ſp ſl ſl
ƙ ƙ ij ß ɇ, ɇ ℞ æ æ æ æ æ 3 ȝ.

ſa b c d e e f g g g h i
o o o p p q r ſ ſ ſ s t v v

Wolffgang fugger

WOLFFGANG FUGGER

1553, NÜRNBERG **Ein nutzlich und wolgegrundt formular**
Useful and Well-grounded Formulary . . .

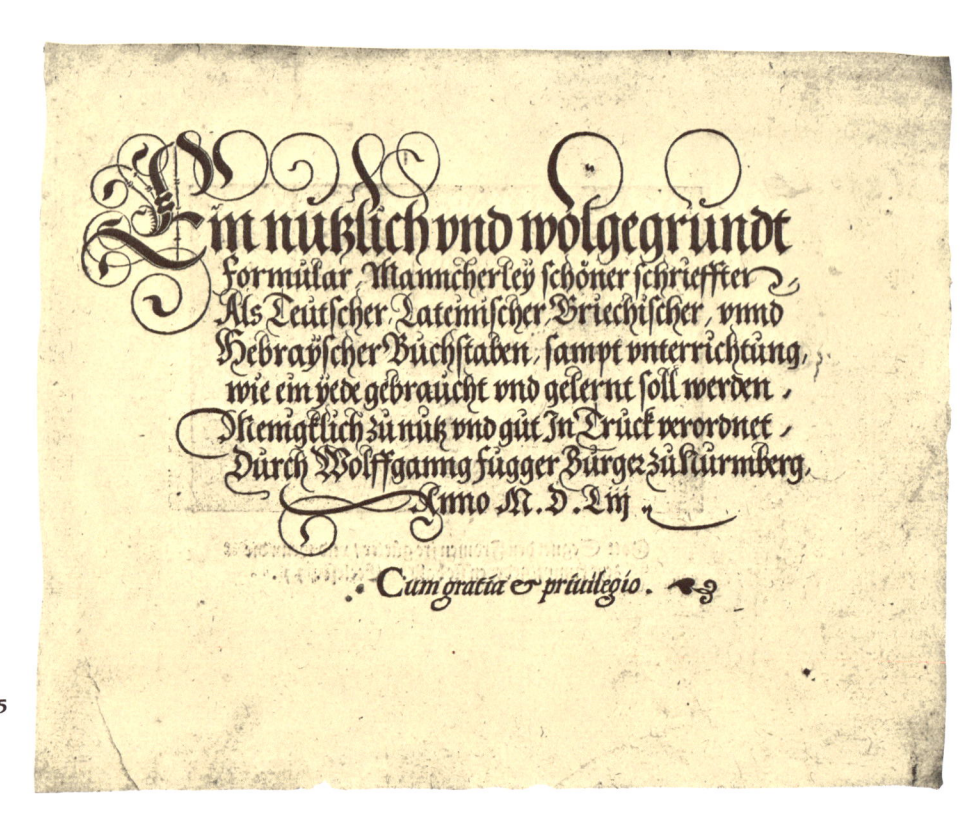

AUTHOR
Origins: b. Nürnberg c. 1515; d. Nürnberg 1568.
Activity: Publisher, printer
Age at edition date: c. 38

BOOK
Publisher: Wolffgang Fugger
Printer: Valentin Geissler
Technique: Metal cut
Size: 7¾" × 6⅛"
Audience: Punchcutters, printers, compositors, "young enthusiasts."
Dedication: Joachim Tetzel

Edition Description: Reproduced with the kind permission of The Newberry Library, Chicago, Illinois, Wing ZW 547.F953, 2 fly leaves, 100 pages printed in black. The blind-stamped black leather cover has a border depicting biblical scenes. There are holes on the edge of the binding indicating that there were once closures. Illustrations include demonstrations of quill-cutting, and arm positions for writing. The writing instruction is written and is always shown on the pages opposite the exemplars. The last twenty-eight pages show the geometrical construction of Roman capitals. Page formats include quotations, alphabets, alphabet stroking order, ligatures, and writing exercises.

Page reduced.

a b c d e f
g h i k l m
n o p q r ſ
s t u x y z

I ij.

25 A useful and well-rounded arrangement of various fine scripts. For instance, German, Latin, Greek, and Hebrew letters, together with instruction on how they are to be learned and used. Arranged in print for the good and use of all by Wolffgang Fugger, citizen of Nürnberg.
In the year 1553.
With grace and privilege.
   Translation by Alexander Nesbitt.

Signature enlarged from 25.

This letter, usually known as *Cursiv,* is a common Roman current, being one of the regular hands. You may see it opposite. How this letter is to be drawn follows hereafter, with texts and instructions. Also how many pieces or matrices are required if you wish to have it cut for print. German does not look well written in Roman letters. Use a pen trimmed towards the right. The capitals used in this alphabet are those of the Roman alphabet.

   (*Translation of facing page. Not shown.*) Translation from Wolffgang Fugger's *Handwriting Manual entitled A Practical and Well-grounded Formulary for Divers Fair Hands,* a translation of the 1553 edition by Frederick Plaat. London: Oxford University Press, 1960. Printed with the kind permission of Oxford University Press, London.

Ferdinandus Ruano

FERDINANDO RUANO

1554, ROME **Sette alphabeti di varie lettere**
Seven Alphabets in Different Lettering

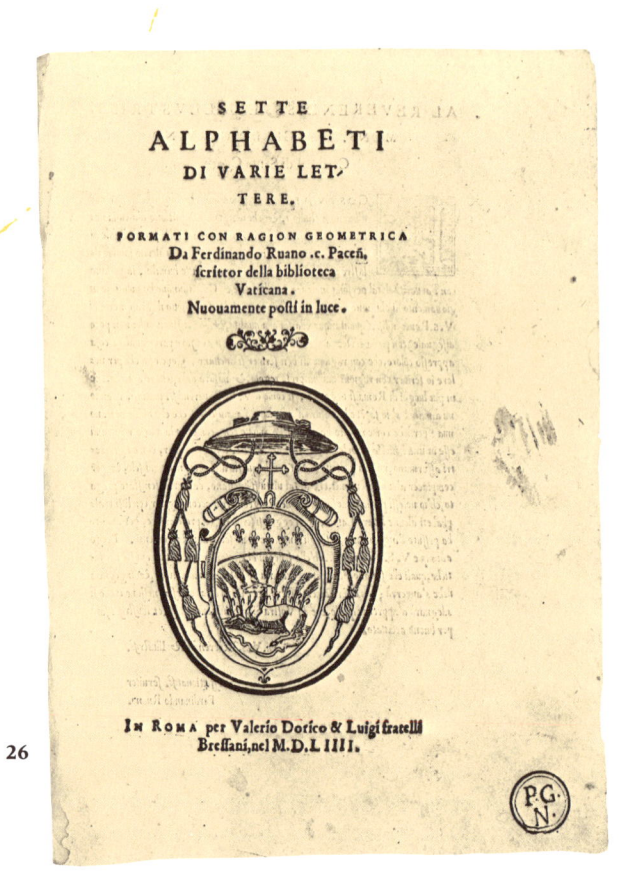

AUTHOR
Origins: b. Badajoz; d. 1560
Activity: Scriptor of the Apostolic Library
BOOK
Printer: Luigi and Valerio Dorico
Technique: Woodcut and type
Size: 7¾" × 10¾"
Dedication: Cardinal Marcello Cervini
Edition Description: Reproduced with the kind permission of The Newberry Library, Chicago, Illinois, Wing ZW f14.R82, 4 fly leaves, 43 pages printed in black. The cover is light-brown leather stamped with gold stars. The spine reads *Ruano, Sette Alphabeti, Roma 1554*. Roman capitals, Rotunda, Versals, Italic and Grotesque alphabets are demonstrated geometrically. The individual letters measure two and a half to four inches and are inserted into columns of instruction. The text for Versal and Grotesque alphabets is missing. Each alphabet is preceded by a page of general instruction in type. The last page shows the stamp of the Dorico printing house.

Signature enlarged from 28.

26 Seven Alphabets of various letters. Formed according to geometrical principles by Ferdinand Ruano, a priest of Badajoz, scribe of the Vatican Library. Newly published. In Rome by Valerio Dorico & Luigi brothers Bressani, in MDLIIII.
Translation by Dom Julian Stead.

27 The letter *a* is constructed within its square, which you should divide up in the way which I told you. To make its bowl, place one leg of the compasses on point a, which lies on line 7 below the diameter and place the other leg at the top of line 6 where another a is marked for you. Then make a half circle terminating at line 3 where you will find another a. Its oval or curve is made with 3 arcs as follows: (1) Place one leg of the compasses on the point marked to which you will find in column 7 beneath the diameter and place the other leg on line 3. Beginning from the diameter marked with another b, come to the middle of the third column (2) Place one leg of the compasses on point c which you will find on the [perpendicular] line which crosses the square on the left-hand side above the diameter, and the other leg on the 3rd line, starting from the diameter go up until you reach the line with which it forms an angle (3) Place one leg of the compasses on the point marked d which you will find on line 5 above the diameter, and the other leg above the same line, and from the first line under that which crosses the square, you will come to the diagonal which joins that of c.

The round part under the letter is constructed by placing one leg of the compasses at point e and the other under line 3: make an arc which meets line 5 below the diameter. You will make another arc above this one fifth of a unit apart, by placing one leg on point f (you will find points *e & f* on the right hand [actually it's the left!]) outside the square and the bowl will be constructed. The downstroke of the letter must be straight and separated from the curve by the space of two units. At its base, make an oblique serif corresponding to the points marked. You should notice that when you have constructed this *a*, you will be able to construct *b,c,d,e,g,h,o,p,q* and *x* with the same points and arcs and, with these examples before you, let this suffice. (*Page reduced.*)
Translation by A. S. Osley, consultation of Barbara Oranger Hawes.

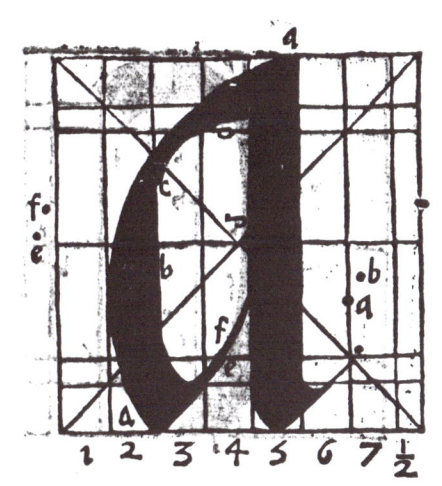

27

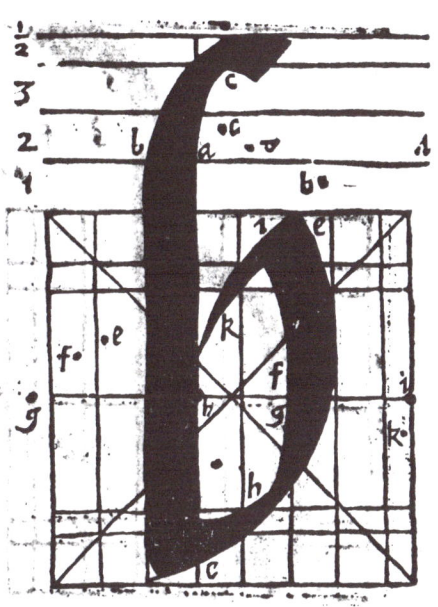

LA lettera .A. si forma nel suo quadro il qual tu partirai come io t'ho detto : & per far il suo caso metterai il compasso nel punto del .a. che sta nella 7. linea sotto il diametro, & risponda sopra la .6. linea doue ti segna un'altra .a. & farai mezo circolo che fornisca alla .3. linea doue trouarai un'altra .a. Il suo ouato, ouer cauo si forma in tre mezi circoli , cioè mettendo il compasso nel punto del .b. che trouarai alla .7. linea sotto il diametro, & risponda alla .3. linea, & cominciarai dal detto diametro doue ti segna .l'altro .b. & uenirà al mezo della terza testa: il secondo sarà il punto del .c. il qual trouarai nella linea che serra il quadro à mano manca sopra il diametro , & risponderà il compasso alla .3. linea cominciando dal detto diametro, et andarà di sopra fin alla linea angolare: il terzo sarà il punto del .d. il qual trouarai nella .5. linea sopra il diametro, & risponda di sopra la medesima linea, & alla prima linea sotto quella del quadro, & uenirà fin alla angolare, che si liga con quella del .c. La sua tondezza di sotto si forma mettendo il compasso nel punto del .e. & risponda sotto la .3. linea, & farai mezo circolo che arriui alla .5. linea sotto il diametro, farai un altro mezo circolo sopra questo, & discosto un quinto mettendo il compasso nel punto del .f. liquali due punti .e. & .f. trouarai a man dritta di fuora al quadro, & sarà formato il caso . La sua gamba uuole esser dritta, et discosta dal detto caso due teste. In loco di base farai una testina sguinza conforme a i punti che trouarai. E te bisogna auuertire che come hai fatto questa .a. farai il b.c.d.e. g.h.o.p.q.x. con quelli medesimi punti, et circoli. Et questo ti basti hauendo l'essemplare inanzi.

LA lettera .B. si forma come l'a, saluo chel suo astillo esce fuora del quadro tre teste , & meza, & della prima testa sopra il quadro farai la sua tondezza con un poco di testina anchora in tondo: & per farla seguirai l'ordine de i punti come nell'a. & questo astillo ti seruirà per d.f.h.l.

te nobis debita nostra, sicut et nos dimittimus debitoribus nostris. Idest hoc roga=
mus, ut sicut nos dimittimus, ita et ipse dimittat nobis. Sicut ipse dominus di=
xit. Si enim remiseritis hominibus peccata eorum, et pater uester coelestis remit=
tet uobis peccata uestra. Si enim non remiseritis, nec Deus dimittet uobis. Et
ne nos inducas in tentationem: hoc est, hoc rogamus, ut nos sua pietas, non plus
permittat tentare, qua nostra fragilitas potest sustinere. Sed libe=
ra nos à malo: idest sua pietas liberet à peccato, à diabo=
lo, ab omni opere malo, vel de inferno:
Amen.

Ferdinandus Ruano . c . Pacen . scriptor Biblio^{cæ} . ap^{cæ}p . Vaticanæ . scribebat
Romæ . anno . D . M . D . LIIII Pont . S^{mi} . D . D . N . Julij tertij . Anno eius qui=
to: v.f.

28 Vat. Lat. 317,258v, *Expositio Rationis Dominicae*, 1554. Reproduced with the kind permission of the Biblioteca Apostolica Vaticana, Rome, Italy.

29 Vat. Lat. 3841,80v, *Epistolae*, 1551. Reproduced with the kind permission of the Biblioteca Apostolica Vaticana, Rome, Italy.

29

Concerning the formal chancery hand.
The Chancery hand is so well known to everyone, I will not in my examples discuss its origin nor even its variations because so many able men have described its practice and the method of forming the letters, and the starting and finishing strokes appropriate to the pen: and since it has always been my plan, from the beginning, not to use the pen but only the compass and the ruler; I will speak of this formal letter. Therefore, if you wish to shape its letters, you must know that a letter must be enclosed in a square which you will divide into seven and a half units and one of these pen widths will constitute the broadest line of the letter and seven and a half units will constitute the height: when you have divided this square lengthwise, you will draw a line from each corner to the corner diagonally opposite crossing in the center of the square and, above the diameter under the line which closes the top of the square, you will make a line one unit below, and next to it you will make another, a half a unit away; these will serve for the upper parts of the letters; you will do the same below, above the line which closes the bottom of the square to form the feet or serifs as needed: in any case, always start with the diameter and this is the rule you must follow in forming this hand. (*Not shown.*)

Translation by A. S. Osley.

GIOVANNI FRANCESCO CRESCI

1560, ROME — **Essemplare di piu sorti lettere**
A Model of Many Kinds of Letters

AUTHOR

Origins: b. Milan, 1534/35; d. c. 1614.
Activity: Copyist, Scriptor to the Apostolic Library and to the Sistine Chapel, writing master
Age at edition date: 25/26

BOOK

Woodcutter: Francesco Aureri da Crema
Printer: Antonio Blado
Technique: Woodcut and type
Size: 8¾" × 6½"
Audience: Secretaries.
Dedication: Cardinal Carlo Borromeo

Edition Description: Reproduced with the kind permission of The Newberry Library, Chicago, Illinois, Wing ZW 535.C86, 2 fly leaves, 47 pages printed in black. The cover is pastel marbled paper with a green cloth spine; the binding is in very delicate condition. All of the writing instruction is set in type in the first twenty-seven pages. The border decorations are of two different types: Exemplar pages have ruled lines bordered by arabesques, and instructional pages have ruled lines bordered by historiations. The last twelve pages are of Roman capitals in reverse. Most exemplar pages have six- to eight-line quotations demonstrating a style of writing. Others are of alphabets alone. Two exemplars show the stroking order of an alphabet. Most of the pages are signed.

Maiuscole cancel.che

A A A B B C C C D D D
e e E F F E G G I J J K L
L M M M N H H O O
P P P Q Q R R R Q R
S S S S T T T V X Y Z

Cres. scrib.at

Aabbccddeffffgggghhbbillllmmno
oopppggrsssstttuxyzℨ.
ßſßſtſtſhℭtℭpfflflggſbstij.
Aaabbccddefffgggghhiyllllmnnoopp
ppppggrrssssttttuxxyz&.
Joannes Franciscus Crescius Romæ Scribebat.

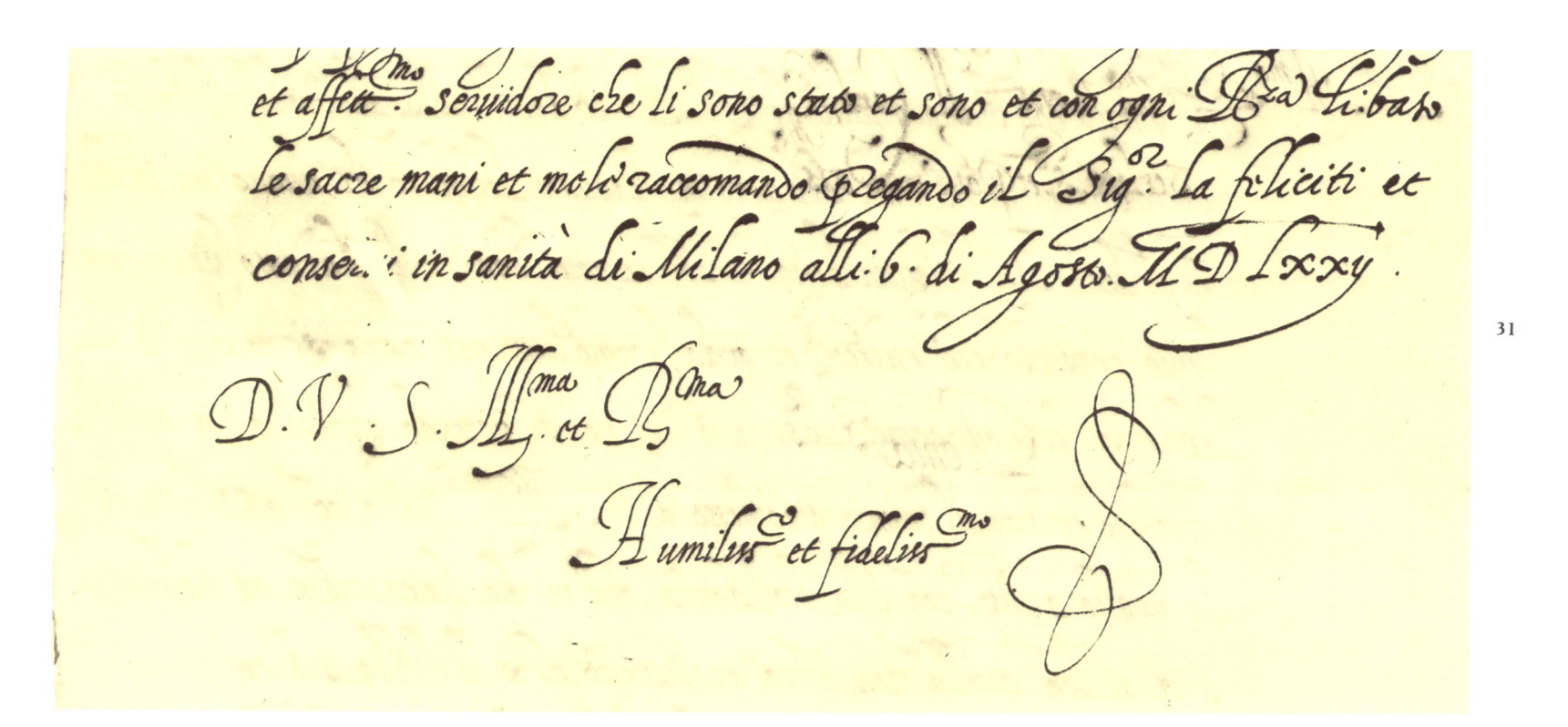

30 A model of many kinds of letters by Master Giovan Francesco Cresci of Milan, Scriptor of the Apostolic Library

In which is displayed the true and new form of cursive chancery script, which he devised himself, and now commonly put into practice by many. With a brief treatise on the ancient Roman capitals, which explains the one rule for forming them according to the art and judgment of the ancients. There is also a description of the practiced experience that a competent writer should have with his pen in regard to aforesaid capitals and other types of letters, newly composed by the aforesaid Author, and published for the common good. In Rome by Antonio Blado at the Author's request MDLX. With a privilege for ten years.
Translation by Dom Julian Stead, recommendations by A. S. Osley.

31 Vat. Lat. 6185,135, *Letter of Gianfrancesco Cresci to Cardinal Guglielmo Sirleto,* 1572.

Reproduced with the kind permission of the Biblioteca Apostolica Vaticana, Rome, Italy.

Signature enlarged from 31. (*Not shown.*)

A good teacher should give a daily lesson to each of his pupils, which should be of medium length, not too long and not too short, but adapted to each according to his abilities. And when his pupil is unable to make an individual letter properly, he should not only repeat orally the construction and shape which that letter should have, but he should write it with his own hand several times in the presence of the pupil. If he is unable by this means to induce the pupil to avoid his error, the master should adopt the following device. With his left hand he should take hold of the right hand of the pupil who is standing by him and receiving the lesson, and make him shape the letter which he does not know how to form; the reason is that the pupil, by feeling the movement of the master's hand, comes to appreciate more readily the details, the subtle points, and the essential shape that this letter, which he is trying to learn, should have. This method is more effective than any other kind of demonstration or instruction which can be employed, not only with beginners, but also with those who have made some progress in the art of writing. (*Not shown.*)
Translation from A. S. Osley's **Scribes and Sources,** *125–6. London: Faber & Faber; Boston: David R. Godine, 1980.*

Translation by A. S. Osley.

P. MORO

FRANCESCO MORO

c. 1560–1570   **Arte Della Strozaria e farsi perfetto stroziero**
The Art of Teaching the Falcon and of becoming a Proficient Falconer

BOOK
Technique: Manuscript
Size: 6″ × 8½″
Dedication: Lorenzo Ridolfi

Description: Reproduced by courtesy of the Trustees of the Victoria and Albert Museum, London, L. 1485–1946, shelf K.R.P.A. 42, 2 fly leaves, 28 vellum pages written on both sides. The original binding in crimson satin cloth over boards is in delicate condition. The book is encased in a green morocco case with the following words tooled in gold on the spine: *P./Artedella/Strozaria/e farsi/Perfetto stroziere.* There is no writing instruction in the manuscript. The text begins with a treatise on hawking and ends with biblical quotations. Individual pages feature a constant and varied assortment of letter forms, sizes, and colors. There is gold on every page and a few have black, green, or red painted backgrounds with gold or silver writing. Letters vary in height from ⅟₃₂″ to ½″. Initial-framed capitals, freely-flourished capitals, and horizontal bars of green, red, or blue embellish the pages.

32 To the most illustrious lord, my lord Lorenzo Ridolfi, ever his most obedient servant, P. Moro. Your Lordship's generosity of heart, my most illustrious Lord, full of courtesy, and your revered conduct, which was always overflowing with honor, penetrated my heart so firmly at the time when I merited to meet your lordly presence, and when you deigned to look at my writings and praise them for my greater glory, that from then on I have always desired and thought of serving you and honoring you with all my strength, although I be of low virtue and little worth. Nonetheless, with a most prompt heart, I have judged that if I cannot serve you in all that I would wish to be able to do: at least I will pay part of that debt which I owe you, for your many merits and illustrious virtues, granting you as much as my low intellect and coarse talent has been able to produce, which will be the present little book made up of that diversity of writings that Your Lordship deigned both to praise and to signify that you would be glad to have them.
May you therefore be pleased to accept it together with my good will: and considering myself highly remunerated by you, your esteemed pleasure will be sufficient reward, with the prestige of your most illustrious name, to which I humbly commend myself and kiss your honorable hand.

Translation by Dom Julian Stead.

Signature reversed from 32.

33 How to give a bird raging hunger. Take the giblets of a hare without the liver, put them in strong vinegar. After they have set well, add a morsel of mare's meat, skin it well, and then give it to the sparrow-hawk to eat. The next day the bird will rage with hunger. If giblets cannot be found, a piece of well beaten bacon will have a similar effect and do him good.

In this instance, my Lord, take spikes of garlic, pierce them in several places, and put them into common oil for three days and three nights. It is a proven fact that if the bird is given one spike of garlic in an empty bag in the evening, it will act as a laxative. (*Excerpt*)

Translation by Dom Julian Stead.

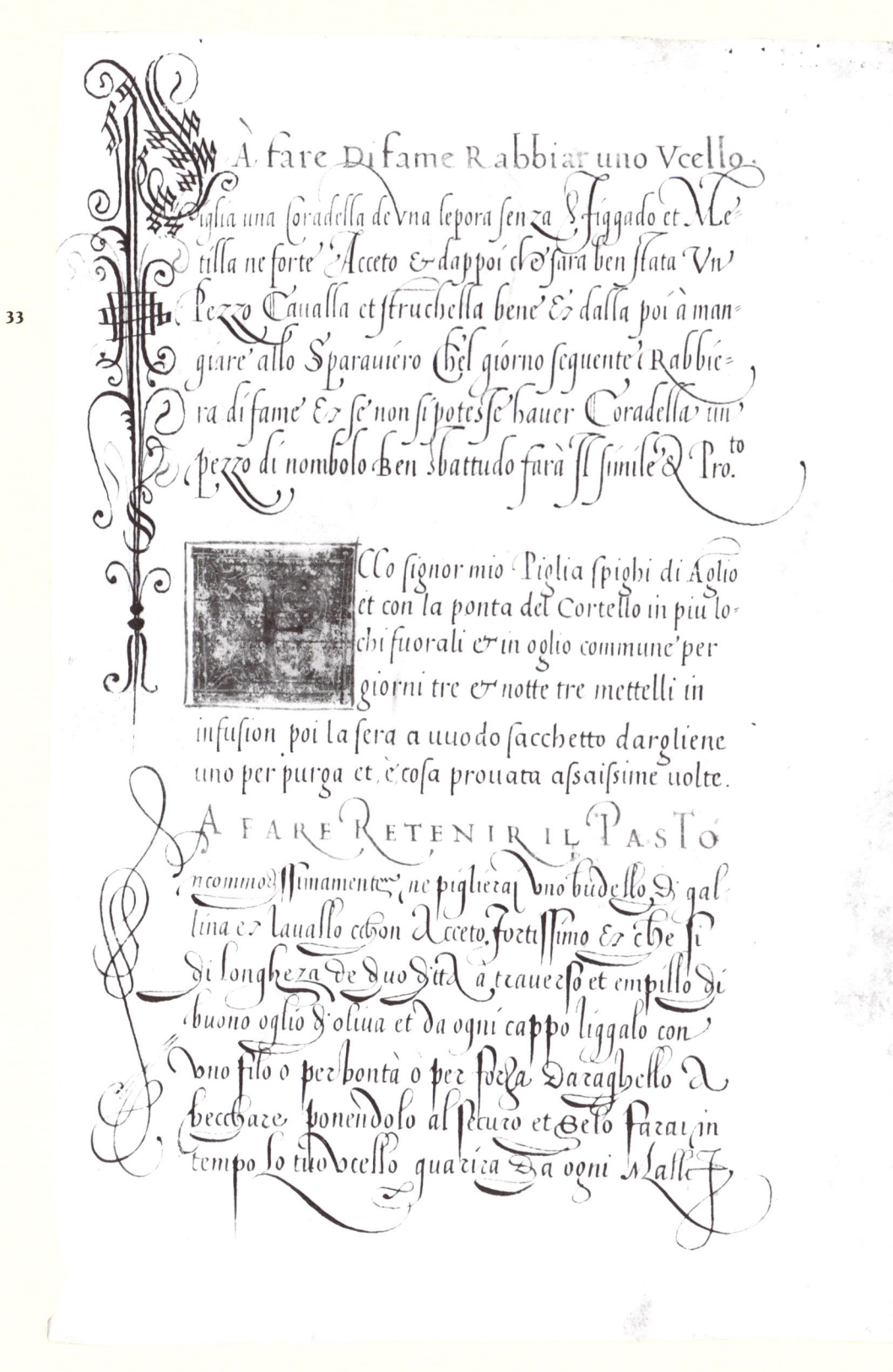

RIMEDIO AL VENENO DELLE SANGUETE

Et quanto tu trouerai. Quando l'ucello si ritroua in qualche loco doue sia aqua et assai sanguette che si attaccano alla persona delli detti sparauieri et gli caua il sangue et gli fauno gran danno et dispiacere se sono in

Acqua morta cioè non sia corrente quella sangueta sié attosicata et è mortale et sono ucelli che si ritrouano musicate dalle ditta et non si ritrouando huomo cosi appresso a darli rimedio lo ucello se l'huomo se ritruoua, a ueder lo ucello con la sanguette attacate ipso fatto piglierai

Una guaibia, ò uero cortello, et pongila sanguetta per mezo acciochè habbia dolore e abbandonerà la impresa poi piglierai questa sangueta, ò uero una altra et mettila

In una lucerna di oglio che sia bellissimo et metti in detta lucerna dui onci uermi et metti a boglire el detto oglio in detta lume et insieme con quelle cose et di quello oglio ongerai la piagha et il core acciochè la mordadura non possi offendere il cuore et bisogna onger una o due uol

TE AL GIORNO ET IN SPATIO
DI TRE GIORNI L'VCELLO
SARA GVARITO ET
QVESTO SECONDO
L'OPPINIONE
DI MICHIEL
GRECO.

34 Into an oil lamp, which holds fine oil, put two ounces of worms and bring both of them to a boil. With this mixture anoint the wound and the heart so that the bite cannot damage the heart. It may be necessary to anoint the wound one or two times a day: but in the space of three days, the bird will be cured. This is according to the opinion of Michiel Greco. (*Excerpt*)

Translation by Dom Julian Stead.

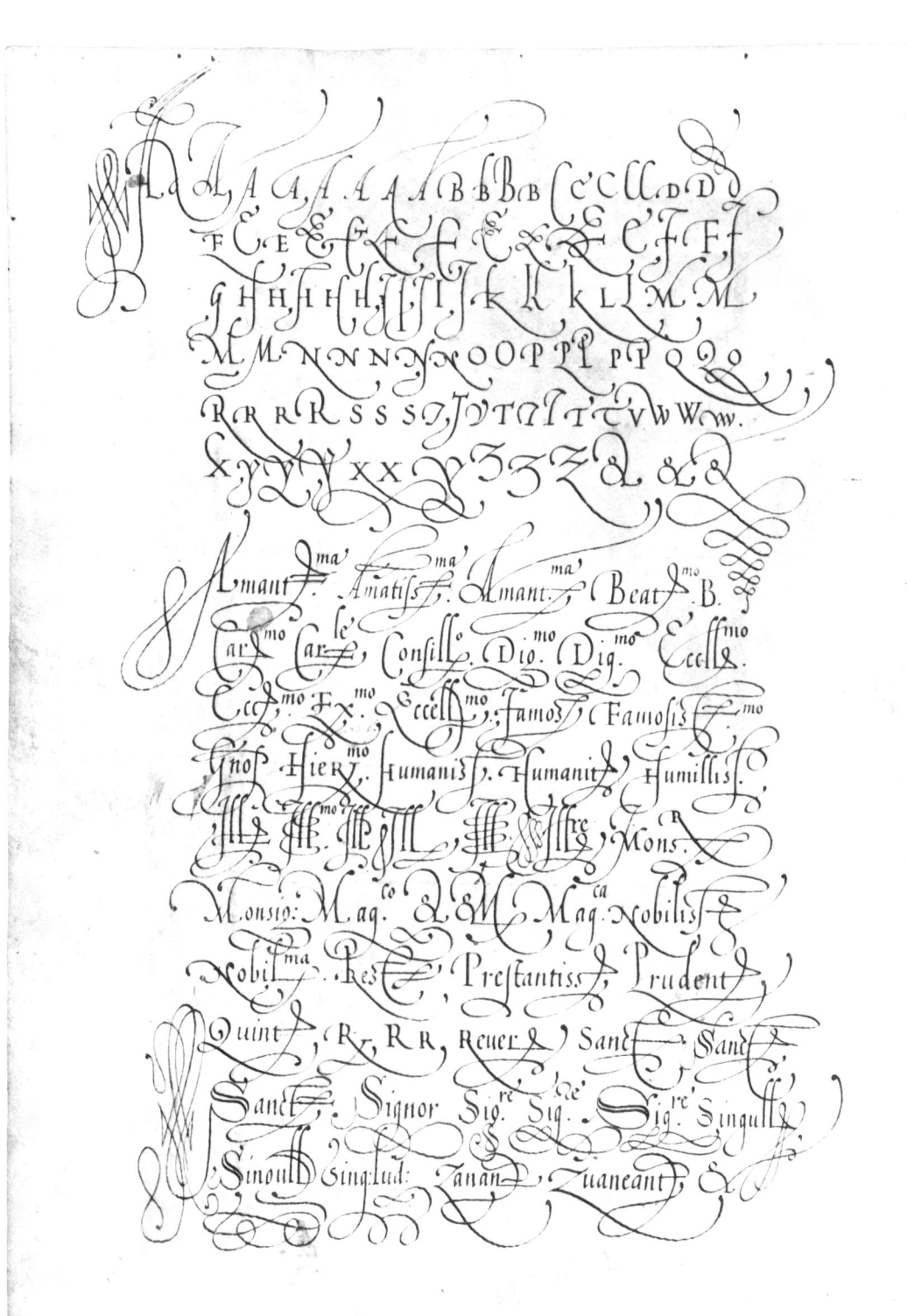

A A A A A A A B B B B C C U D D
E E E E E E E E E E F F f
G H H H H I I I J K K k L M M
M M N N N N O O P P p P Q Q
R R R R S S S S J J T A I I T U W W w
X Y Y V x x Y 3 3 Z Q & Q

Amant.mo Amatiss.ma Amant.ma Beat.mo B.
Car.mo Car.le Consil.o Dig.mo Dig.mo Eccell.mo
Eccell.mo Ex.mo Eccell.mo Famos. Famosis.mo
Ill.mo Hier.mo Humaniss. Humanit. Humillis.
Ill. Ill. Ill.mo Ill. Ill.re Mons.
Monsig: Mag.co Mag. Mag.ca Nobiliss.
Nobil.ma Res. Prestantiss. Prudent.
Quint. R. R R. Reuer.d Sanct. Sanct.
Sanct. Signor Sig.re Sig. Sig.re Sig.re Singull.
Singull. Sing. lud: Zanan. Zuaneant.

DON AVGVSTINO DA SCIENA

AUGUSTINO DA SIENA

1573, VENICE (FIRST EDITION, c. 1565)   **Opera . . . nella quale si insegna a scrivere**
A Work for Teaching How to Write

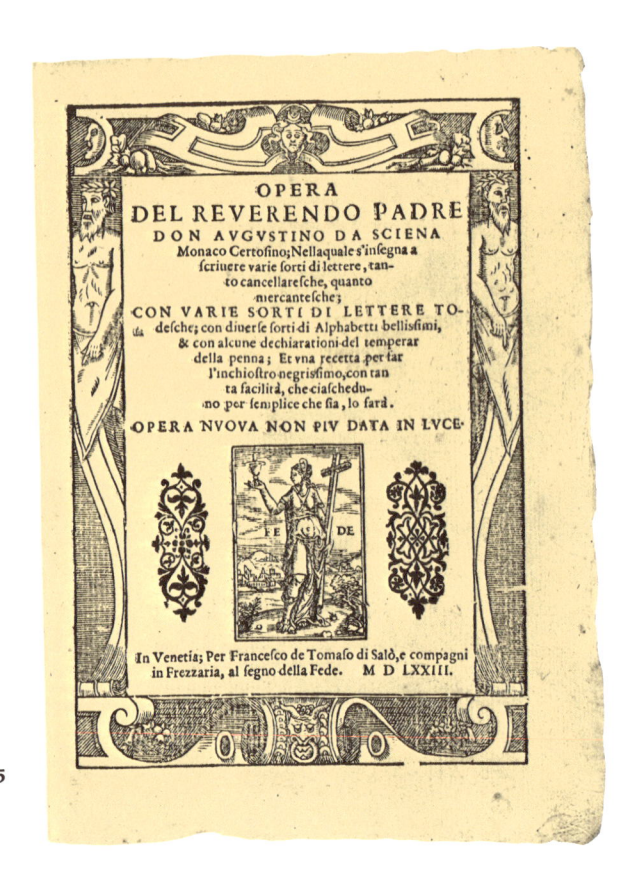

AUTHOR

Activity: Carthusian monk

BOOK

Woodcutter: Francis de Tomaso of Salo

Publisher: Possibly Matteo Pagano

Technique: Woodcut and type

Size: 6¼" × 8½"

Audience: "Gentlemen and young men of good families and those who, because of their parentage, do not occupy so high a position in society, and those of lowly birth."

Edition Description: Reproduced with the kind permission of The Newberry Library, Chicago, Illinois, Wing ZW 535.A923, 3 fly leaves, 36 pages with deckle edges, printed in black. The binding is a marbled paper of blue, green, and beige with brown leather corners and spine.

The entire book is written, with the exception of the first and last pages which are set in type. Half-inch to three-quarter-inch historiated borders dominate all the pages. Many borders show two hands clasped and the word *fides*. Small birds and plants decorate areas close to the text. The page formats include quotations and alphabets with a title to designate the writing style, writing instruction, and demonstrations, and alphabets only.

35 The work of Reverend Father Don Augustine da Siena, Carthusian monk: for teaching how to write various sorts of letters, both chancery and commercial; with various kinds of germanic letters; with divers types of beautiful alphabets, and some explanations of cutting the quill and a prescription for making the blackest ink, with such great ease that anybody, however simple he may be, can do it. A new work not hitherto published. Venice by Francis de Tomaso of Salo, and company in the Frezzaria, at the sign of Faith. MDLXIII
Translation by Dom Julian Stead.

Signature enlarged from 35.

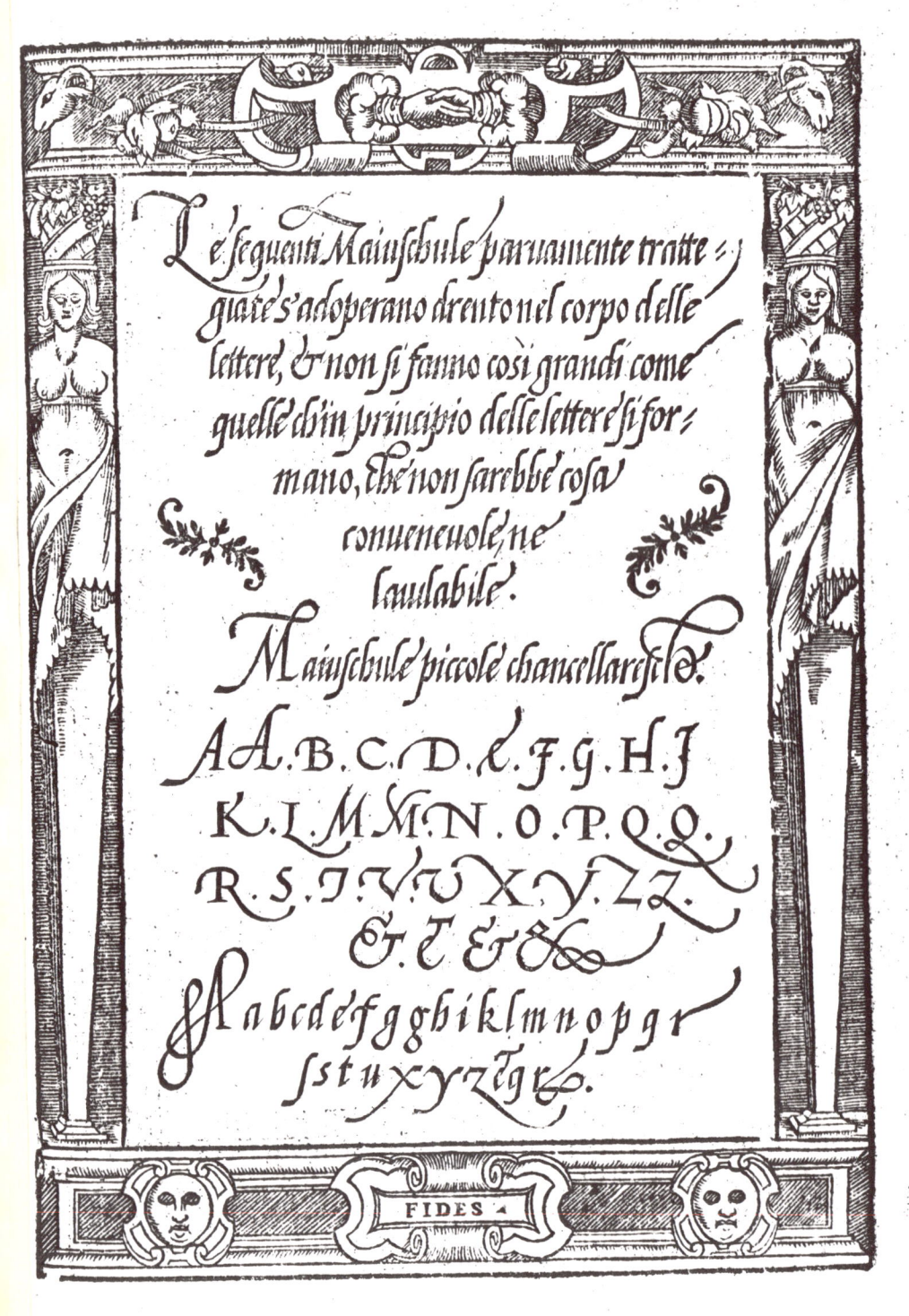

36 The following capitals, lightly flourished are used within the body of a letter, and are not made so large as those formed at the beginning of letters, which would not be the fitting or praiseworthy thing. Small Chancery capitals.

Translation by Dom Julian Stead.

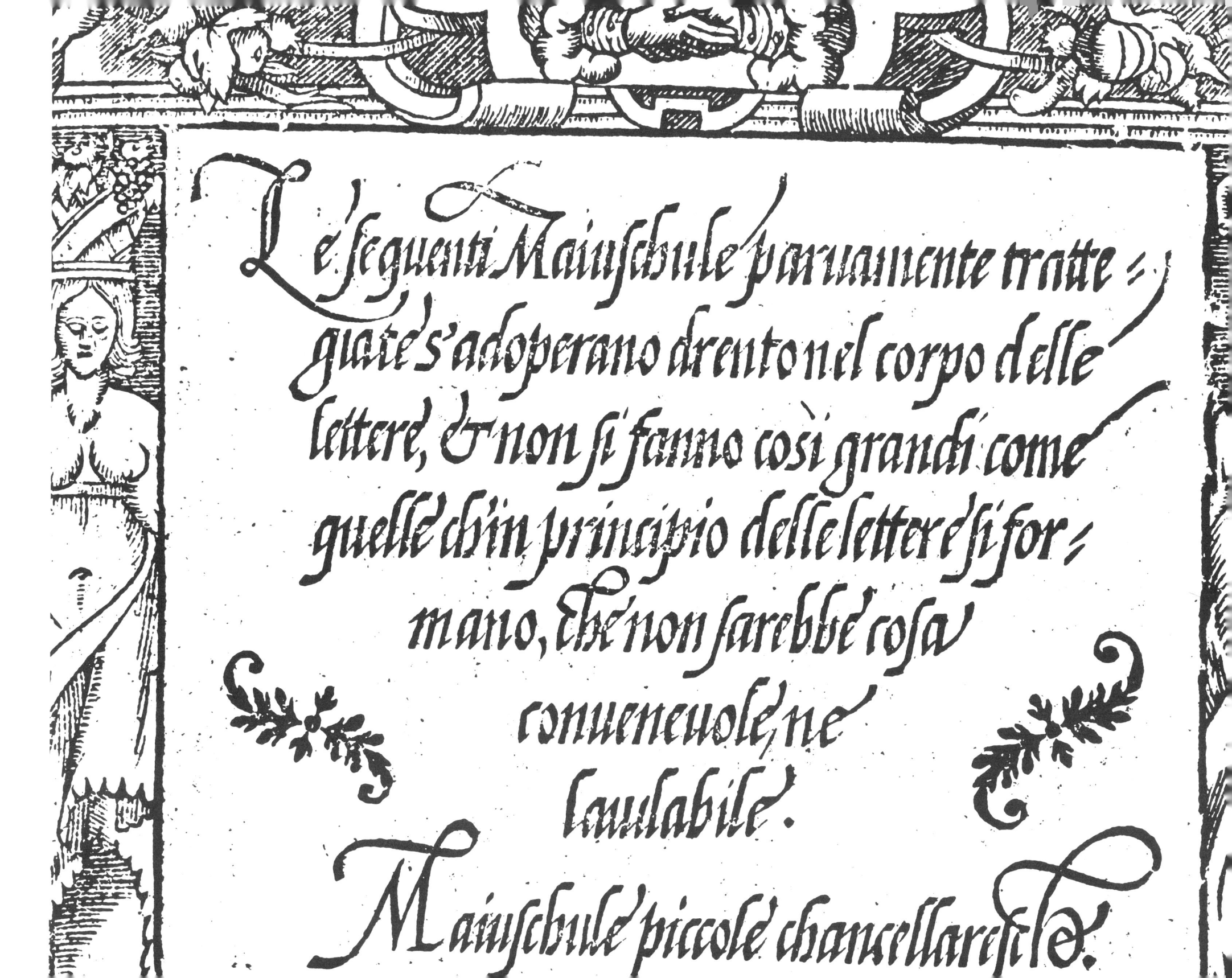

Le seguenti Maiuschule paruamente tratte=
giate s'adoperano drento nel corpo delle
lettere, & non si fanno così grandi come
quelle ch'in principio delle lettere si for=
mano, che non sarebbe cosa
conueneuole, ne
lauulabile.

Maiuschule piccole chancellaresche.

Jaques de La Rue

JACQUES DE LA RUE

c. 1565, PARIS (FIRST EDITION, PARIS, 1565) **Exemplaires de plusieurs sortes de lettres...**
Examples of Several Sorts of Letters

AUTHOR

Activity: Scribe at the University of Paris, schoolmaster

BOOK

Publisher: Claude Micard

Technique: Woodcut

Size: 7 9/16" × 5 1/16"

Audience: Young people.

Dedication: The Duc d'Anjou

Edition Description: Reproduced with the kind permission of The Newberry Library, Chicago, Illinois, Wing ZW 539.L322, 2 fly leaves, 22 pages printed in black. The cover is goatskin parchment. Two editions are bound together: *Exemplaires . . .* , featured here, and *Alphabet de dissemblables sortes de lettres italiques* (not shown), 19 pages. The title page is in red and black. There is no writing instruction in the book. Illustrations include Claude Micard's printing house mark on the title page, nine identical marks on as many pages, and two printing devices on page Fi. Letters range in height from one eighth of an inch to one and three-eighths of an inch. Four pages are in reverse. Page formats include: alphabets, quatrains and alphabets, single line salutations, and three- to four-line quotations with titles.

abcdefghiklmn opqrstvuxyz&.

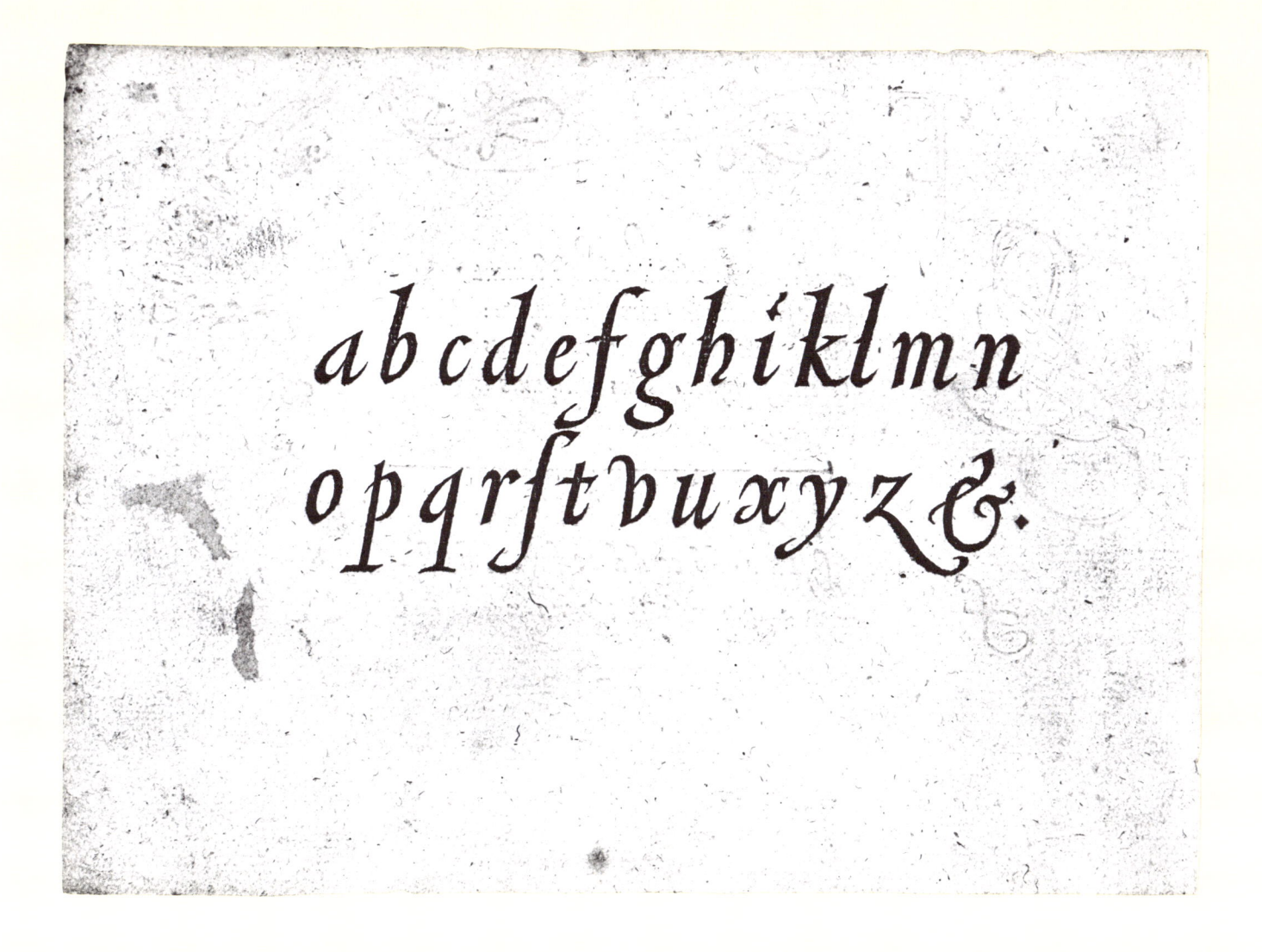

37 Examples of several sorts of letters, by the hand of Jacques de la Rue, teacher of handwriting and arithmetic in Paris at Claude Micard's rue Saint de Latran at the pulpit.
  Translation by Miltiades B. Hatzopoulos.

Signature enlarged from 37.

38 How happy is the rustic shepherd
 Making merry with his fold on the high mountains!
 Neither worry nor rancor enrage him
 Nor any of the passions which are your companions in the big cities.
 Translation by Miltiades B. Hatzopoulos.

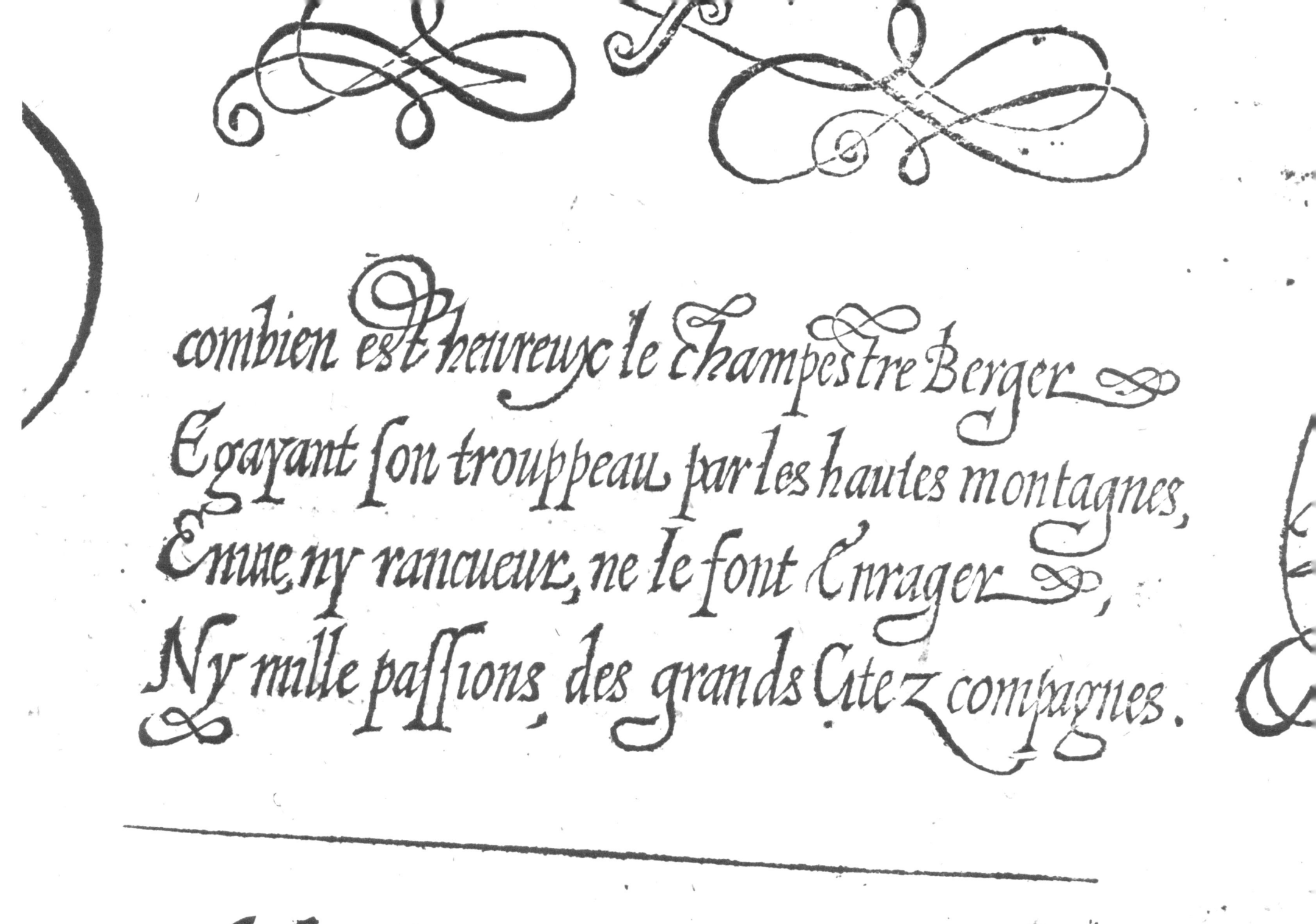

combien est heureux le champestre Berger
Egayant son trouppeau par les hautes montagnes,
Enuie, ny rancueur, ne le font Enrager
Ny mille passions, des grands Citez compagnes.

A B C D E F G H I K L M N
abcdefghiklm

Clementis Perreti

CLÉMENT PERRET

1569, BRUSSELS   **Exercitatio alphabetica nova et utilissima**
New and Practical Exercise in the Alphabet

AUTHOR

Origins: b. 1552

Activity: Scribe, possibly employed in Queen Elizabeth's Chancellery

Age at edition date: In his 18th year

BOOK

Publisher: Probably Christopher Plantin

Engraver: Cornelius de Hooghe engraved the writing

Technique: Copperplate engraving

Size: 12³⁄₈" × 9³⁄₁₆"

Edition Description: Reproduced with the kind permission of The Newberry Library, Chicago, Illinois, Wing ZW f5465.P426, 1 fly leaf, 34 numbered plates printed on one side. The cover and spine are vellum over pasteboards. The words *Clément Perret, 1569* are written in red on the spine. Elaborate cartouche borders of maskes, floral designs, cherubs, and architecture dominate every page. Roman numerals appear on the center of each plate. There is no writing instruction in this edition. Most pages have five-line quotations, an alphabet, embellished capitals, and a final large knot. Plate XXXIIII and the title page are signed on the border by the engraver, Cornelius de Hooghe.

Page reduced.

39 New and practical exercise in the alphabet printed in various languages and characters adorned with rare pictoral and architectural decorations, chiaroscuro and perspectives never published before. Through the industry of Clément Perret of Brussels, who has not yet passed his 18th year. In the year 1569.

Translation by Dom Julian Stead, recommendations by A. S. Osley.

Signature enlarged from 39.

XIX

Rimuoui da te la prauità de la bocca, et la peruersità de la labra
discosta da te Gliocchi tuoi risguardino al dritto, et le palpebre
tue dirizzino auanti à te, Pondera la strada de piedi tuoi, et
co'tutte le vie tue siano stabilite. Non declinare à la dextra,
ne à la senestra, ma rimuoue el piede tuo dal male.

A a.b.c.d.e.f.g.h.i.kl.m.n.o.p.q.r.s.ſ.st.t.u.v.x.y.yz.z.&.

40 XIX. Remove from yourself depravity of speech, and put away perversity from your lips. Let your eyes look straight and your eyelids be fixed in front of you. Weigh the path of your feet, and let all your ways be established. Do not turn away to the right, nor to the left, but remove your foot from evil. (*Page reduced.*)
Translation by Dom Julian Stead.

41 MS. Pembroke 113, Ortelius: *Album Amicorum*, 1596.
Reproduced with the kind permission of the Masters and Fellows of Pembroke College, Cambridge, England.

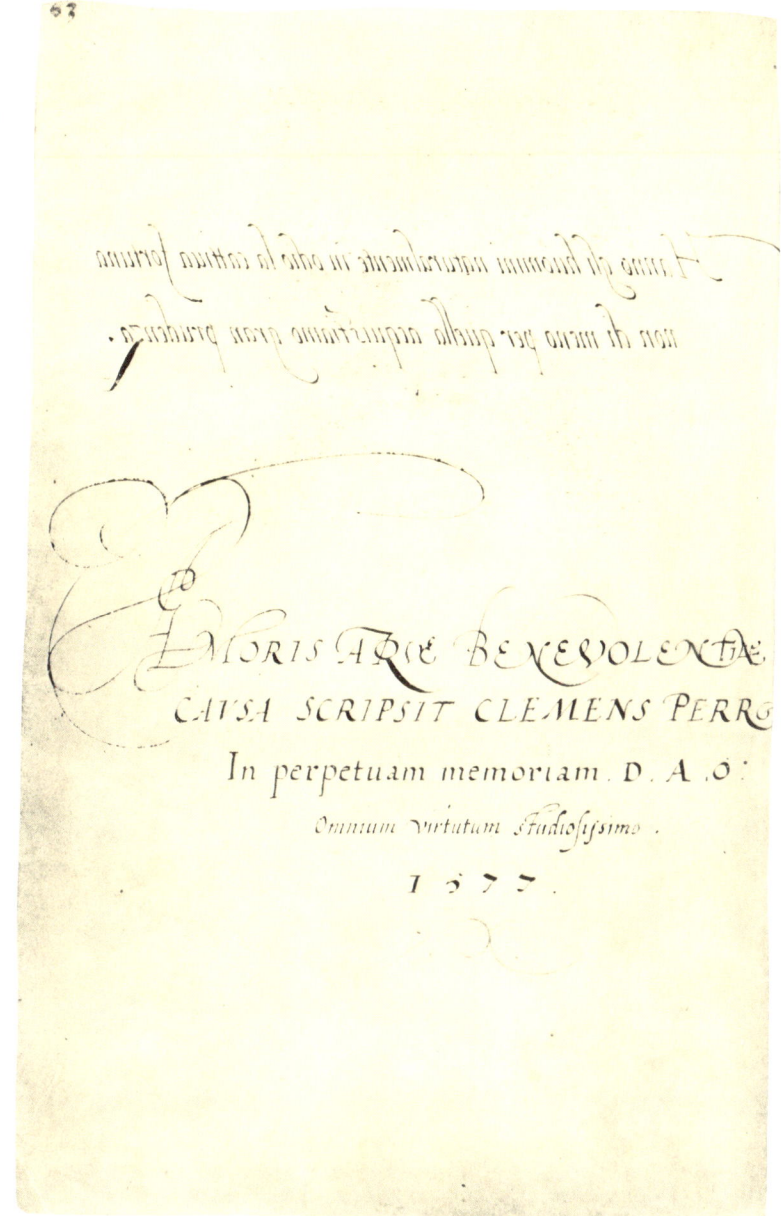

Fran.co Lucas

FRANCESCO LUCAS

1580, MADRID (FIRST EDITION, TOLEDO, 1571)

Arte de Escrevir
The Art of Writing

AUTHOR

Origins: b. 1530s, Seville

Activity: Writing master in Seville, opened a writing-school in Madrid, (probably) tutor to Prince Don Fernando, resident in the court of His Majesty Philip II of Spain

Age at edition date: In his 40s

BOOK

Printer: Francesco Sanchez

Technique: Woodcut and type

Size: 5⅜" × 7¹³⁄₁₆"

Dedication: Philip II of Spain

Edition Description: Reproduced with the kind permission of The Newberry Library, Chicago, Illinois, Wing ZW 540.L96, 1 fly leaf, 59 pages of text, 59 pages of exemplars printed in black. The cover is black Spanish leather with a gilt-tooled border and *Biblioteca de Salva* stamped in the center. The words on the spine read, *Lucas/Arte de Escribir/1580*. The writing instruction is set in type thoughout the book. Borders appear on all the exemplars either as ruled lines or as elaborate historiations. Many pages are reverse. All the pages are signed and many are dated. Individual letters vary in height from ⅛" to 1".

42 The Art of Writing of Francesco Lucas, divided into four parts. Included in this latest edition are certain previously unprinted plates, corrected and amended by the author himself. Dedicated to the Christian Royal Majesty of King Philip II, Our Lord. Printed under privilege in Madrid in the House of Francesco Sanchez, Printer, Year 1580.

Translation by James Teixeira, recommendations by A. S. Osley.

Signature enlarged and reversed from 43.

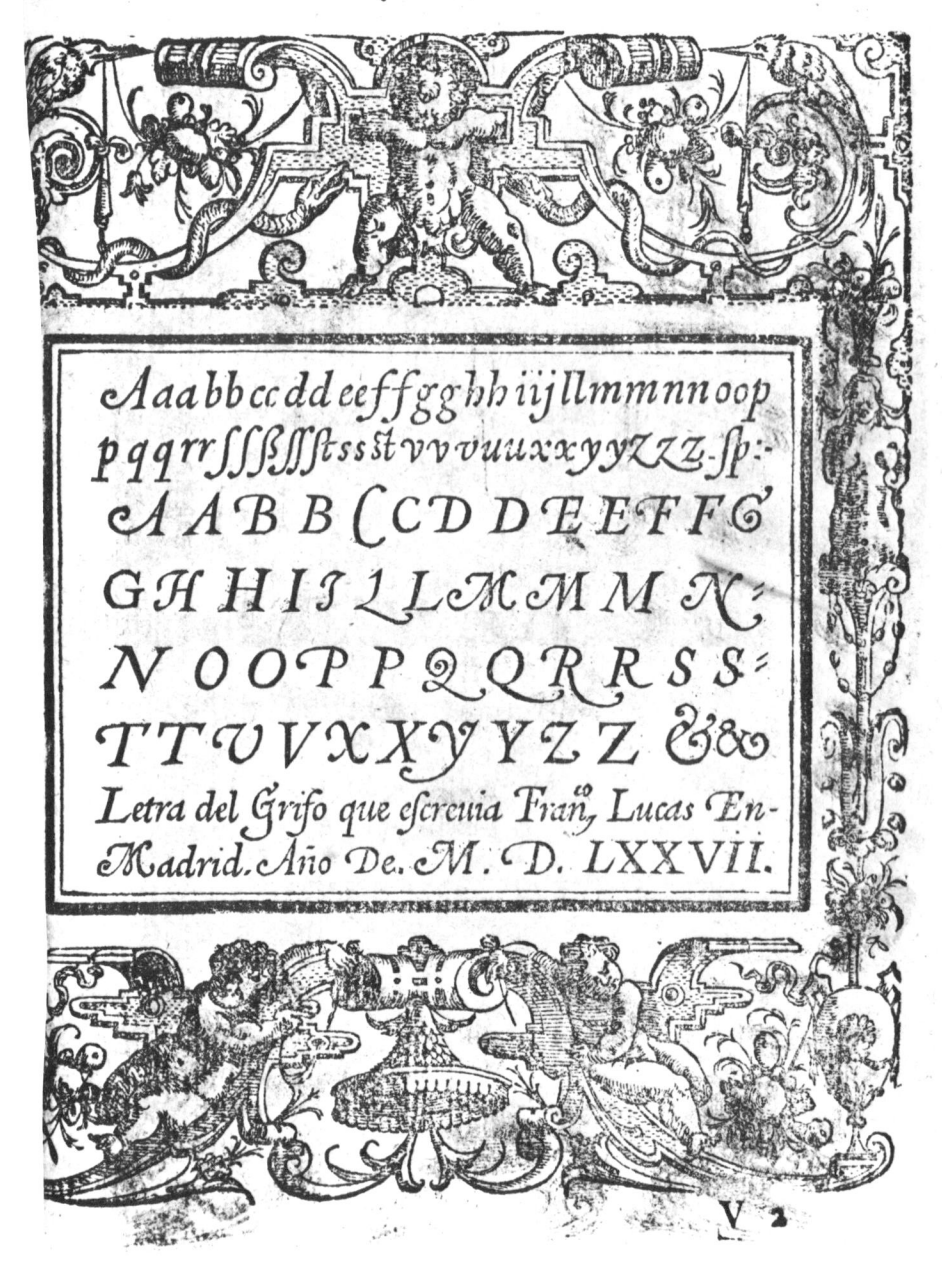

And the master who writes in such a way (especially if he has mastered all the letters) should rightfully be esteemed. It is a pity that when one reaches this point, which costs him the better part of his life, that he is hardly differentiated from those who never knew how to write or even made any effort to know how. For this reason there are fewer scribes who want to strive to become skilled writers and they are partly right, because although it is a very necessary skill, it is one of those that brings least honor and profit among the various crafts and arts that there are in the world, as experience clearly demonstrates. As for my part, I hold that one of the principal causes of this is that the art is little favored among princes and lords who, as they are not in need of writing well, neither learn this skill from masters nor care much that there should be good scribes who would teach it. And I believe it is certain that, if they did, there would exist in Spain more and better scribes than elsewhere in the world, for with all this lack of favor there are many who write with excellence. (*Not shown.*)

Translation by James Teixeira. Text from the Preface of *Arte de Escrevir*.

Aa bb cc dd ee ff gg hh ij ll mm
p qq rr ſſ ſſ ſſ ſt ss st t vv vu xx yy zz

A A B B C C D D E F
G H H I J L L M M M M
N O O P P Q Q R R S
T T U X X Y Y Z Z

Letra del Grifo que escreuia Fran.co Luca

Johann Neudörffer

JOHANN NEUDÖRFFER THE YOUNGER*

1578, NÜRNBERG **Kurtze Fürweisung**
A Brief Display

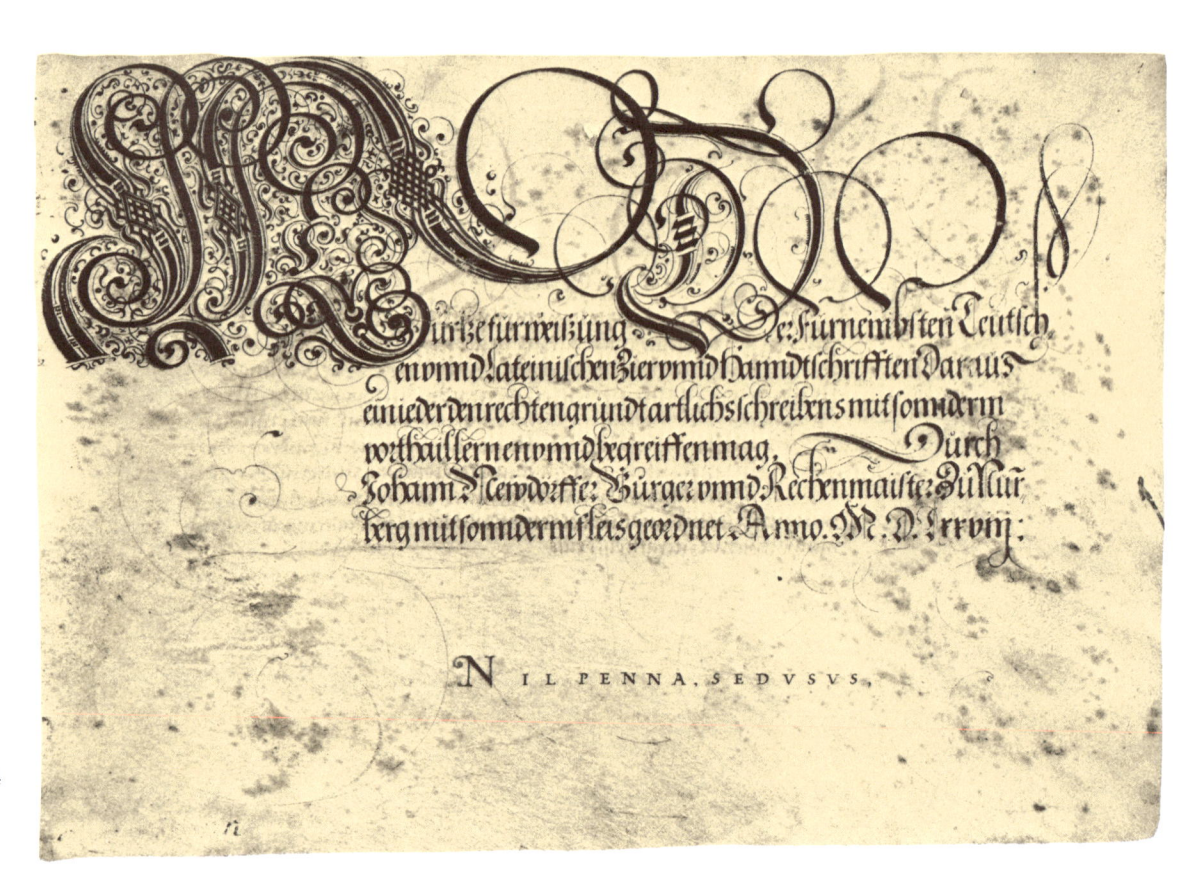

AUTHOR

Origins: b. Nürnberg, 1543; d. Nürnberg, 1581.
Activity: Printer, writing master
Age at time of the MS: 35
Technique: Manuscript
Size: 9" × 6¼"
Audience: "Everyone."

Description: Reproduced with the kind permission of The Newberry Library, Chicago, Illinois, Wing ZW 547.N391, 15 vellum leaves written in brown and gold on both sides. The cover is vellum over boards with *Johann Newdorffer Kurtze Furweisung* written in black in the center and on the spine. This is clearly the most elegant manuscript book in this series. It is beautifully written and designed. There is no writing instruction. Each page follows the same format with an embellished initial letter, seven- to ten-line quotations, and decoration in the form of loose flourishing or two horizontal lines filled with gold. All the pages are written in brown with gold embellishments.

*The title page gives no indication that this is the MS of Johann Neudörffer the Younger. However, Johann Neudörffer the Elder died in 1563, and the date of *Kurtze Fürweisung* is 1578.

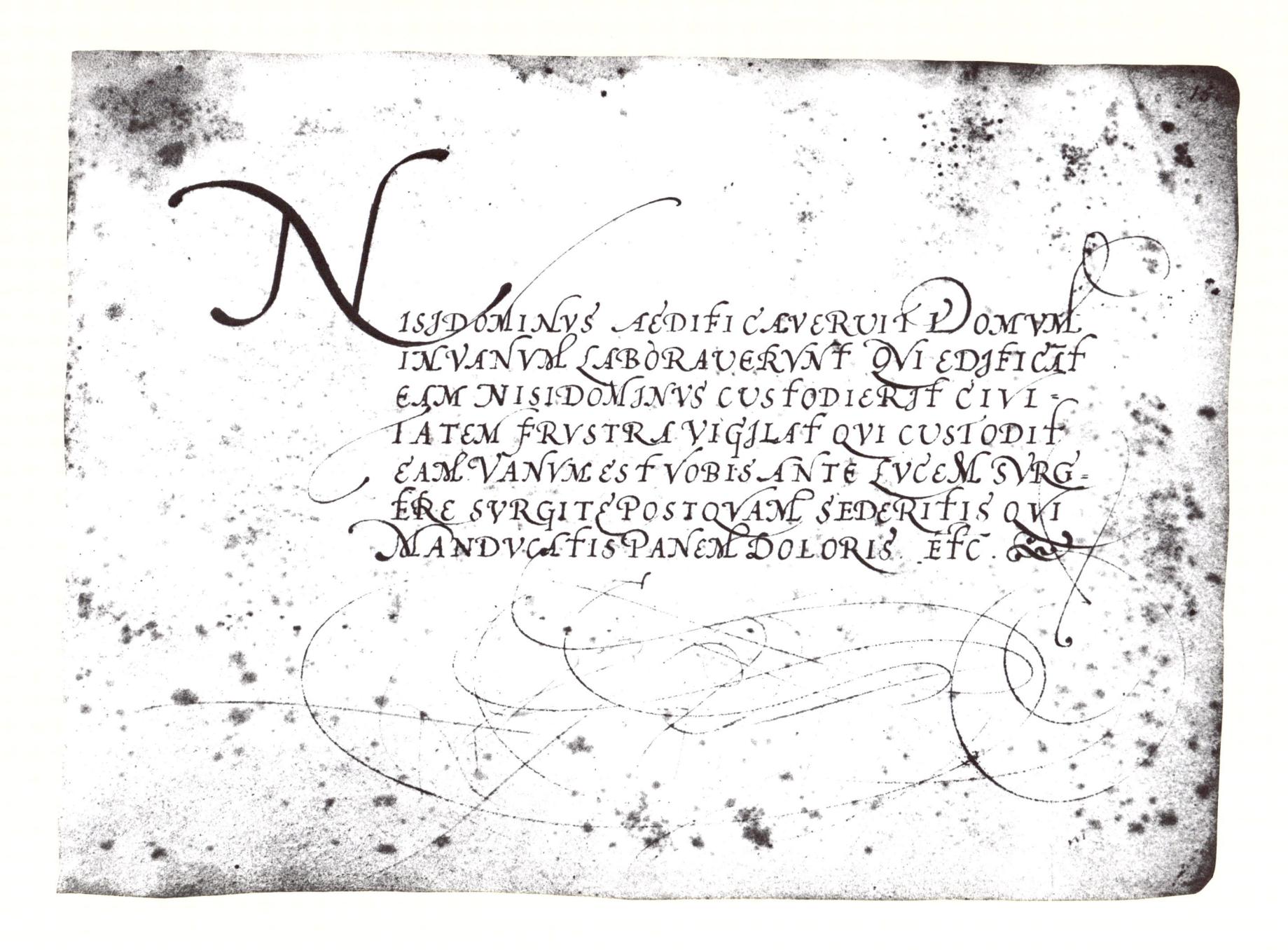

44 A brief display of the most important German and Latin decorative and writing hands from which everyone, with special benefit, may learn and understand the correct basis for writing well. Arranged with special diligence by Johann Neudörffer, citizen and arithmetic teacher of Nürnberg. In the year 1578. Not the pen, but the practice.

Translation by Alexander Nesbitt.

Signature enlarged from 44.

45 In thee, O Lord, do I put my trust, let me never be put to confusion. Deliver me in thy righteousness, and cause me to escape: incline thine ear unto me, and save me. Be thou strong habitation, whereunto I may continually resort: thou hast given commandment to save me, for thou art my rock, and my fortress. Deliver me, O my God, out of the hand of the wicked, out of the hand of the unrighteous, and cruel man. For thou art my hope, O Lord God: thou art my trust from my youth. By thee have I been holden up from the womb: thou art He that took me out of my mother's bowels, my praise shall be continually of thee. I am as a wonder to many, *etc.* (Psalm 70:1–7)

Translation by Dom Julian Stead.

on confundar in eternum, in iustucia tua libe
aurem tuam, & salua me Esto mihi in De
um, Vt saluum me facias. Quoniam firmam
nes tu. Deus meus eripe me de manu peccat
tis et iniqui. Quoniam tu es patientia mea D
te mea. In te confirmatus sum ex Vtero,
r meus In te cantatio mea semper, tanq prod

De Andres Brun

ANDRES BRUN

1583 & 1612, SARAGOSSA

Arte muy provechosa para aprender de escrivir perfectamente
A Very Beneficial Art for Learning to Write Perfectly

AUTHOR
Origins: b. Saragossa, 1552; d. 1612.
Activity: Writing master, engraver, nobleman
Age at edition dates: 31 and 60
BOOK
Publisher: Jean de Larumbe
Woodcutter: Andres Brun
Technique: Woodcut and type
Size: 8 11/16" × 12"
Audience: Young people and others who do not wish to go to a writing master.

Edition Description: Reproduced with the kind permission of Kunstbibliothek Berlin with Museum of Architecture, Fashion, and Graphic Design of the state museum, C31M15.TP.8470248, 2 fly leaves, 10 pages printed in red and black on both sides. This is a collection of existing pages, not a complete book. The binding is of black leather with delicate gold tooling on edges of cover and back border. The spine also has gold inlay decoration and the words, *Maestro Andres Brun, 1583.* The endpapers are a marbled paper with a deep red background and swirled accents of blue, green, gold, and white. Written on the endpapers is the following statement: "To Stanley Morison with kindest regards from Maggs B., Nov. 1927. Transferred to the British Museum. SM March 1928." These ten leaves are in delicate condition with tears, writing, and uneven printing on almost every page. The majority of the pages are reverse red on beige and include multiple woodblock sections. All writing instruction is given in type in the opening pages of the book. At least fourteen pages are signed. Exemplar formats include liners for writing, alphabets for tracing with stroking sequences, alphabets, writing exercises and quotations. All the pages have borders; some are framed by ruled lines while others have wide borders with foliated designs.

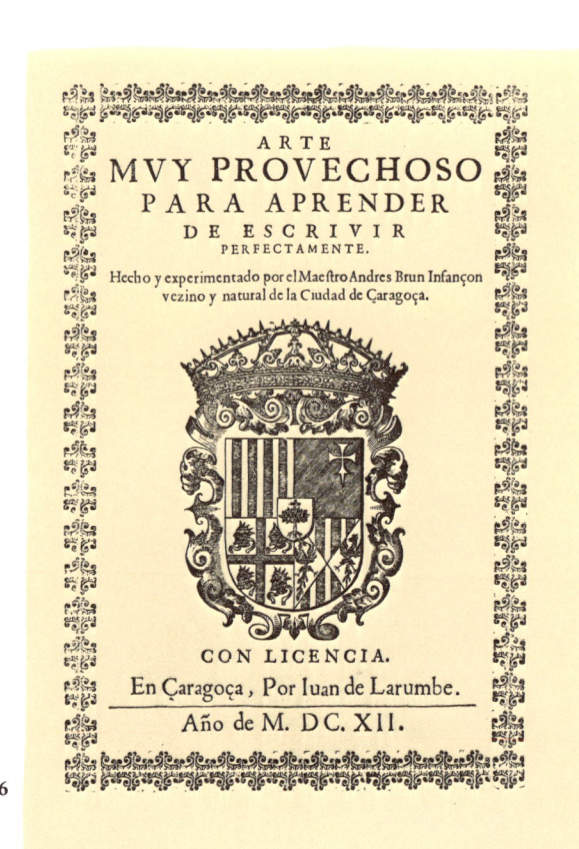

47

Page reduced.

The photographs shown on these pages were reproduced in *Andres Brun, Calligrapher of Saragossa, Some Account of His Life and Work,* published in 1929 by Pegasus Press in Paris, and are the property of the Kunstbibliothek in Berlin. I did not see the original leaves in Berlin. However, I did see ten leaves in the collection of the British Library, one of which is reproduced here as #48.

46 The Very Beneficial Art of Learning how to Write Perfectly, composed and tested by Master Andres Brun, nobleman, resident and native of the City of Saragossa. Published under authority in Saragossa by Jean de Larumbe in the year 1612.
 Translation by A. S. Osley and Douglas Fenner.

Signature reversed from 47.

... I am accustomed to teaching handwriting with large letters because they are more useful at the outset; and all the other masters who teach well-made letters follow the same practice. For this reason, I have made one alphabet in a large size, in which you have the beginnings, middle portions, and endings of all the letters, and other models to be practiced; these are in the two styles now in common use throughout our land of Spain: namely, the redonda and the bastarda, so that anyone can choose whichever he prefers. The background of the paper is colored and the letter consists of that part of the paper which has been left white, with the idea that you should make each letter by covering the white space with ink. It is necessary to fill in the white part of the letter completely, without however making corrections; in completing the large alphabet, you will have the letters which are made in one stroke *a b c e g h i l m n o q r s u v y z*, and those which must be made in two *d p t x*. By practicing on these sheets in the given order, you can learn to write and develop a nicely shaped letter.

    Translation from A. S. Osley's *Scribes and Sources,* 182. London: Faber
       & Faber; Boston: David R. Godine, 1980. (*Not shown.*)
    Translation by A. S. Osley.

48 C31m15.TP.8470248. Reproduced with the kind permission of the British Library, London.

48

El Maestro Andres Bruny menestril de Caragoça, lo escriuia y cortaua, en el Año de, 1583.

Judoco Hondio

JODOCUS HONDIUS

1594/95, AMSTERDAM

Theatrum artis scribendi
Theatre of the Art of Writing

AUTHOR

Origins: b. Flanders, 1563; d. 1611.

Activity: Punch-cutter, engraver, writing master, cartographer, map publisher

Age at edition date: 31

BOOK

Engraver: Jodocus Hondius

Technique: Copperplate engraving

Size: 12½″ × 9⅛″

Audience: Children and young students.

Edition Description: Reproduced with the kind permission of The Newberry Library, Chicago, Illinois, Wing ZW 4546.H755, 42 plates printed on one side in black. The cover is marbled paper over board with a vellum spine. The words *I. Hondii, Theatrum Artis Scribendi, 1594* are written in black on the spine. This is an anthology featuring the writing of Solomon Henrix, van den Velde, Felix Van Sambix, Curione, M. Martin, Beauchesne, Houthusius, P. Goos, Jacomina Hondius, and Peter Bales. All the plates are signed. The writing instruction is set in type and appears on the first four pages. Elaborate historiated borders dominate each plate. Although the pages were written by different scribes, they follow the same format. Each page begins with a title showing a particular style of writing followed by a four- to five-line quotation and ending with an alphabet and the scribe's signature.

49 Theatre of the Art of Writing containing a variety of examples by the greatest craftsmen of our time, engraved in nine different languages. Jodocus Hondius was the engraver.
   Translation by Dom Julian Stead.

Signature enlarged from 49.

50 Old Formal Italic. Blessed are they which are presecuted for righteousness' sake; for theirs is the kingdom of heaven. Blessed are ye, when men shall revile you, and persecute you and shall say all manner of evil against you falsely for my sake. Rejoice and be exceeding glad: for great is your reward in heaven, *etc.* Hondius wrote this. *(Page reduced.)*
   Translation by Dom Julian Stead.

Alphabetum Capitalium Curs:

A A A B B B B C D D D E E F
F G G G H H I I I K K K L L L
M M M M M N N N O O P P P
P O Q R R R R S S S T T T T
V V V W X X X Y Y Y Z Z Z

Sequuntur Capitales litteræ unico ductu scribendæ
A B C D E F G H I K L M N O P Q R S T V X Y

Hondius scrip.

A A A B B B C D
F F G G G H H H I I I K
M M M M M N N N
P Q Q Q R R R S S S
V V V V W W X X X Y

Sequuntur Capitales litteræ unius d...
A B C D E F G H I K L M N O P Q

JEAN DE BEAUCHESNE

c. 1610, ENGLAND **Gift to Princess Elizabeth I**
(untitled)

AUTHOR

Origins: b. Paris c. 1538; d. Black Friars, 1620.

Activity: Author, writing master to Princess Elizabeth and Prince Charles of England

Age at time of the MS: 72½

BOOK

Technique: Manuscript

Size: 6½″ × 4⅞″

Dedication: Princess Elizabeth, daughter of James I, England

Description: Reproduced with the kind permission of The Newberry Library, Chicago, Illinois, Wing ZW ZIV 639 B382, 3 fly leaves, 28 leaves written on one side; 14 leaves are written on vellum, the other 14 leaves are written on paper. The binding is blind-stamped calves' leather with gilt fillers. This untitled manuscript is signed by Jean de Beauchesne. It is undated, but Beauchesne states that he is seventy-two and a half years old. With the exception of the dedication, each page has five to six lines of text. The writing is all cursive and varies in height from ⅛″ to ¼″. The text is written in black ink and the initial letters are in gold. Fine red lines frame each text and extend to the edge of each page. Lovely, loose knots ornament the margins.

A Madame **E**lizabeth, fille vnique du **R**oy de la grand **B**retaigne.

L'honneur qui se doit rendre aux merites des grands
Donnent mille proiects a vn gentil courage,
Pour se manifester par vn beau tesmoignage,
De ce qu'il a compris dans les arts florissans.
Le zele que ie dois aux effects paroissans
Des vertus qui vous font vn Phœnix de vostre aage,
Me pousse a vous offrir ce mien petit ouurage,
Tesmoin de l'exercice ou i'ay passé mes ans.
Receuez d'vn bon œil PRINCESSE, ie vous prie,
L'ouurage & l'ouurier de qui le cœur n'oublie
Les tres-humbles respects qui par luy vous son deus :
A vous donc il consacre & sa main & sa plume
Sans la plume les noms des Princes ne sont leus,
Et le temps rauissant dans l'oubly les consume.

51 Final leaf.

Signature enlarged from 51.

52 To Madam Elizabeth, only daughter of the King of Great Britain. The honor which is due to the merits of the princess inspires a thousand projects to a noble heart, to manifest itself in a beautiful token of what it has learned in the flourishing arts. The affection that I owe to the manifest effects of the virtues that make you a Phoenix of your times incites me to offer you this little work of mind, evidence of the efforts in which I have spent my years. Accept favorably, Princess, I pray you, the work and the worker whose heart forgets not the very humble respects which he owes to you: to you then he devotes both the hand and the pen; without the pen the names of the Princes are not read and time, sweeping them away, consumes them in oblivion.

Translation by Miltiades B. Hatzopoulos.

53 Comme il n'y a point de vuide en nature, non plus y en a il es choses spirituelles; chaque vaisseau est plein, sinon de liqueur, aumoins d'air: ainsi en est il du cœur de l'homme, quoy que par nature vuide de grace, tousiours plein d'hipocrisie & d'iniquité, mais qui se remplit de grace a mesure qu'il se vuide de ses mauuaises humeurs; comme en vn vase autant qu'il y entre d'eau, autant d'air il en sort: mais le cœur de l'homme est vn &c.

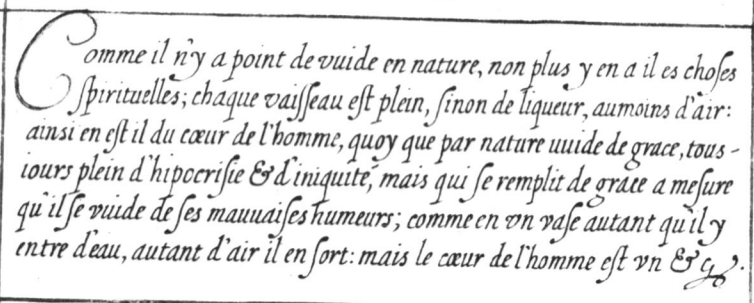

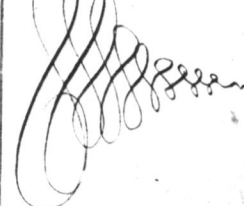

53 As there is no vacuum in nature, there is none in things spiritual; each vessel is full, if not of a liquid, at least of air. It is the same with the heart of man: although by nature empty of grace, always full of hypocrisy and iniquity, it is filled with grace as fast as it is emptied of its bad humors; as with a vase, as much water goes in so much air goes out; but the heart of man is an, *etc*.

Translation by Miltiades B. Hatzopoulos.

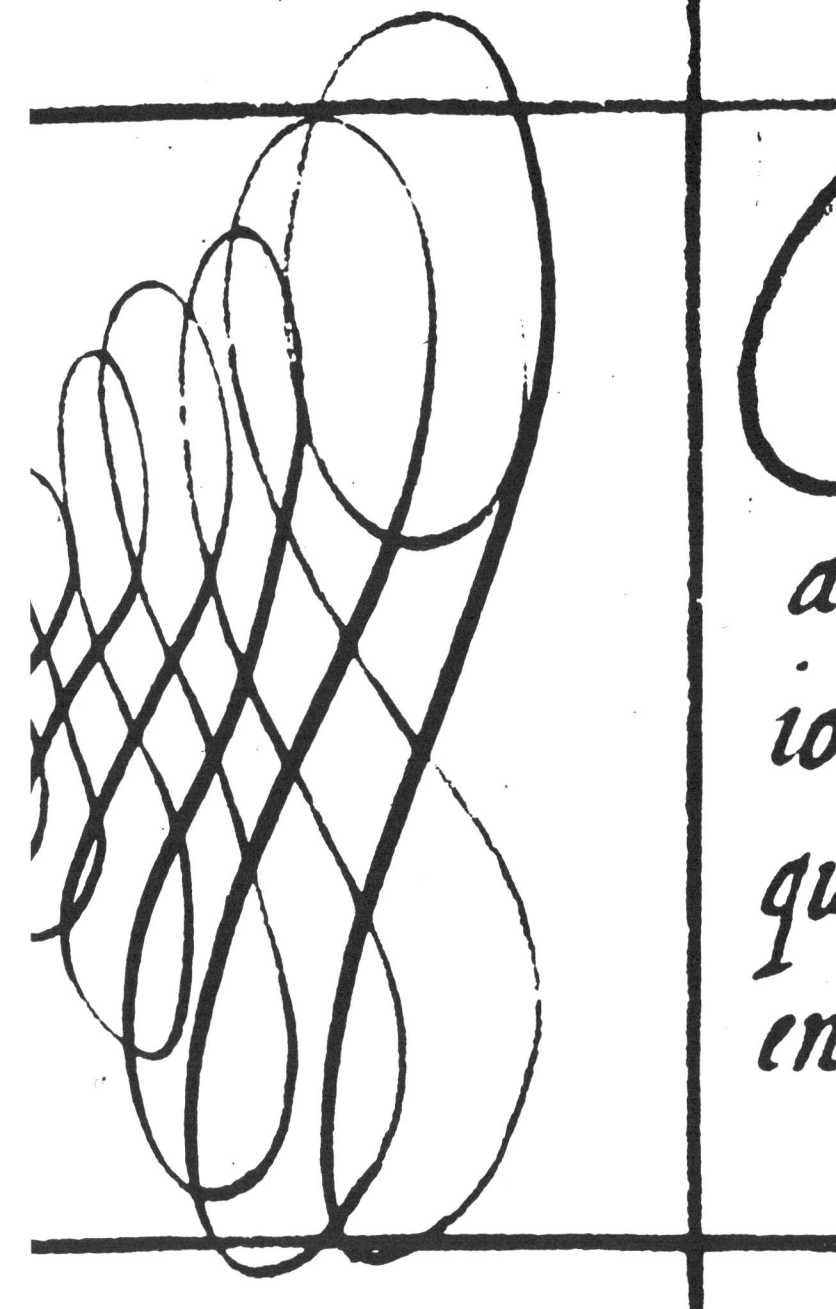

Comme il n'y a point de vuide
spirituelles; chaque vaisseau est
ainsi en est il du cœur de l'homme, qu
iours plein d'hipocrisie & d'iniquité,
qu'il se vuide de ses mauuaises humeu
entre d'eau, autant d'air il en sort: m

LETTER STUDY

Letter Study is a continuation of *Primary Sources* with an emphasis on individual letters rather than on individual pages and translations. It is a collection of italic majuscule and minuscule from the exemplars in *Primary Sources*. They are arranged in alphabetical and chronological order. No attempt has been made to show them to size. Every letter has been enlarged by different percentages according to the needs of individual and facing pages. Some letters have suffered distortions in the enlargement process, while others have improved considerably. The exact shape of every letter has been retained, but all extraneous woodcut chips and inkblots inside and around the letters have been painted out.

    Woodcut and manuscript letters are shown, as well as an assortment of italic variations. All letters are identified with the scribe's name near the letter. All letters are identified according to source by the following code. If the letter has: *No mark*, it is a woodcut or a manuscript featured in *Primary Sources*; *Number + WC*, it is a woodcut shown in part or not at all; *Number + MS*, it is a manuscript shown in part or not at all. In this manner all letters are identified according to scribe, date, library, and library number.

2MS	Arrighi, 11.A.19, signature: XV D 6, Universiteits-Bibliotheek, Amsterdam.
3MS	Tagliente, *Consiglio di X,* Misti, filza 5, carta 127, Archivio di Stato, Venezia.
4MS	Palatino, MS. Canon. Ital. 196, Bodleian Library, Oxford.
5MS	Mercator, MS. Pembroke 113, Pembroke College, Cambridge.
7MS	Amphiareo, MS. Typ 13, The Houghton Library, Cambridge, Massachusetts.
7WC	Amphiareo, Wing zw 535.v63, The Newberry Library, Chicago.
12AMS	Ruano, Vat.Lat.3841,80v, Biblioteca Apostolica Vaticana, Rome.
12BMS	Ruano, Vat.Lat.317,258v, Biblioteca Apostolica Vaticana, Rome.
13AMS	Cresci, Vat.Lat.569, Biblioteca Apostolica Vaticana, Rome.
13BMS	Cresci, Vat.Lat.6185,135, Biblioteca Apostolica Vaticana, Rome.
16WC	de la Rue, 1267a24(1) f8r 8470248, The British Library, London.
17MS	Perret, MS. Pembroke 113, Pembroke College, Cambridge.
22MS	Beauchesne, MS.FR.e.1. 5r, Bodleian Library, Oxford.
22WC	Beauchesne, Don.e.379. Bodleian Library, Oxford.

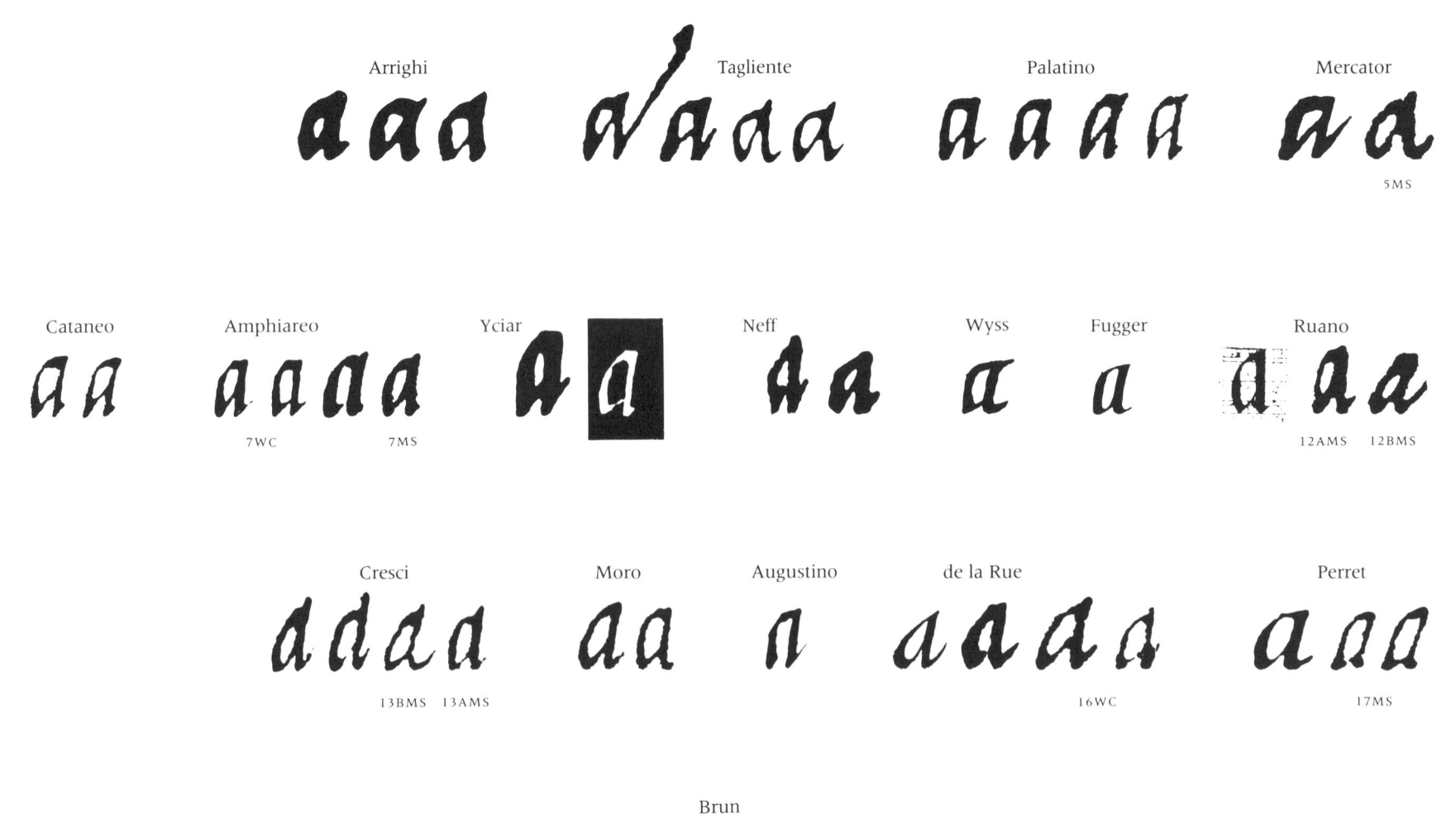

Arrighi	Tagliente	Palatino	Mercator

Cataneo	Amphiareo	Yciar	Neff	Wyss	Fugger	Ruano

Cresci	Moro	Augustino	de la Rue	Perret

		Brun		
Lucas	Neudörffer		Hondius	Beauchesne

105

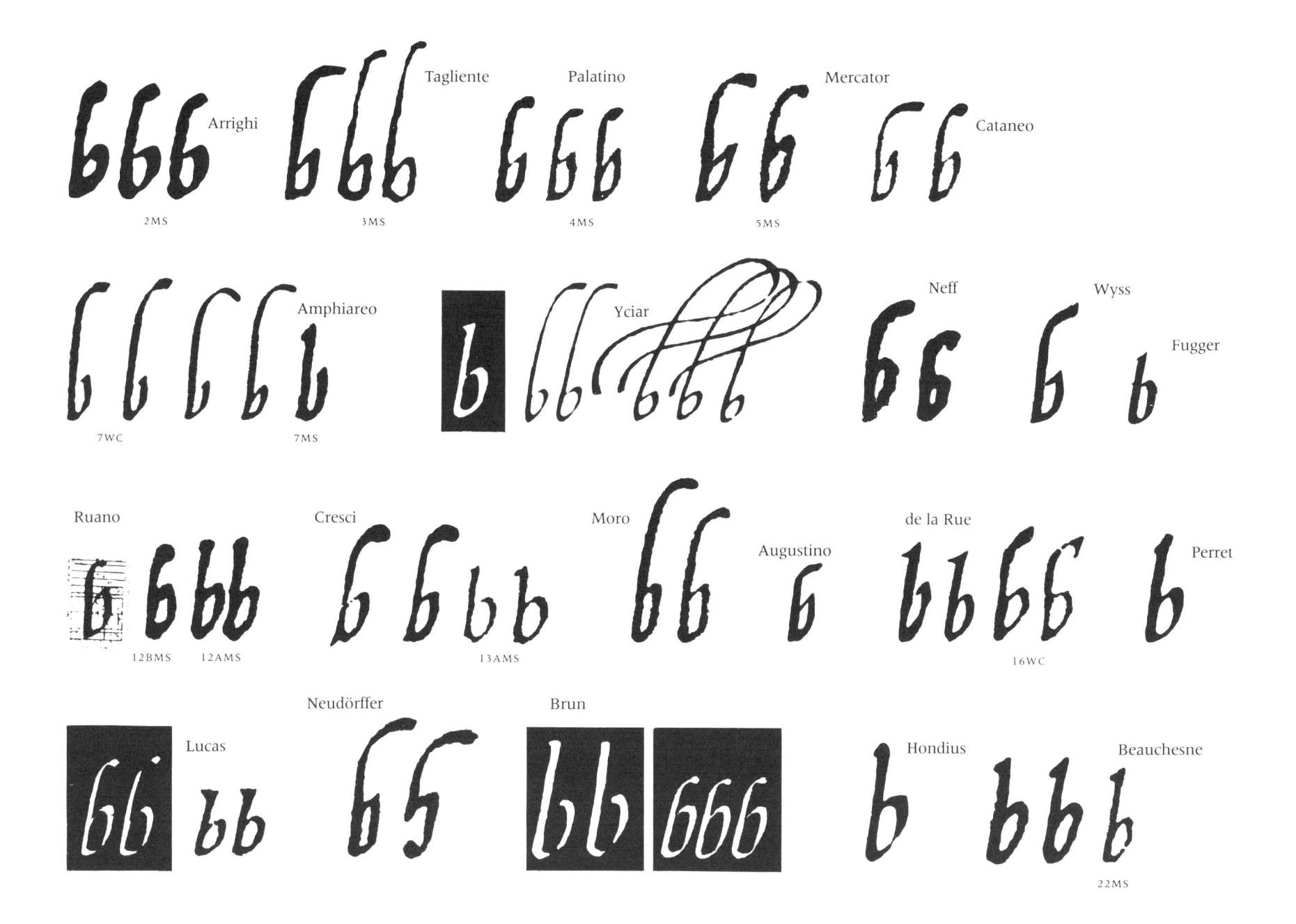

Arrighi	Tagliente	Palatino	Mercator	Cataneo
2MS	3MS	4MS	5MS	

Amphiareo	Yciar		Neff	Wyss / Fugger
7WC 7MS				

Ruano	Cresci	Moro / Augustino	de la Rue	Perret
12BMS 12AMS	13AMS		16WC	

Lucas	Neudörffer	Brun	Hondius	Beauchesne
				22MS

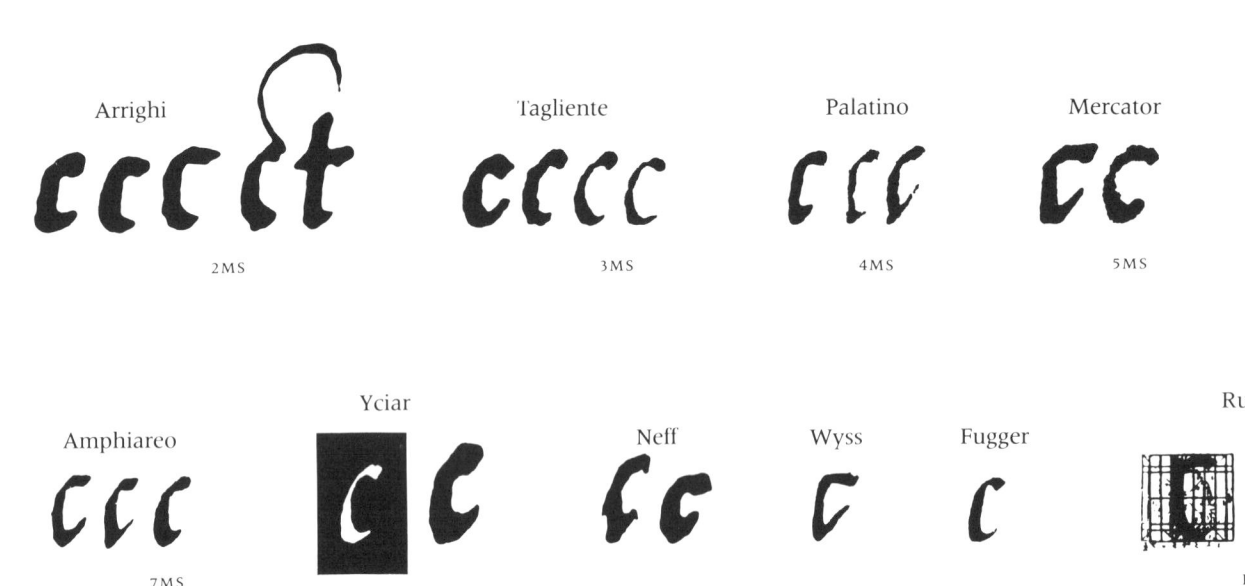

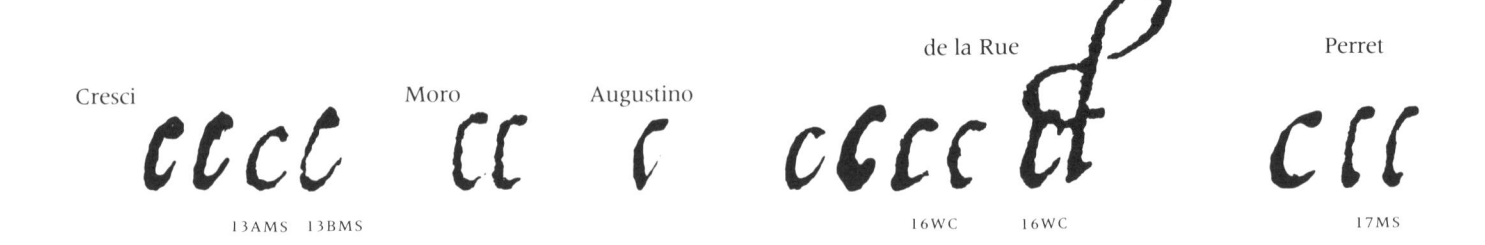

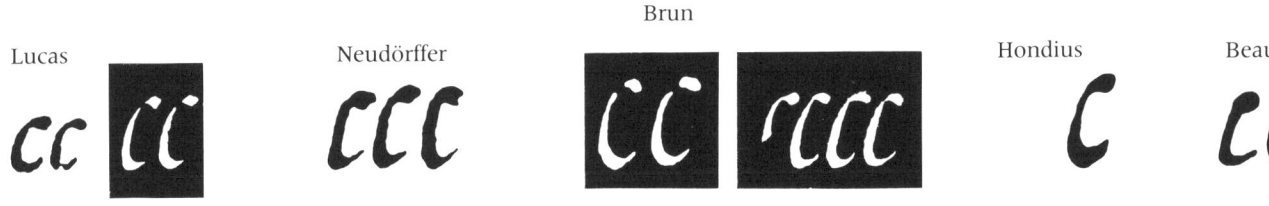

Arrighi	Tagliente	Palatino	Mercator	Cataneo
cccct	cccc	ccc	cc	cc
2MS	3MS	4MS	5MS	

Amphiareo	Yciar	Neff	Wyss	Fugger	Ruano
ccc	c c	cc	c	c	c cc
7MS					12AMS 12BMS

Cresci	Moro	Augustino	de la Rue	Perret
ccct	cc	c	cccc f	ccc
13AMS 13BMS			16WC 16WC	17MS

Lucas	Neudörffer	Brun	Hondius	Beauchesne
cc cc	ccc	cc cccc	c	ccc
				22MS

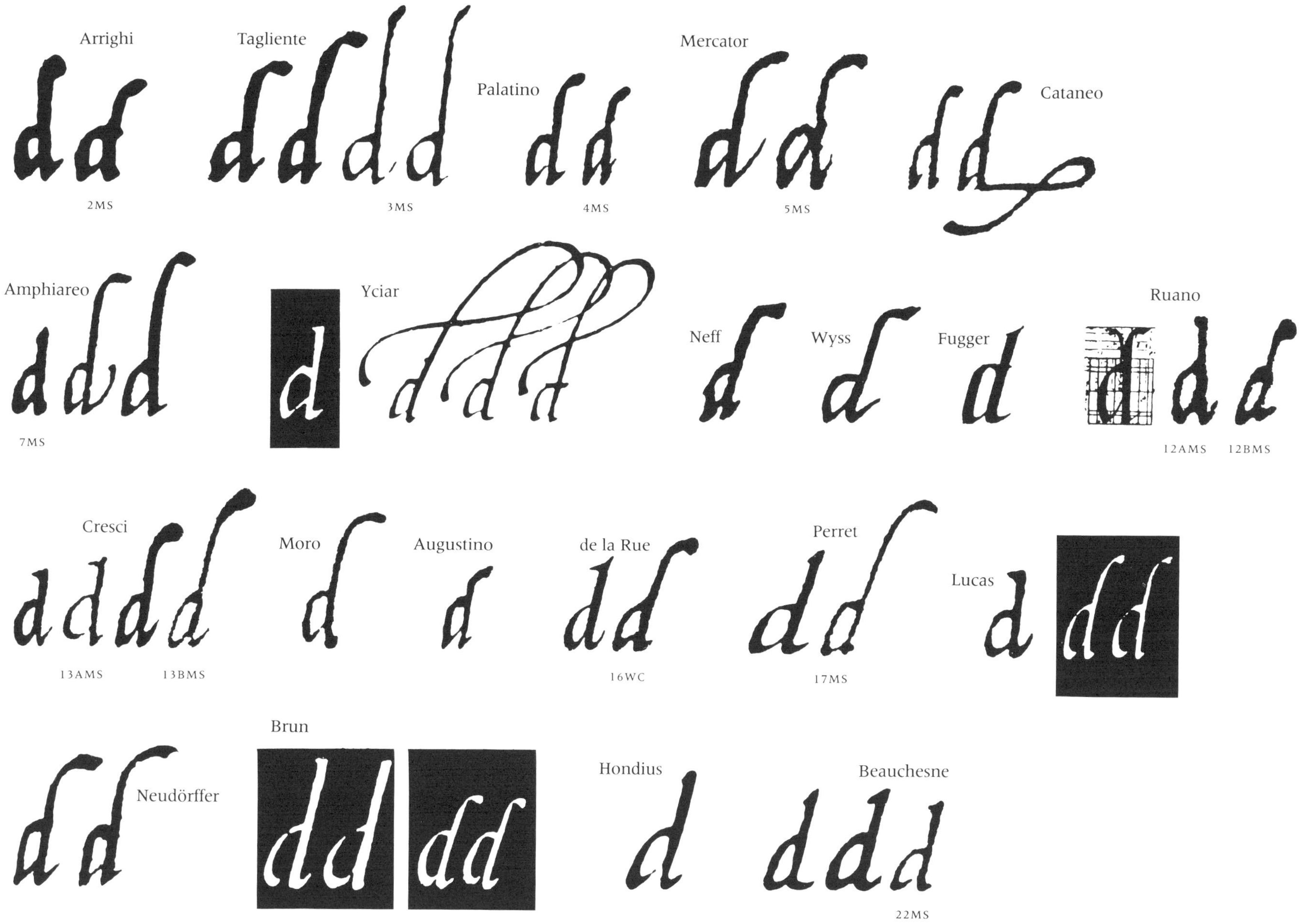
Arrighi
2MS
Tagliente
3MS
Palatino
4MS
Mercator
5MS
Cataneo
Amphiareo
7MS
Yciar
Neff
Wyss
Fugger
Ruano
12AMS
12BMS
Cresci
13AMS
13BMS
Moro
Augustino
de la Rue
16WC
Perret
17MS
Lucas
Neudörffer
Brun
Hondius
Beauchesne
22MS

108

Arrighi	Tagliente	Palatino	Mercator
2MS	3MS	4MS	5MS

Cataneo	Amphiareo	Yciar	Neff	Wyss	Fugger	Ruano
						12AMS 12BMS

Cresci			Moro	Augustino	de la Rue	Perret
13AMS	13BMS				16WC	17MS

Lucas	Neudörffer	Brun	Hondius	Beauchesne
				22MS

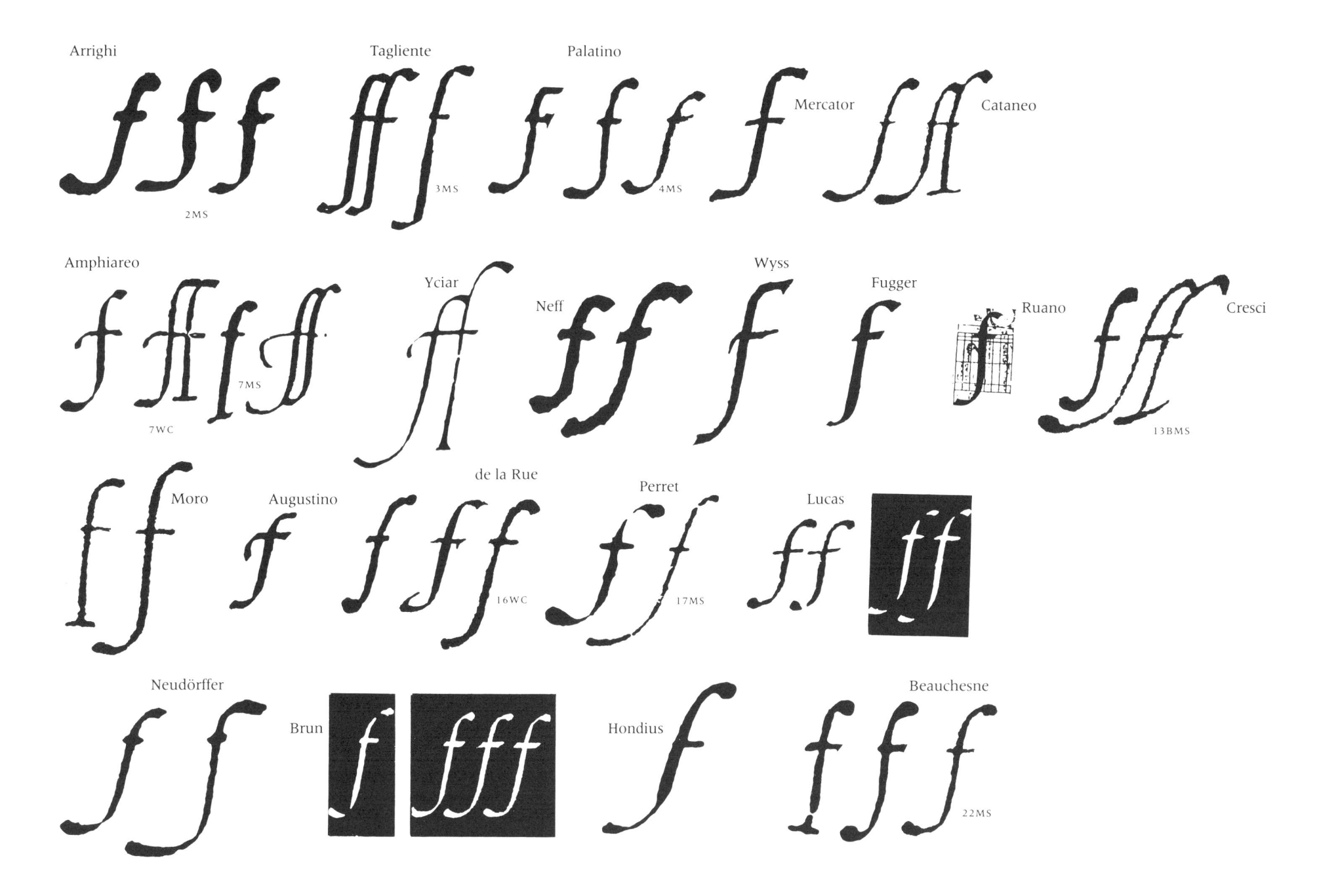

Arrighi	Tagliente	Palatino	Mercator	Cataneo
Amphiareo	Yciar	Wyss / Neff	Fugger	Ruano / Cresci
Moro	Augustino	de la Rue	Perret	Lucas
Neudörffer	Brun		Hondius	Beauchesne

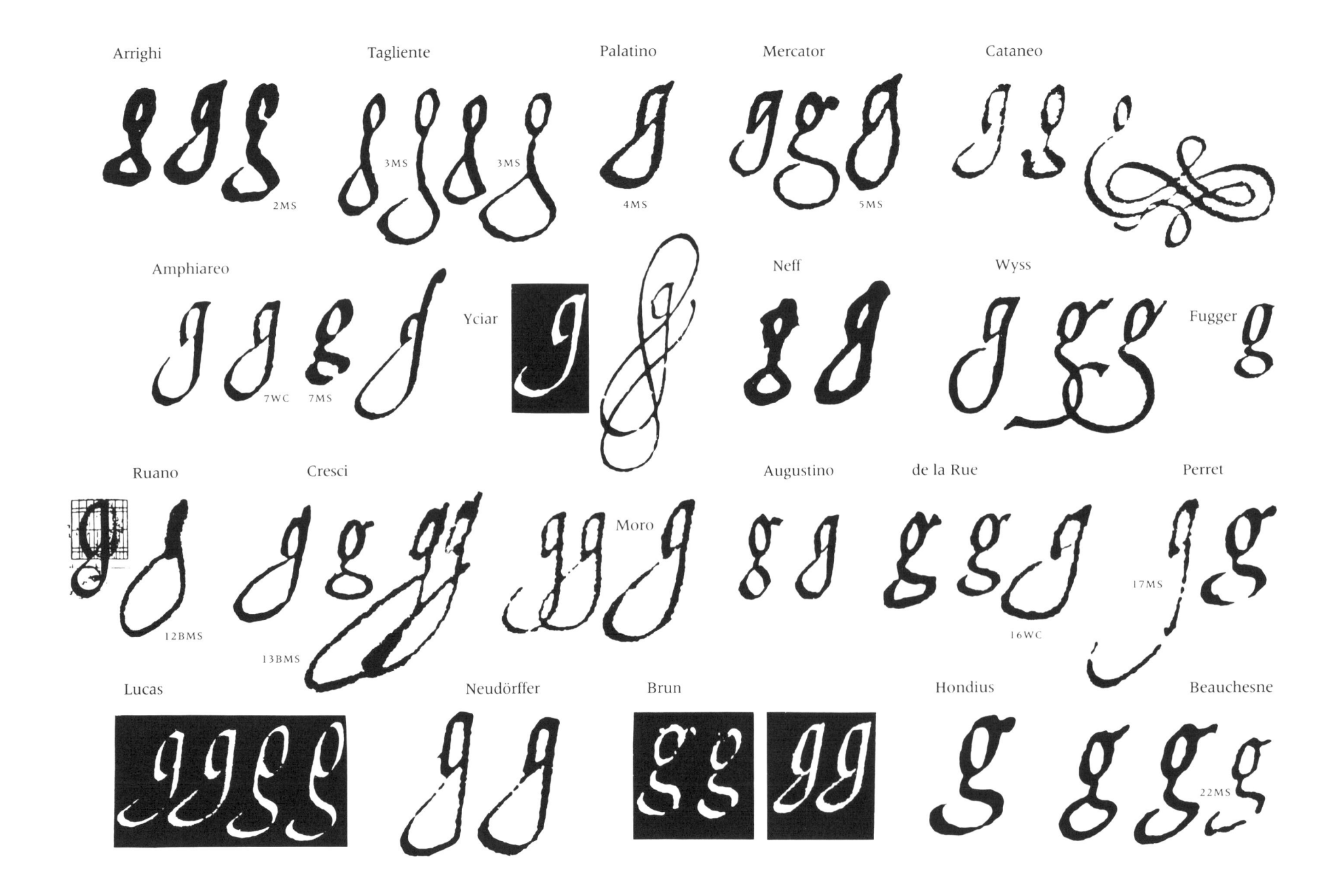

Arrighi	Tagliente	Palatino	Mercator	Cataneo
Amphiareo	Yciar		Neff	Wyss / Fugger
Ruano	Cresci	Moro / Augustino	de la Rue	Perret
Lucas	Neudörffer	Brun	Hondius	Beauchesne

111

Arrighi Tagliente Palatino Mercator

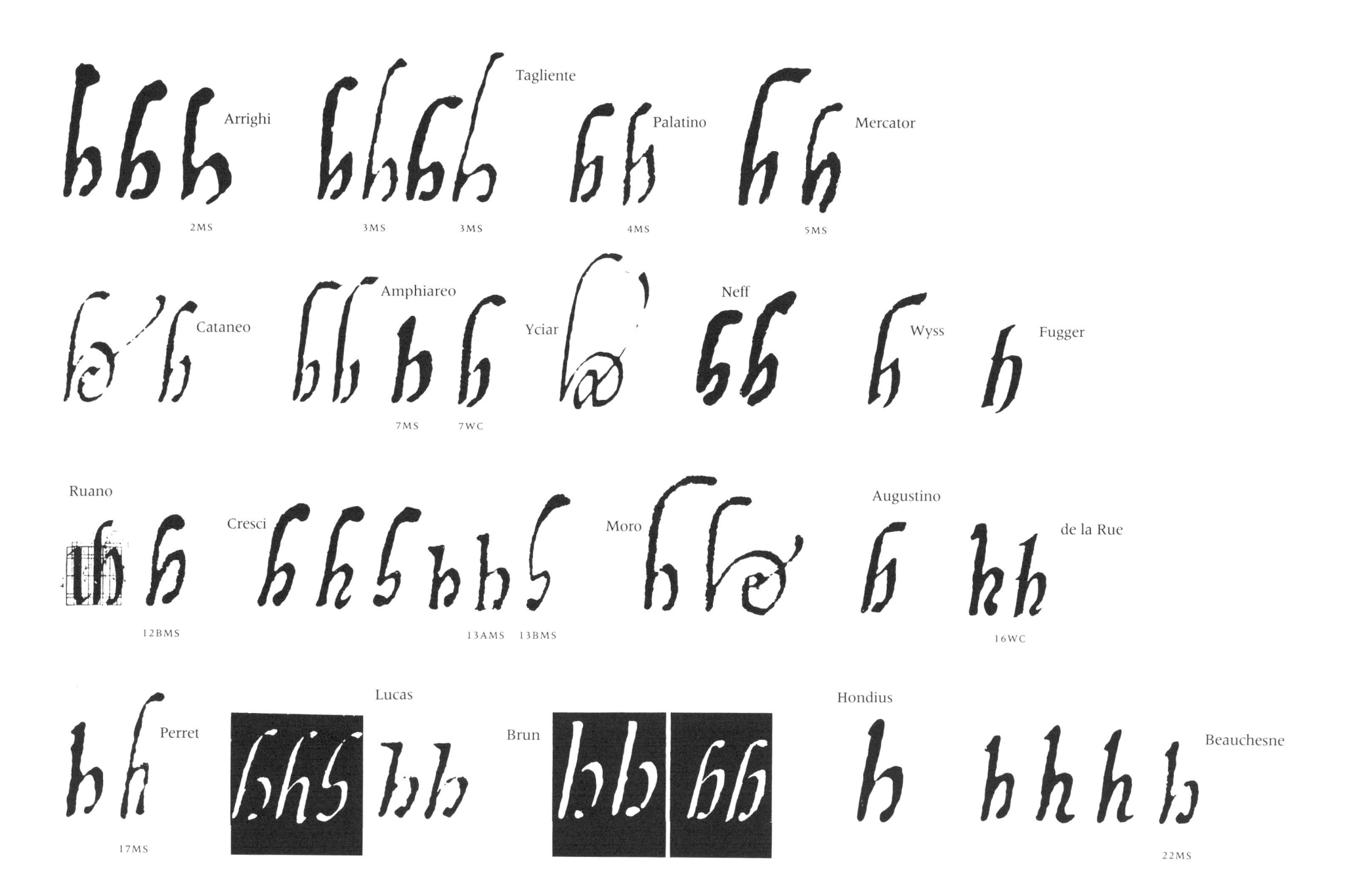

2MS 3MS 3MS 4MS 5MS

Cataneo Amphiareo Yciar Neff Wyss Fugger

7MS 7WC

Ruano Cresci Moro Augustino de la Rue

12BMS 13AMS 13BMS 16WC

Perret Lucas Brun Hondius Beauchesne

17MS 22MS

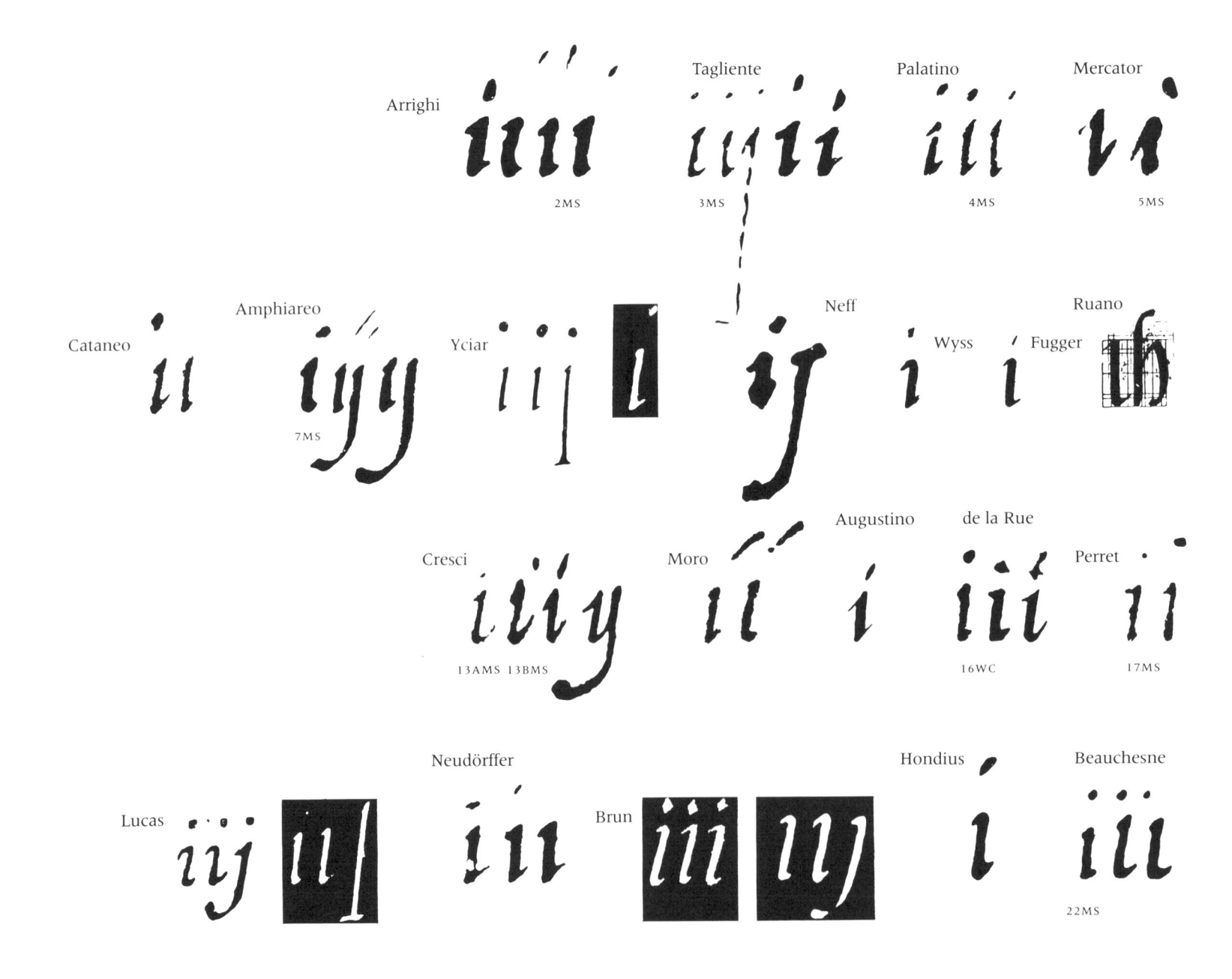

		Tagliente	Palatino	Mercator
Arrighi	iiii	iijii	iii	ii
	2MS	3MS	4MS	5MS

Cataneo	Amphiareo	Yciar	Neff	Wyss	Fugger	Ruano
ii	iyy	iiij	l	ij	i	i	th
	7MS					

Cresci	Moro	Augustino	de la Rue	Perret
iiiy	ii	i	iii	ii
13AMS 13BMS			16WC	17MS

Lucas	Neudörffer	Brun	Hondius	Beauchesne
iij	iil	iii	iiii	iij	i	iii
				22MS

113

k Arrighi *k* Tagliente *k* Palatino

k Mercator *k* Amphiareo *k* *k* Yciar *k*

k k Neff *k k* Wyss *k* Fugger

Ruano de la Rue *k* Augustino *k k* *k* Perret *k* Hondius

114

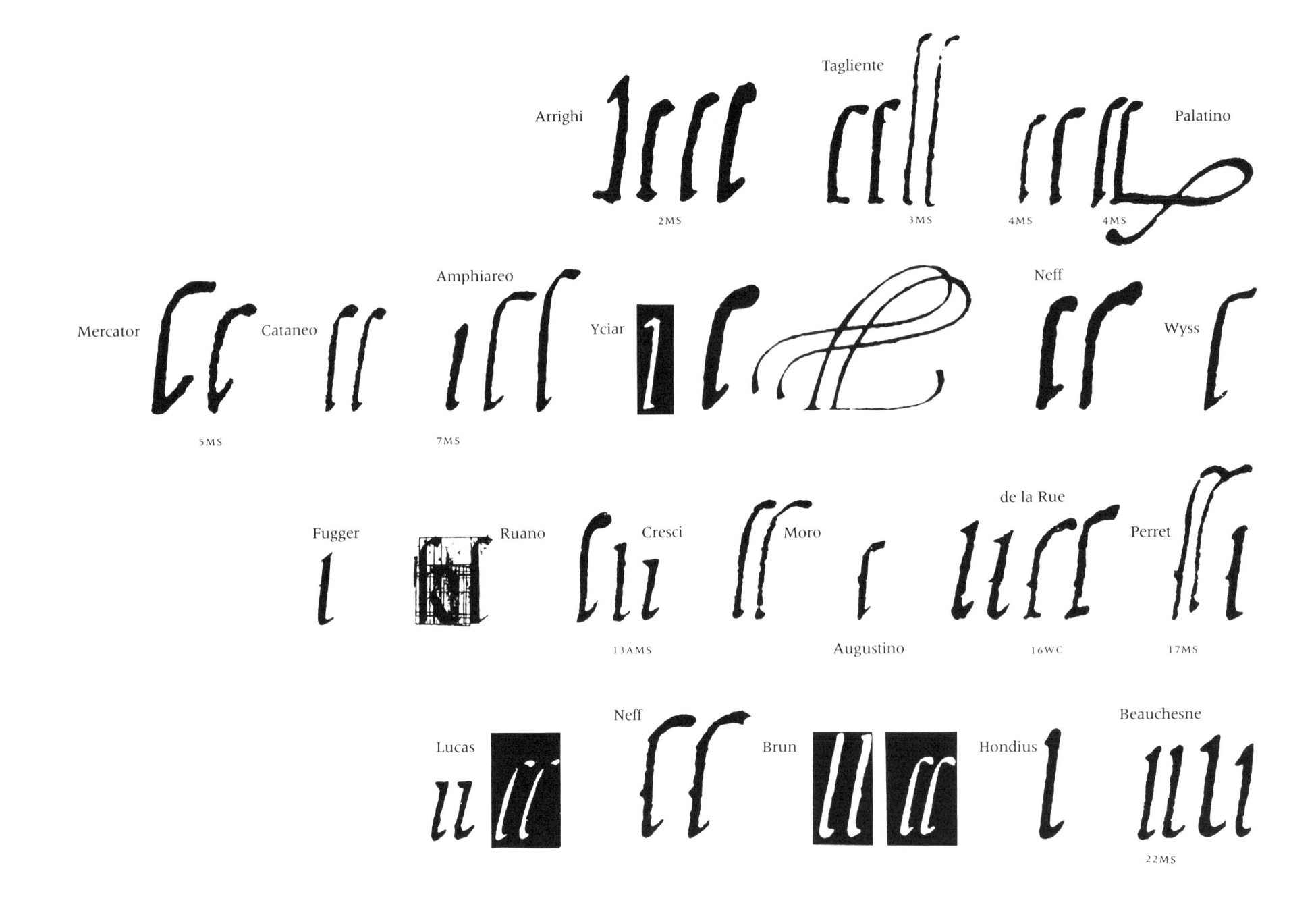

Arrighi Tagliente Palatino
2MS 3MS 4MS 4MS

Mercator Cataneo Amphiareo Yciar Neff Wyss
5MS 7MS

Fugger Ruano Cresci Moro de la Rue Perret
13AMS Augustino 16WC 17MS

Lucas Neff Brun Hondius Beauchesne
22MS

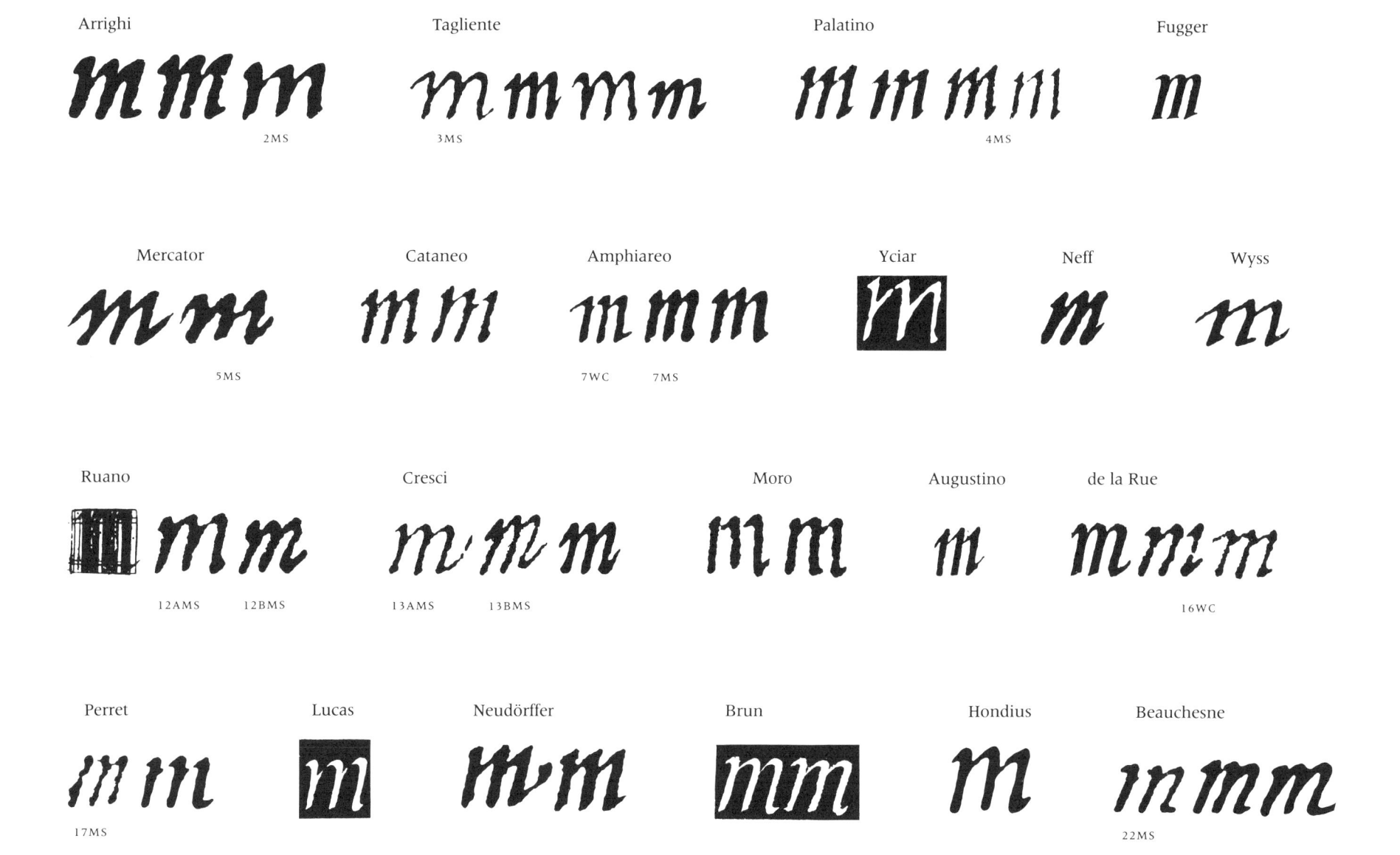

Arrighi	Tagliente	Palatino	Fugger
2MS	3MS	4MS	

Mercator	Cataneo	Amphiareo	Yciar	Neff	Wyss
5MS		7WC 7MS			

Ruano	Cresci	Moro	Augustino	de la Rue
12AMS 12BMS	13AMS 13BMS			16WC

Perret	Lucas	Neudörffer	Brun	Hondius	Beauchesne
17MS					22MS

	Arrighi	Tagliente	Palatino	Mercator
	2MS	3MS	4MS	5MS

Cataneo	Amphiareo	Yciar	Neff	Wyss	Fugger
	7MS 7WC				

Ruano	Cresci	Moro	Augustino	de la Rue	
12AMS 12BMS	13AMS			16WC 16WC	

Perret	Lucas	Neudörffer	Brun	Hondius	Beauchesne
					22MS

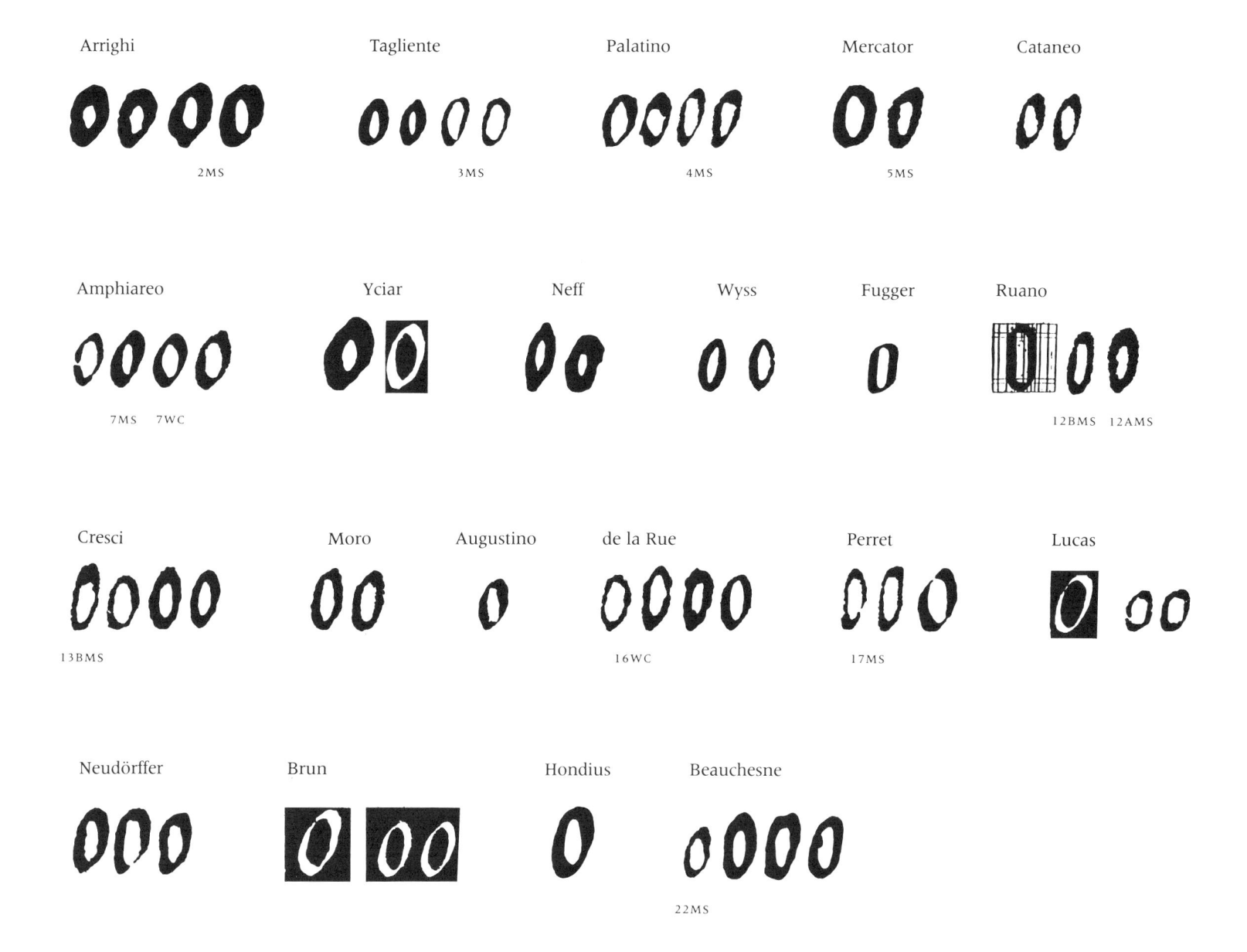

Arrighi	Tagliente	Palatino	Mercator	Cataneo
2MS	3MS	4MS	5MS	

Amphiareo	Yciar	Neff	Wyss	Fugger	Ruano
7MS 7WC					12BMS 12AMS

Cresci	Moro	Augustino	de la Rue	Perret	Lucas
13BMS			16WC	17MS	

Neudörffer	Brun	Hondius	Beauchesne
			22MS

118

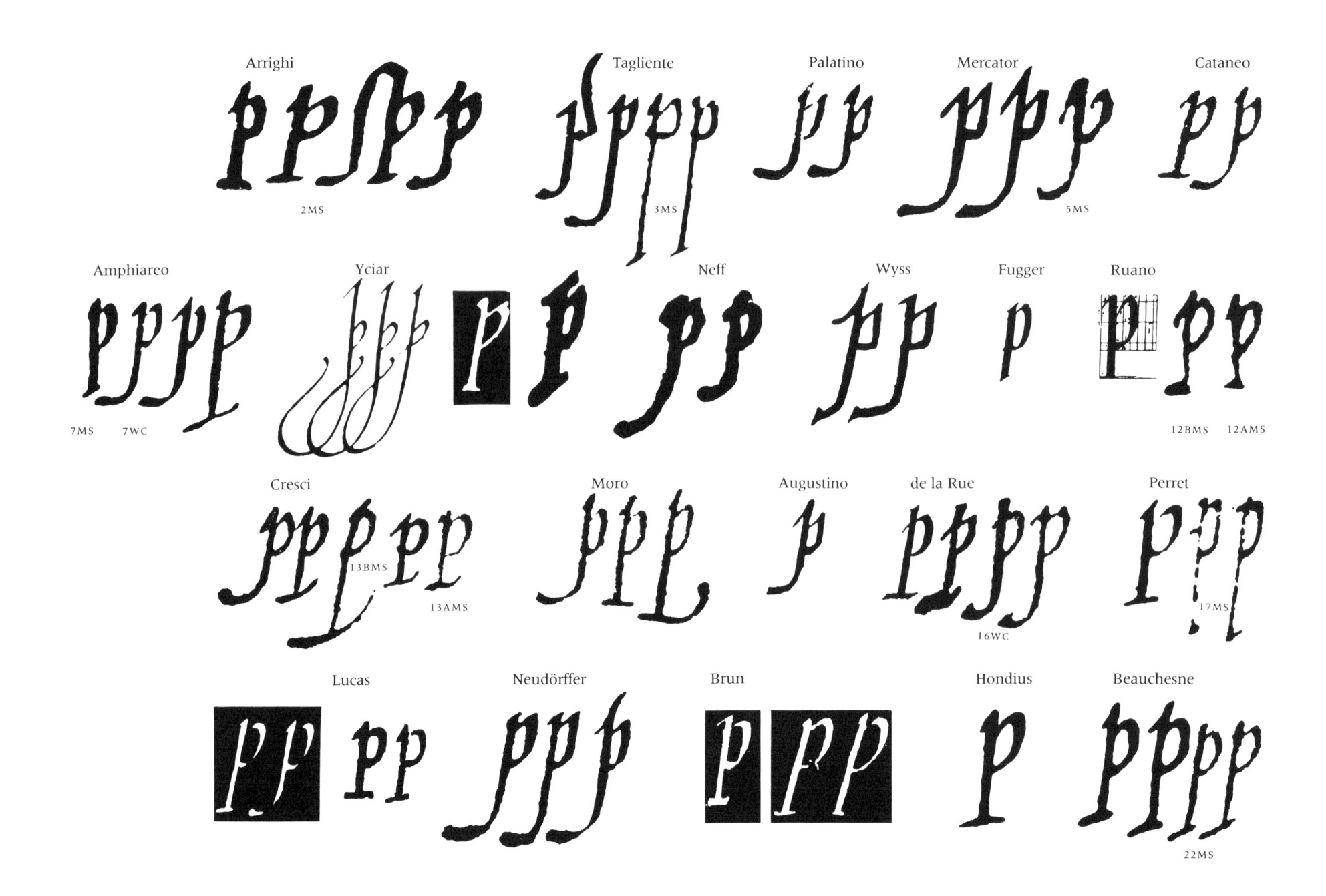

Arrighi	Tagliente	Palatino	Mercator	Cataneo
2MS	3MS		5MS	

Amphiareo	Yciar		Neff	Wyss	Fugger	Ruano
7MS 7WC						12BMS 12AMS

Cresci	Moro	Augustino	de la Rue	Perret
13BMS 13AMS			16WC	17MS

Lucas	Neudörffer	Brun	Hondius	Beauchesne
				22MS

Arrighi	Tagliente	Palatino	Mercator
Cataneo	Amphiareo	Yciar	Neff	Wyss	Fugger
Ruano	Cresci	Augustino	de la Rue	Perret	Lucas
Neudörffer	Brun	Hondius	Beauchesne

119

Arrighi	Tagliente	Palatino	Mercator	Cataneo
2MS	3MS	4MS	5MS	

Amphiareo	Yciar	Neff	Wyss	Fugger	Ruano
7WC 7MS					12AMS 12BMS

Cresci	Moro	Augustino	de la Rue	Perret
13BMS 13AMS			16WC	17MS

Lucas	Neudörffer	Brun	Hondius	Beauchesne
				22MS

121

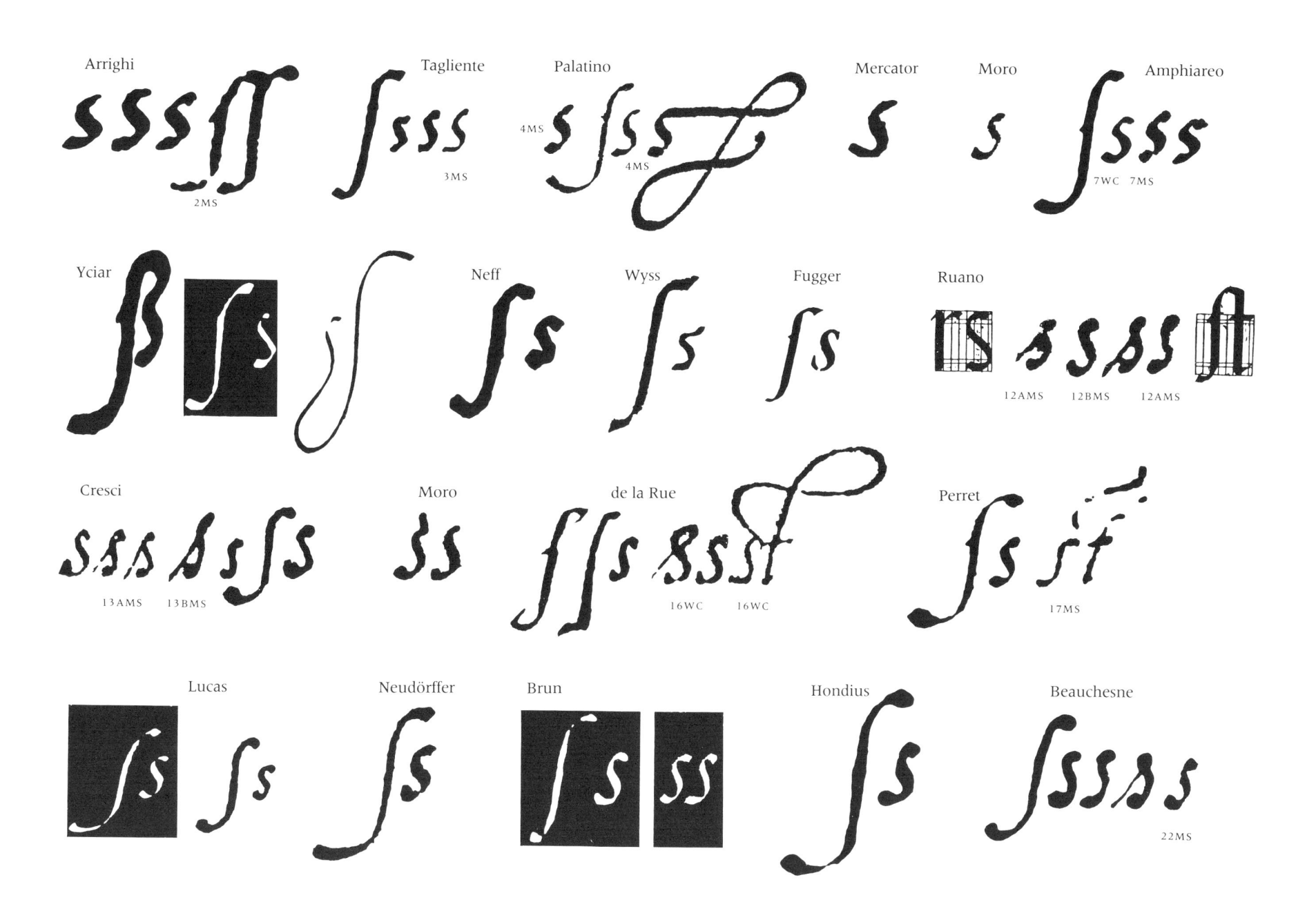

Arrighi	Tagliente	Palatino	Mercator	Moro	Amphiareo
Yciar		Neff	Wyss	Fugger	Ruano
Cresci	Moro	de la Rue		Perret	
Lucas	Neudörffer	Brun		Hondius	Beauchesne

122

Arrighi	Tagliente	Palatino	Mercator
2MS 2MS	3MS	4MS	5MS

Cataneo	Amphiareo	Yciar	Neff	Wyss	Fugger	Ruano
	7WC 7MS					12BMS

Cresci	Moro	Augustino	de la Rue	Perret
13AMS 13BMS			16WC	17MS

Lucas	Neudörffer	Brun	Beauchesne
			22MS

Arrighi	Tagliente	Palatino	Mercator	Cataneo
2MS	3MS	4MS	5MS	

Amphiareo	Yciar	Neff	Fugger	Ruano	Cresci
7AMS 7WC				12BMS 12AMS	13AMS 13BMS

Cresci	Moro	Augustino	de la Rue	Perret	Lucas
			16WC	17MS	

Neudörffer	Brun	Hondius	Beauchesne
			22MS

	Arrighi	Mercator	Yciar

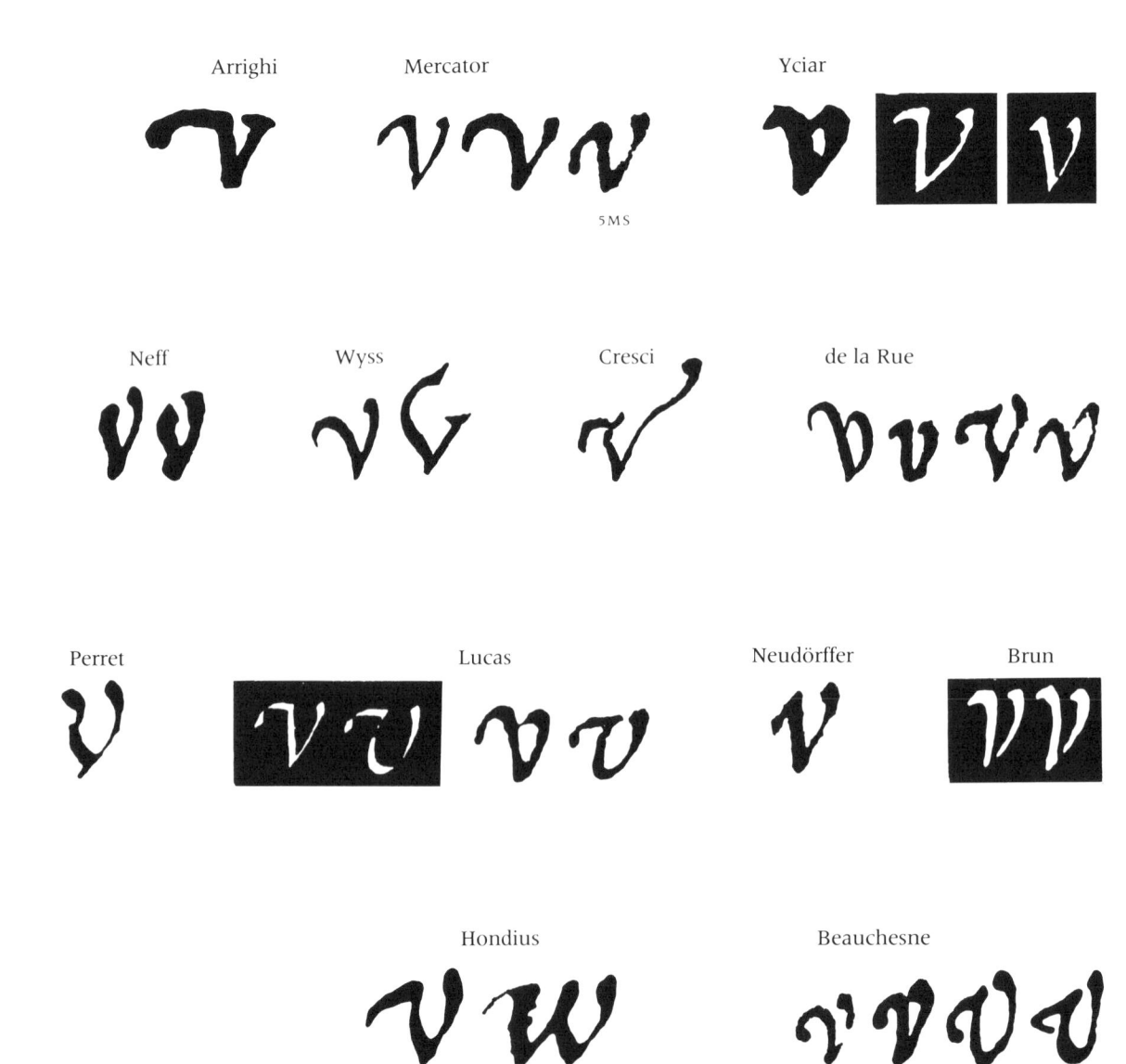

	Neff	Wyss	Cresci	de la Rue

5MS

	Perret	Lucas	Neudörffer	Brun

	Hondius	Beauchesne

22MS

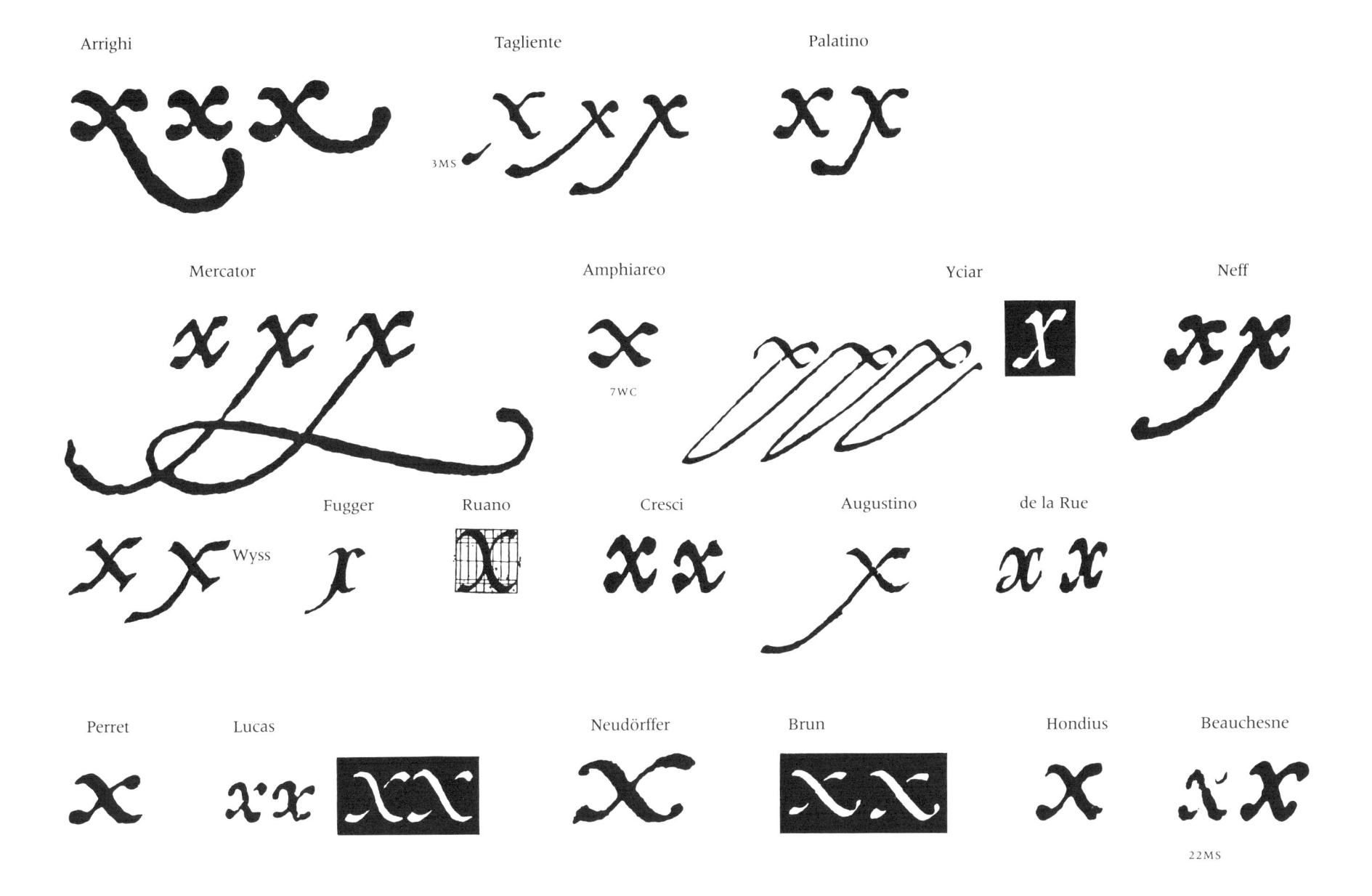

Arrighi	Tagliente	Palatino
Mercator	Amphiareo	Yciar · Neff
Fugger Ruano	Cresci Augustino de la Rue
Wyss	
Perret Lucas	Neudörffer Brun Hondius Beauchesne

| | Arrighi | Tagliente | Mercator | Mercator |

| Amphiareo | | Yciar | Neff | Fugger | Ruano |

| Cresci | Augustino | de la Rue | Perret | Lucas | |

| Brun | | | Hondius | Beauchesne |

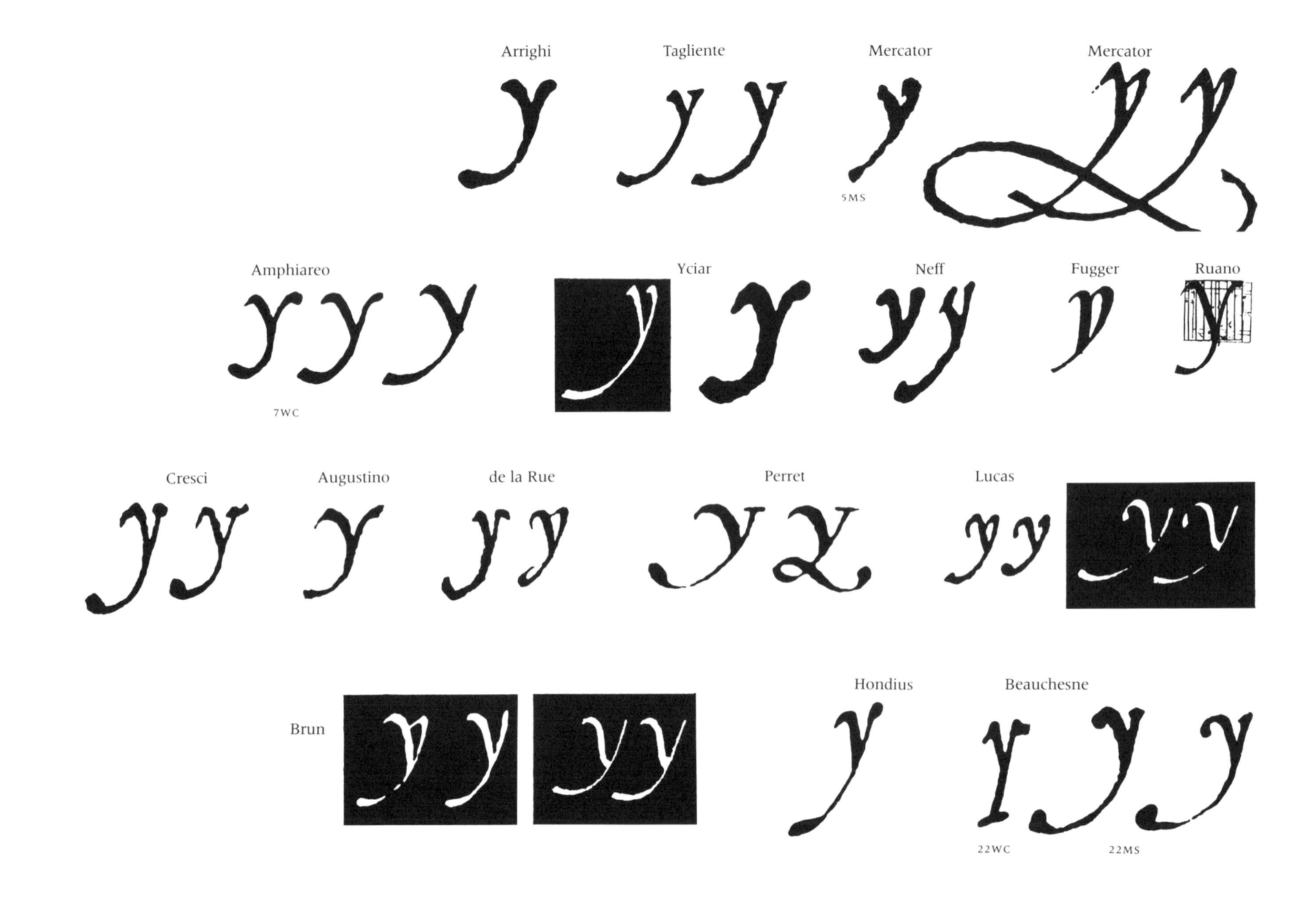

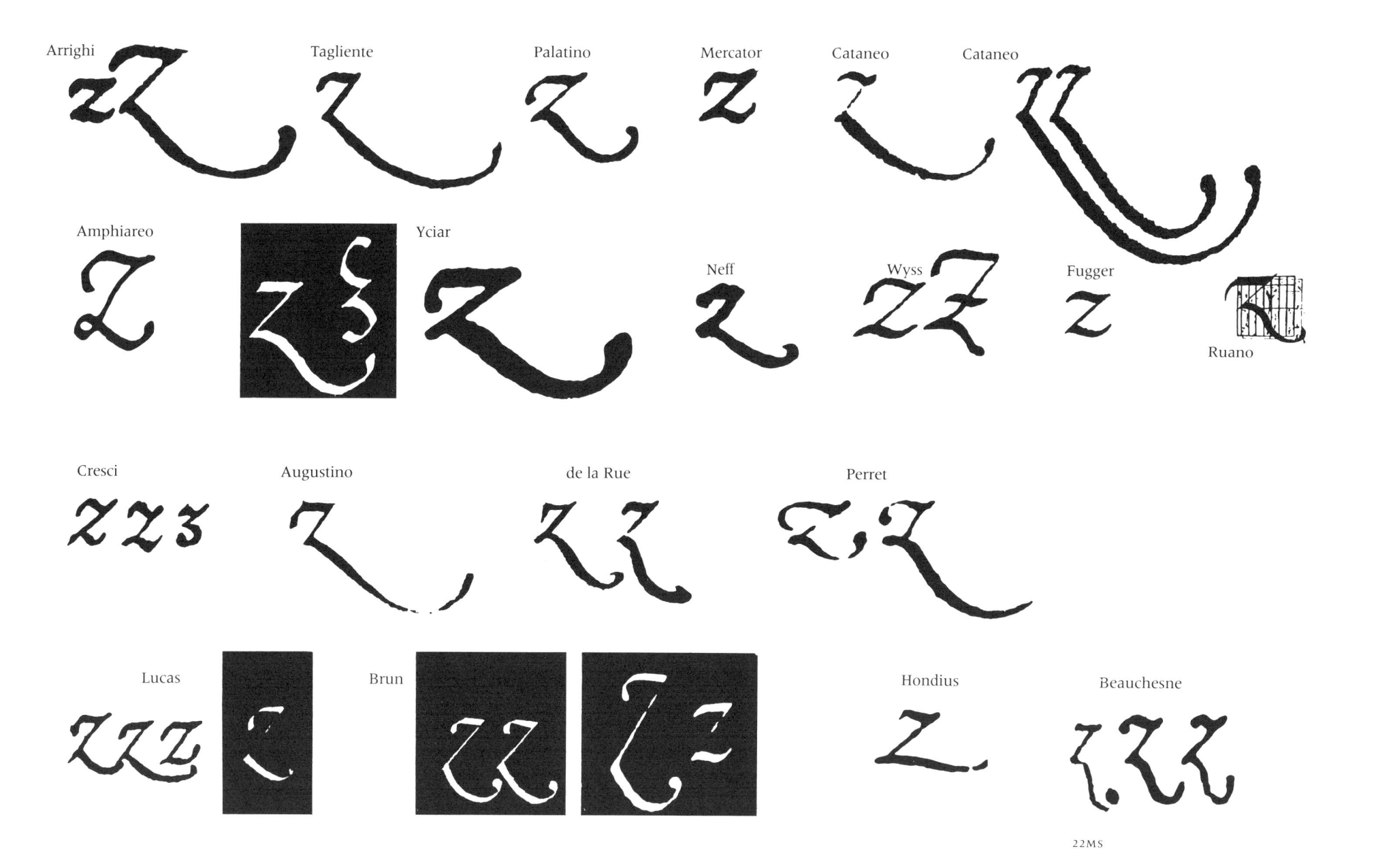

Arrighi	Tagliente	Palatino	Mercator	Cataneo	Cataneo

Amphiareo	Yciar	Neff	Wyss	Fugger

Ruano

Cresci	Augustino	de la Rue	Perret

Lucas	Brun	Hondius	Beauchesne

22MS

128

Fanti

Arrighi

Tagliente

Palatino
4MS

Mercator
5MS

Cataneo

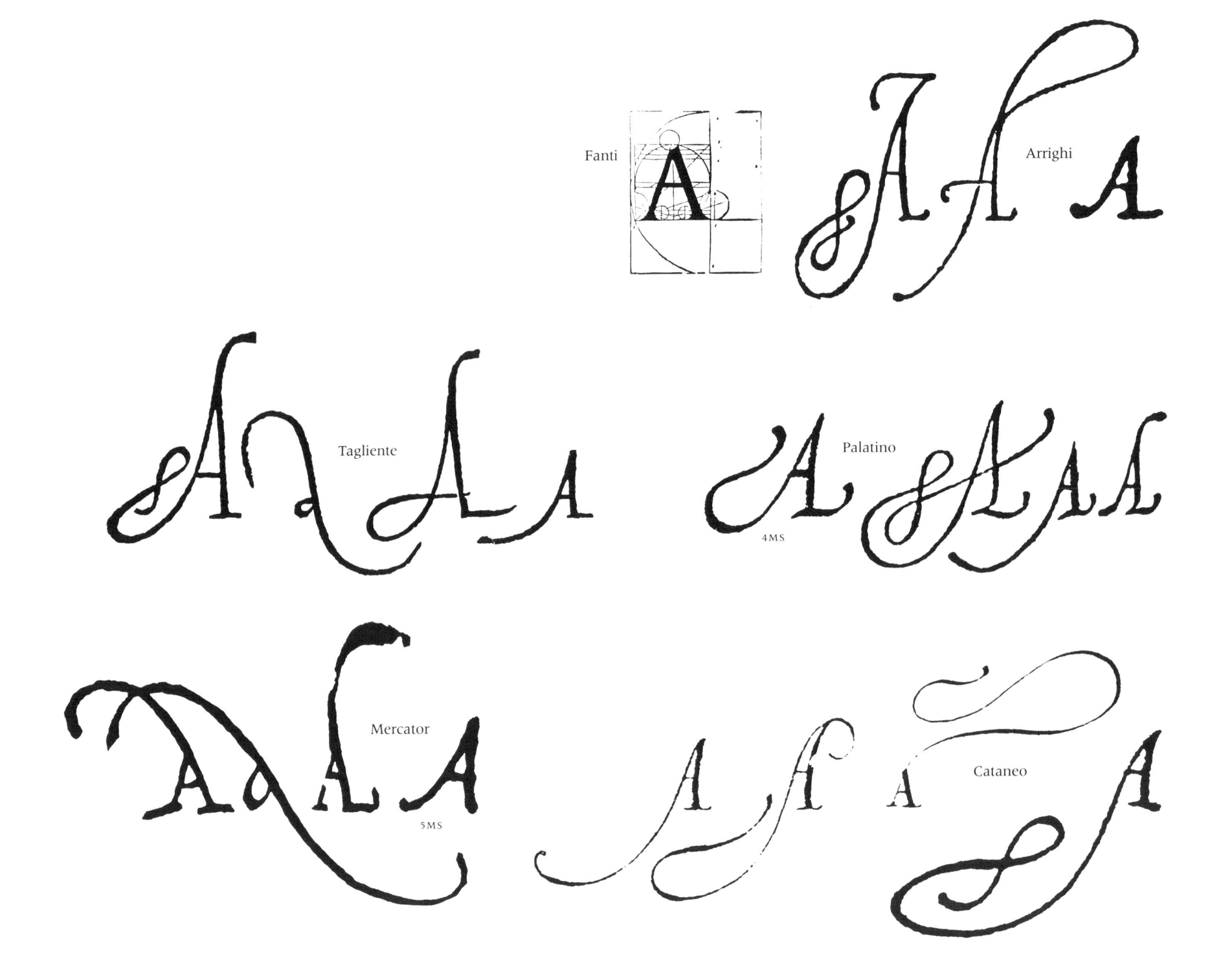

Amphiareo Yciar

Yciar Neff

Wyss Fugger Ruano Cresci

Cresci

Moro

Augustino

de la Rue

Perret

Perret   Lucas   Neudörffer

Brun   Hondius

Hondius   Beauchesne

Arrighi

Tagliente

Palatino

Mercator

Amphiareo

Cataneo

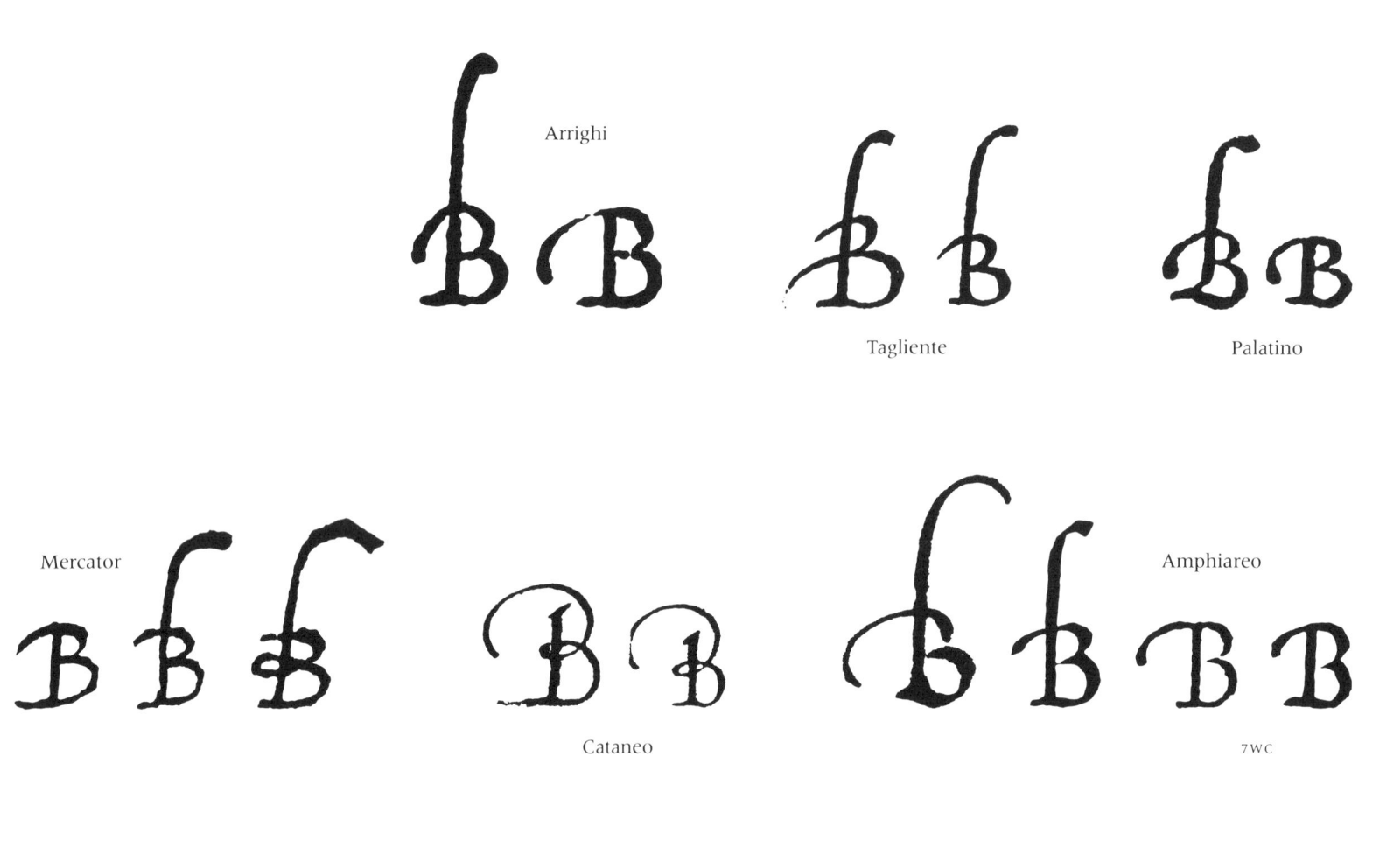

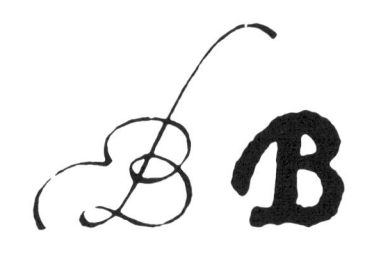

7WC

Yciar

Neff

Wyss

Ruano

Fugger

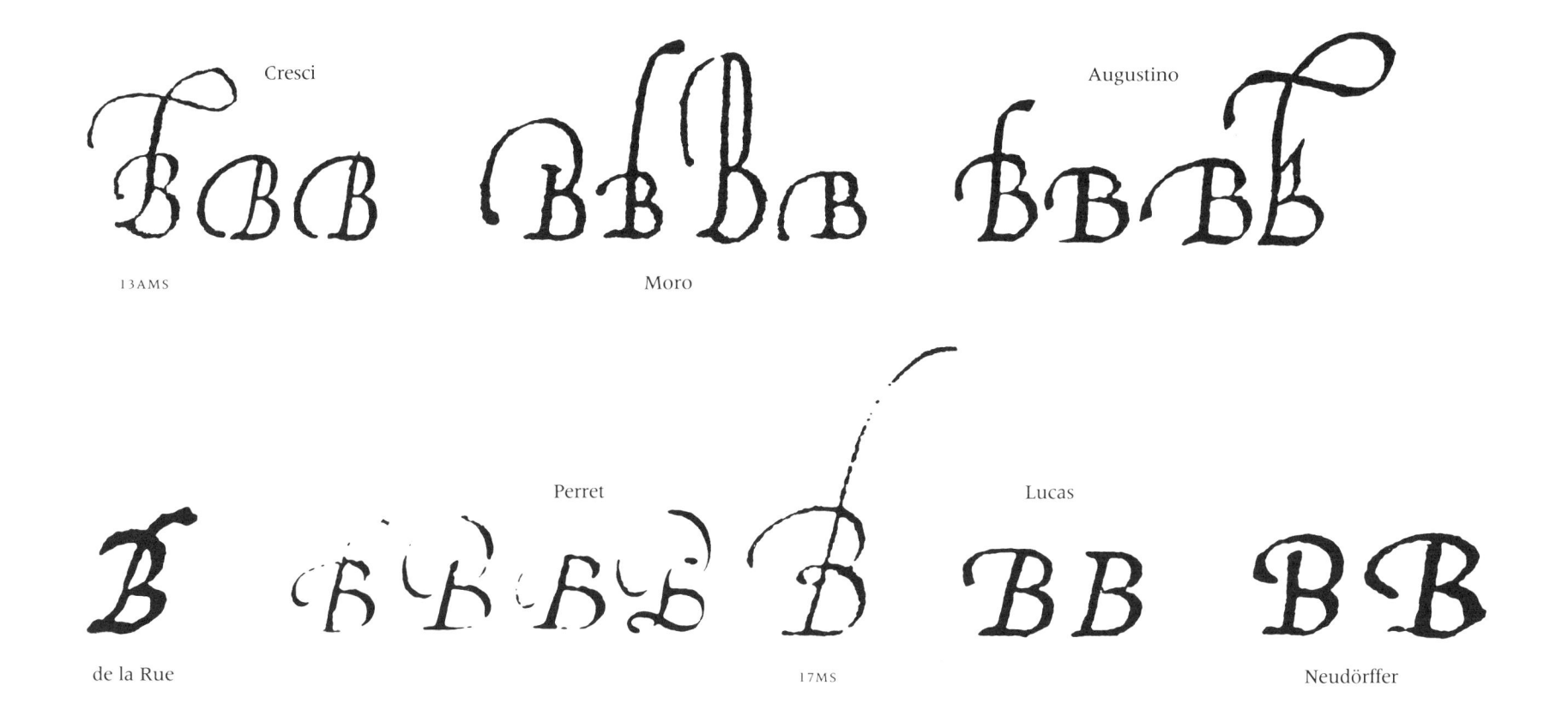

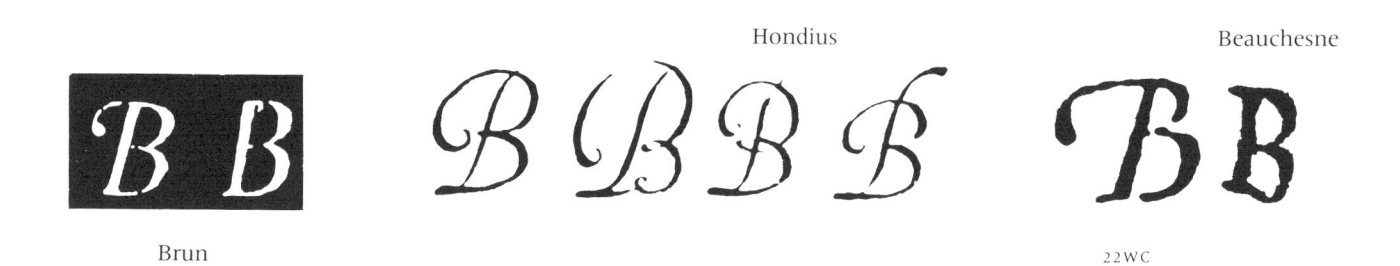

Cresci　　　　　　　　　　　　　　Augustino

13AMS

Moro

Perret　　　　　　　　　Lucas

de la Rue　　　　　　　　　　　17MS　　　　　　　　Neudörffer

Hondius　　　　Beauchesne

Brun　　　　　　　　　　22WC

Arrighi

Tagliente

3 MS

Palatino

Mercator

Amphiareo

4 MS

Cataneo

7 WC

Amphiareo

7 WC

Yciar

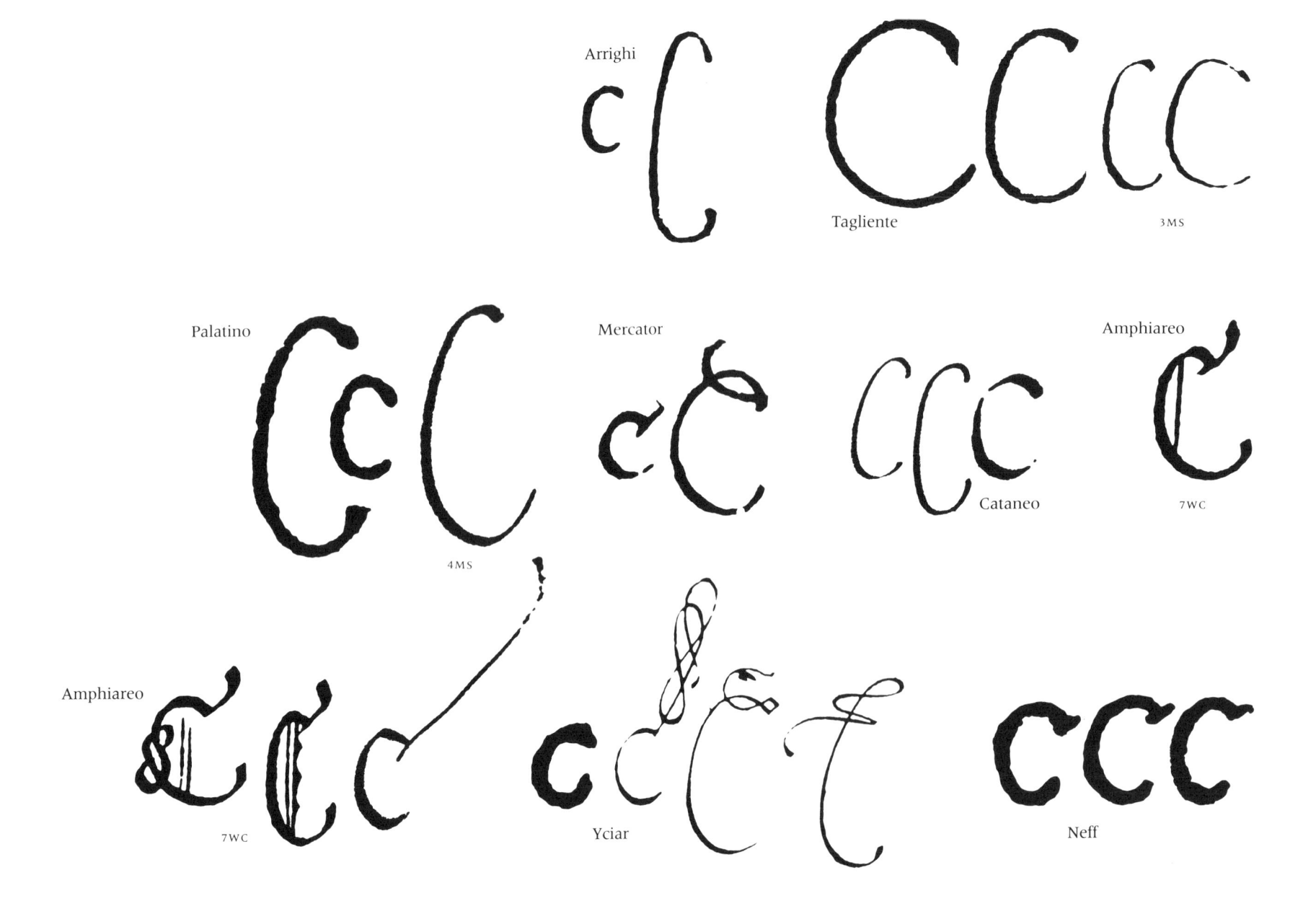

Neff

Wyss   Cresci

                    Ruano   Fugger
                                    13AMS

                            Augustino
                                        Perret

        Moro   de la Rue
                                    17MS

Lucas   Hondius   Beauchesne

        Neudörffer   Brun
                                22WC   22MS

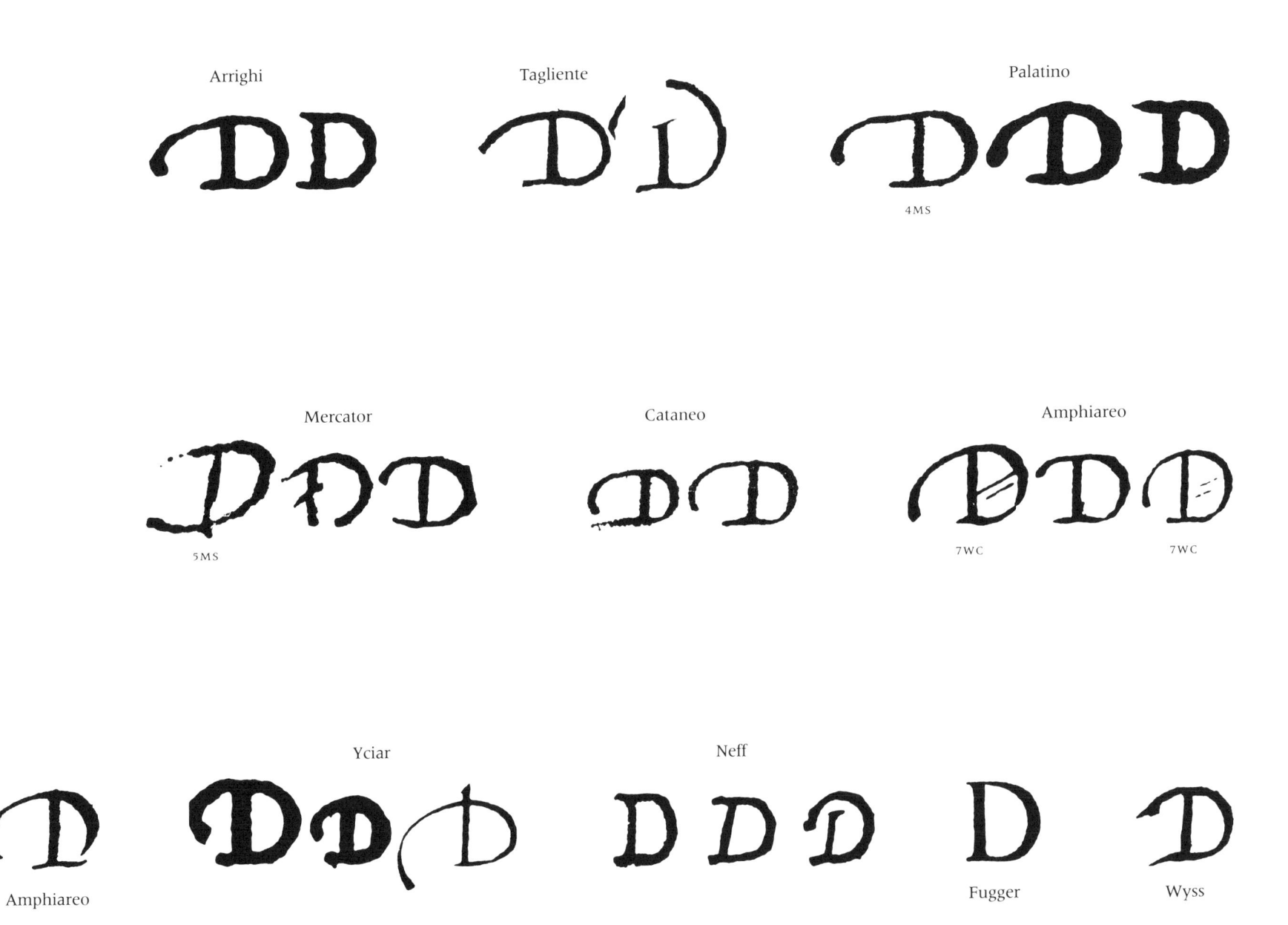

Arrighi	Tagliente	Palatino
Mercator	Cataneo	Amphiareo
Yciar	Neff	Fugger Wyss
Amphiareo		

Ruano

Cresci

Augustino

12AMS

13AMS

de la Rue

Perret

Lucas

Neudörffer

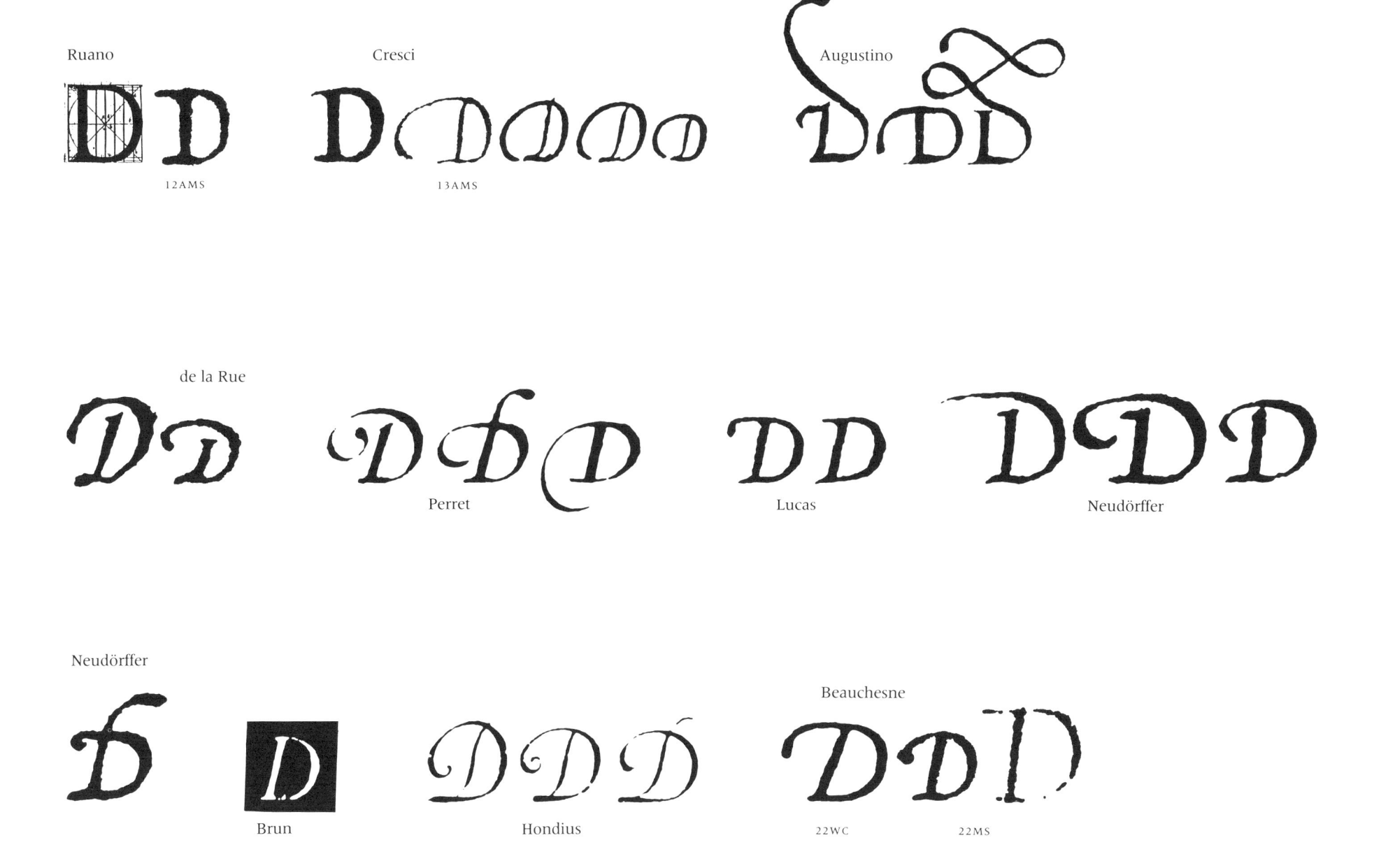

Neudörffer

Beauchesne

Brun

Hondius

22WC 22MS

138

Arrighi

Palatino

Tagliente

Mercator

Cataneo

Amphiareo

7WC 7WC

Yciar

Wyss

Neff

Fugger

139

Ruano

Cresci

Moro

Augustino

de la Rue

Perret

Neudörffer

Lucas

Brun

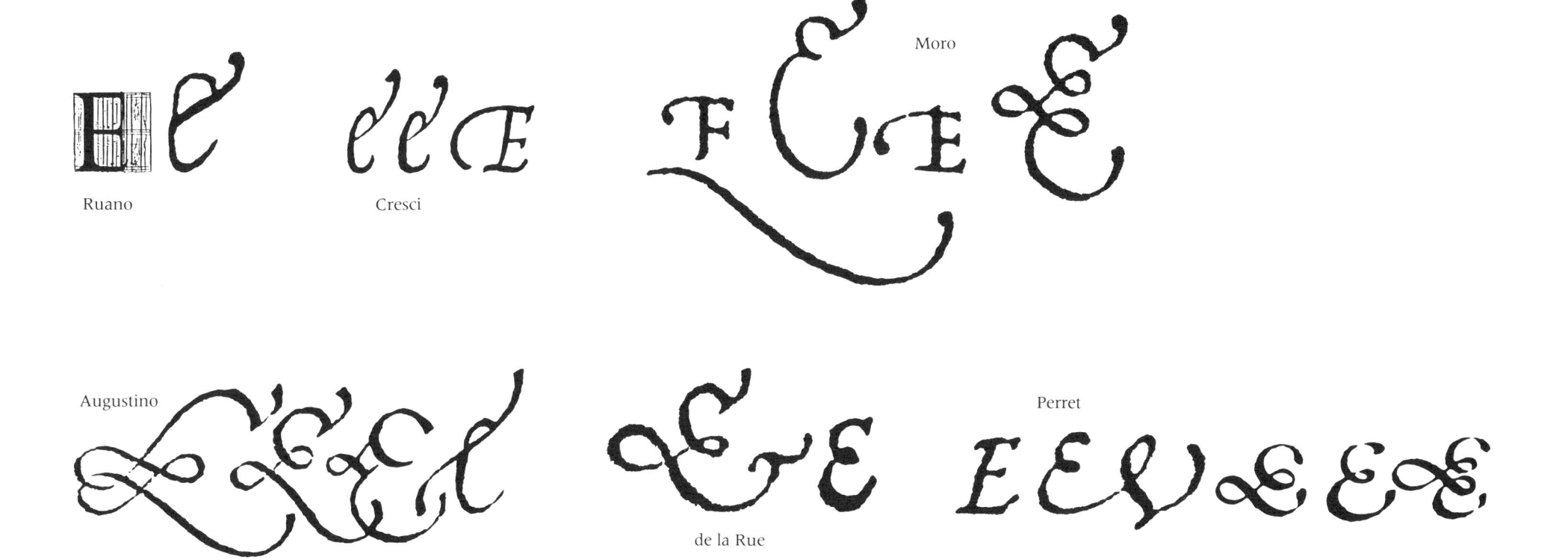

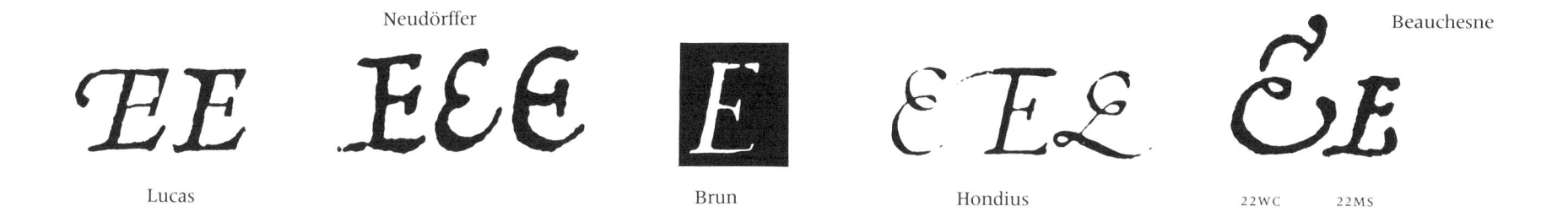

Hondius

Beauchesne

22WC 22MS

Arrighi

Tagliente

Palatino

Cataneo

Amphiareo

Mercator

7WC

Yciar

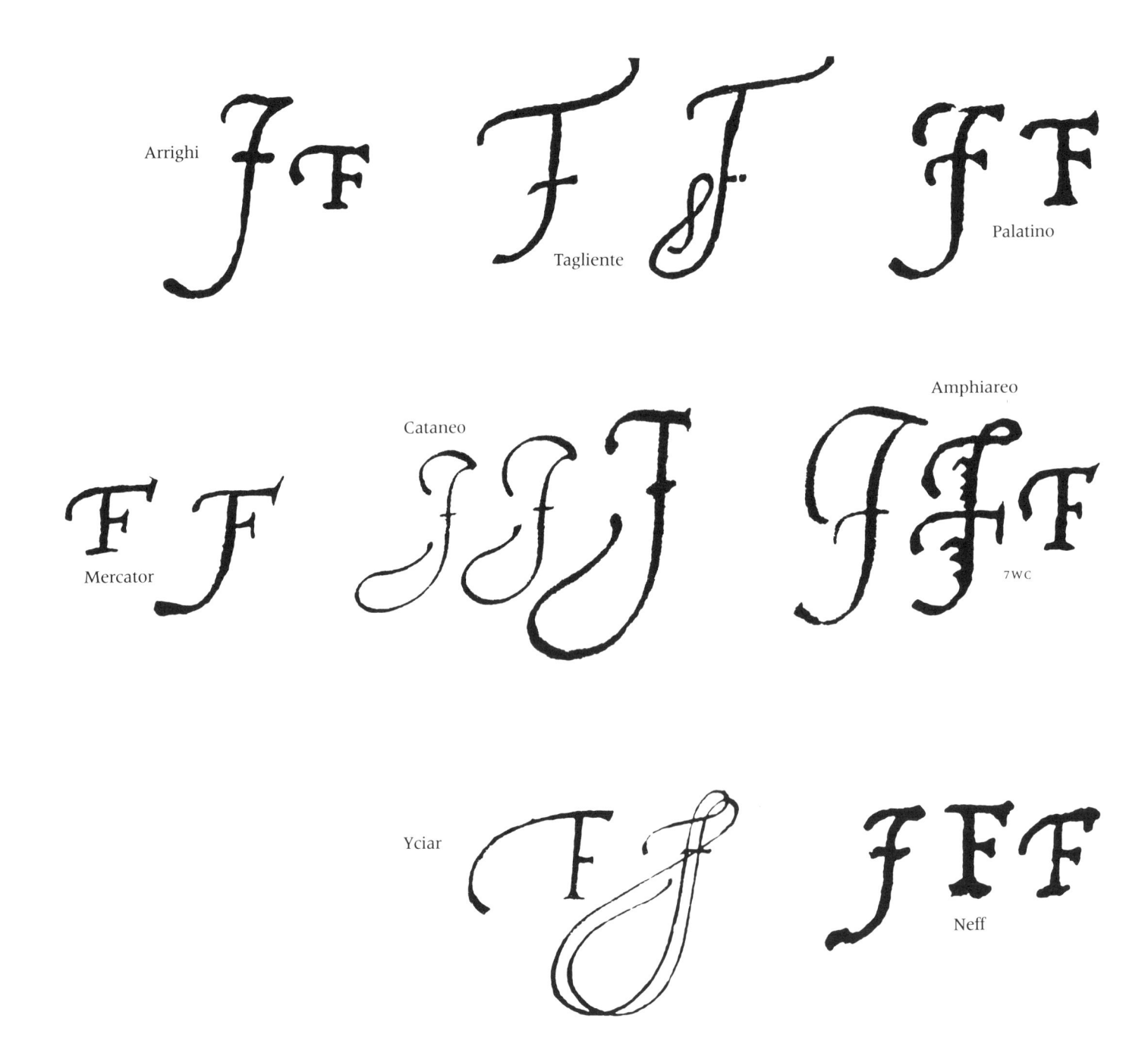

Neff

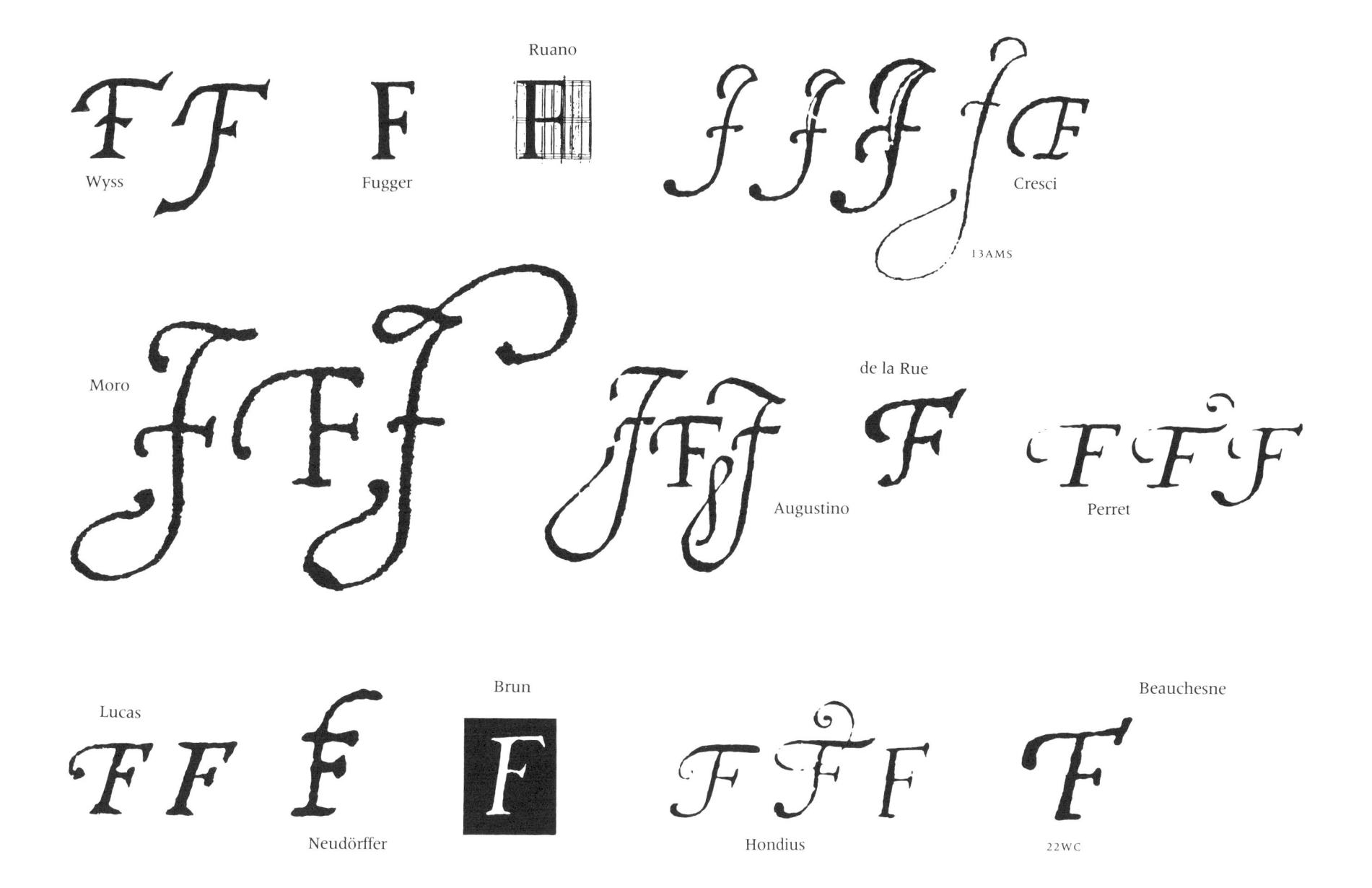

141

Wyss

Fugger

Ruano

Cresci

13AMS

Moro

de la Rue

Augustino

Perret

Lucas

Neudörffer

Brun

Hondius

Beauchesne

22WC

Arrighi   Tagliente   Palatino

Mercator   Cataneo   Amphiareo

Amphiareo   Neff

Yciar

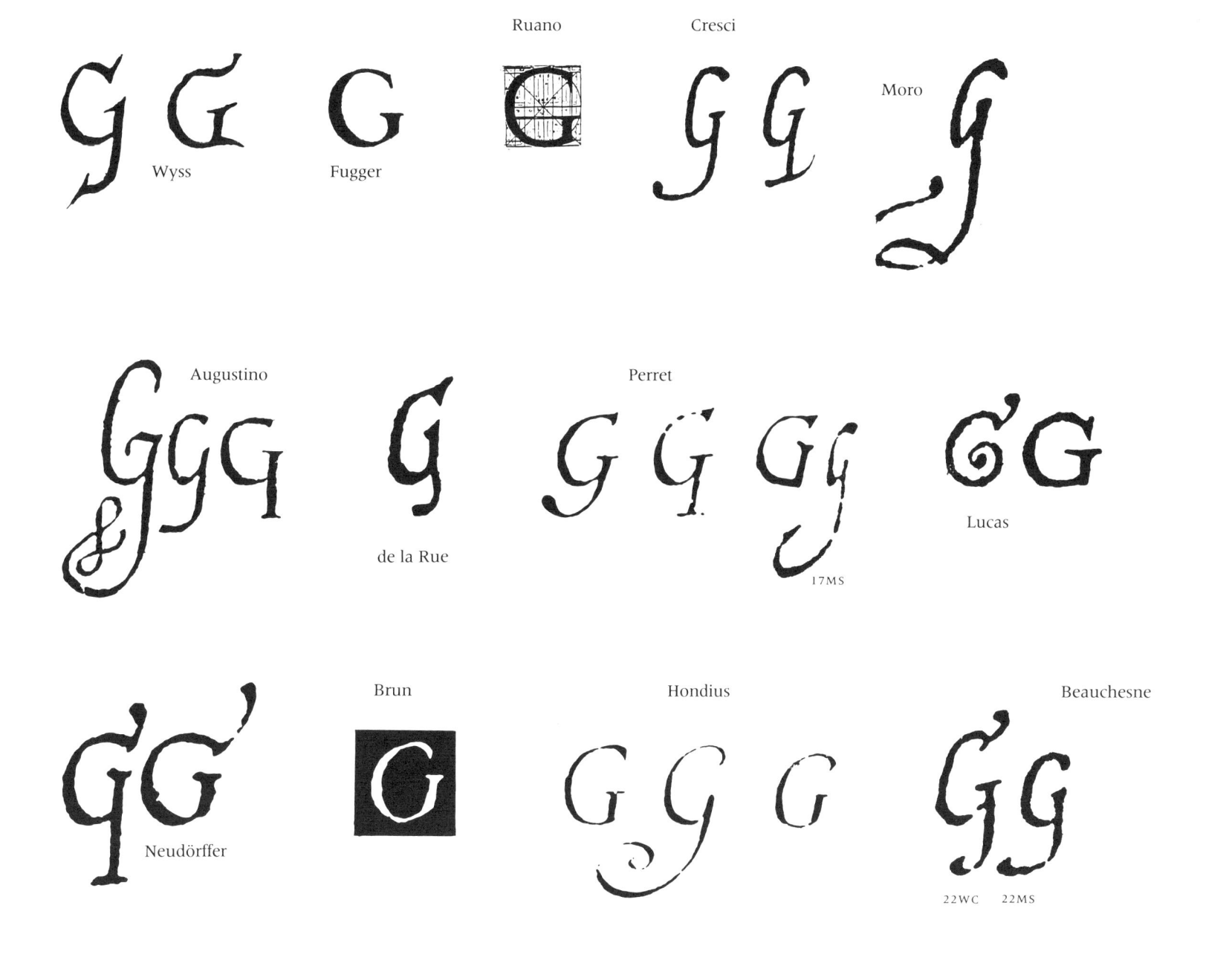

Wyss Fugger Ruano Cresci Moro

Augustino de la Rue Perret Lucas

Neudörffer Brun Hondius Beauchesne

144

Arrighi Tagliente

Palatino   4MS

3MS

Mercator Cataneo Amphiareo   7WC   7WC

Yciar

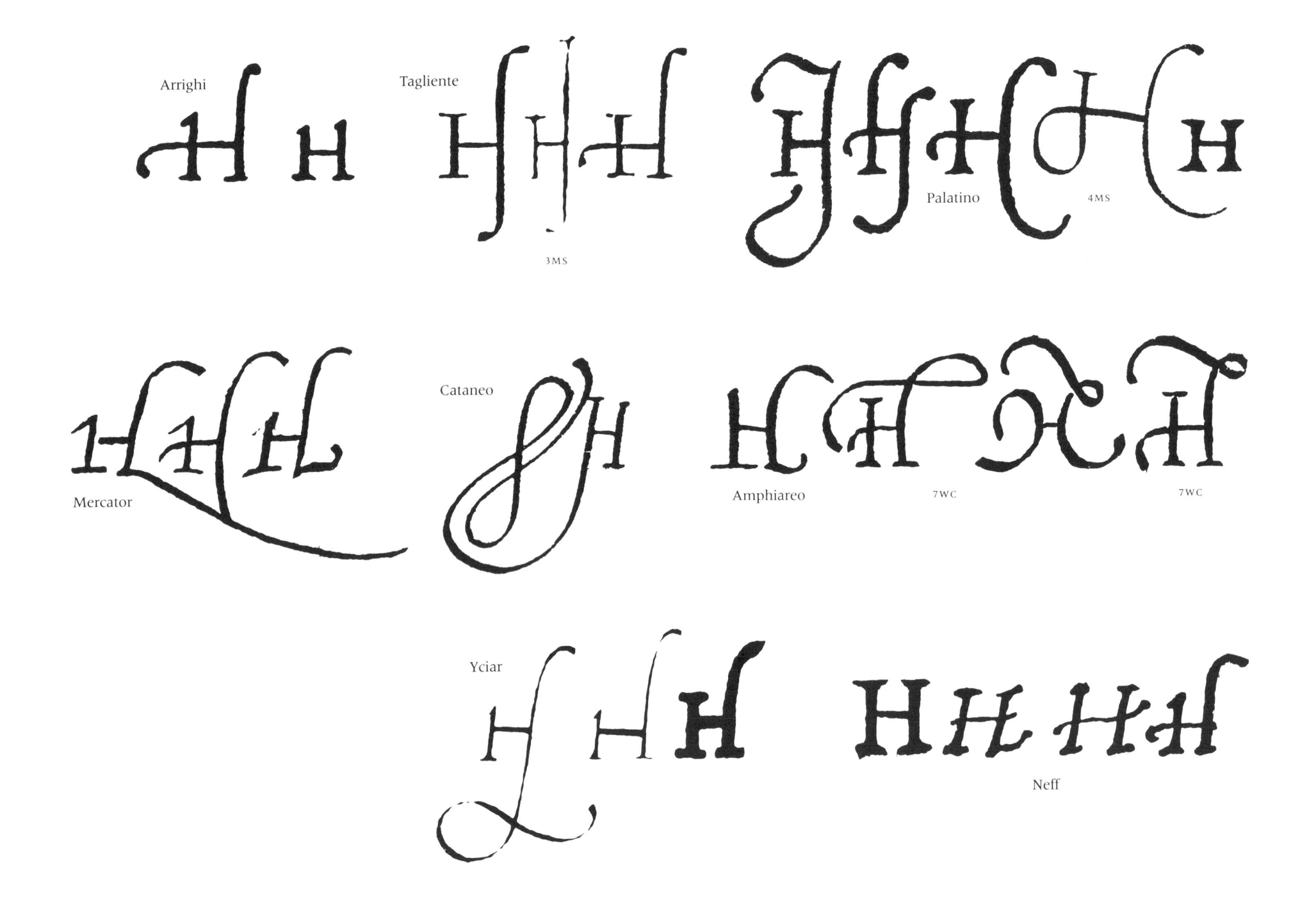

Neff

145

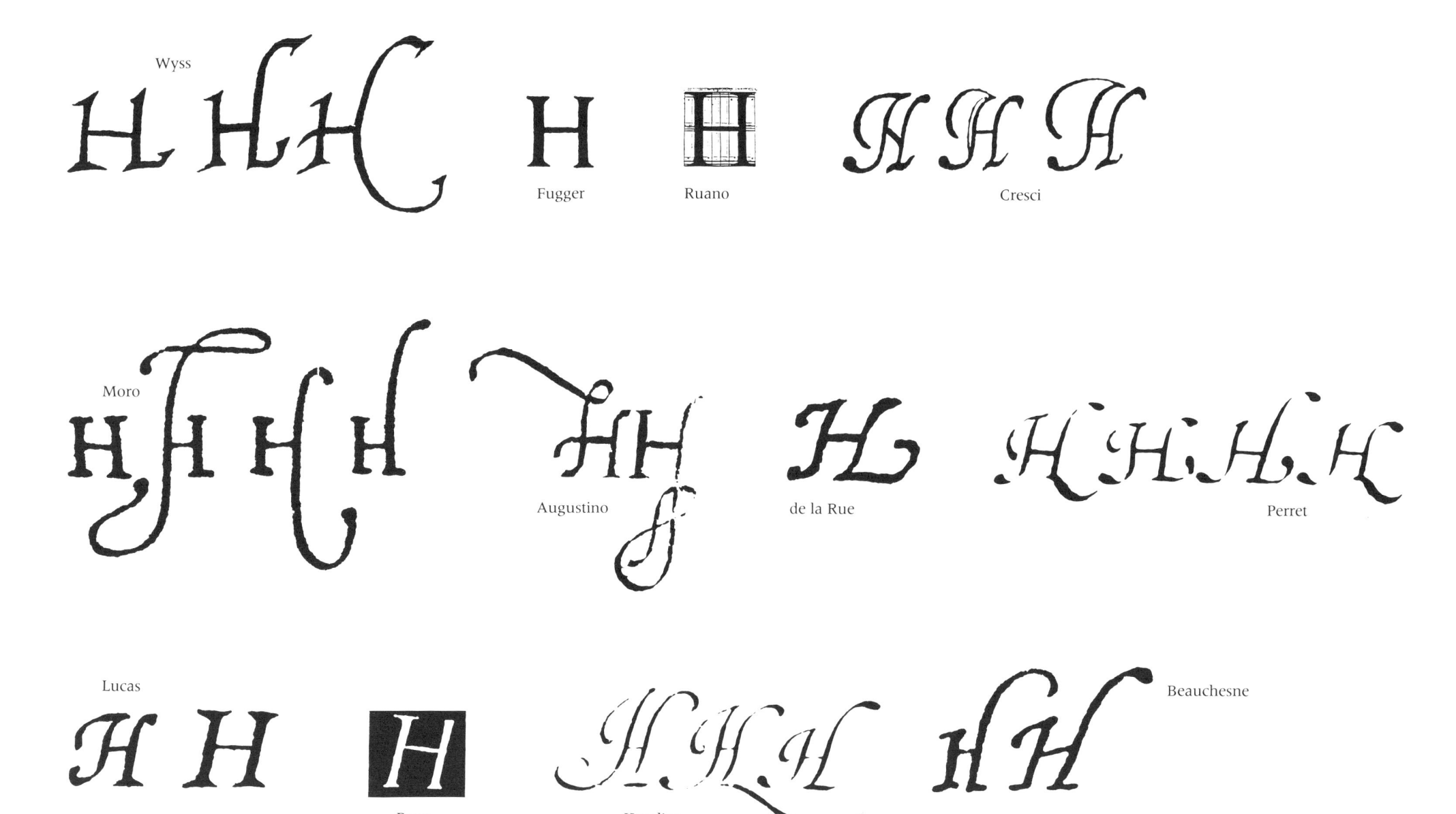

Wyss

Fugger　Ruano　Cresci

Moro

Augustino　de la Rue　Perret

Lucas　　　　　　　　　　　　　　　　　　　　Beauchesne

Brun　Hondius　22MS　22WC

146

Arrighi

Tagliente

Palatino

3MS

4MS

4MS

Mercator

Cataneo

Amphiareo

Yciar

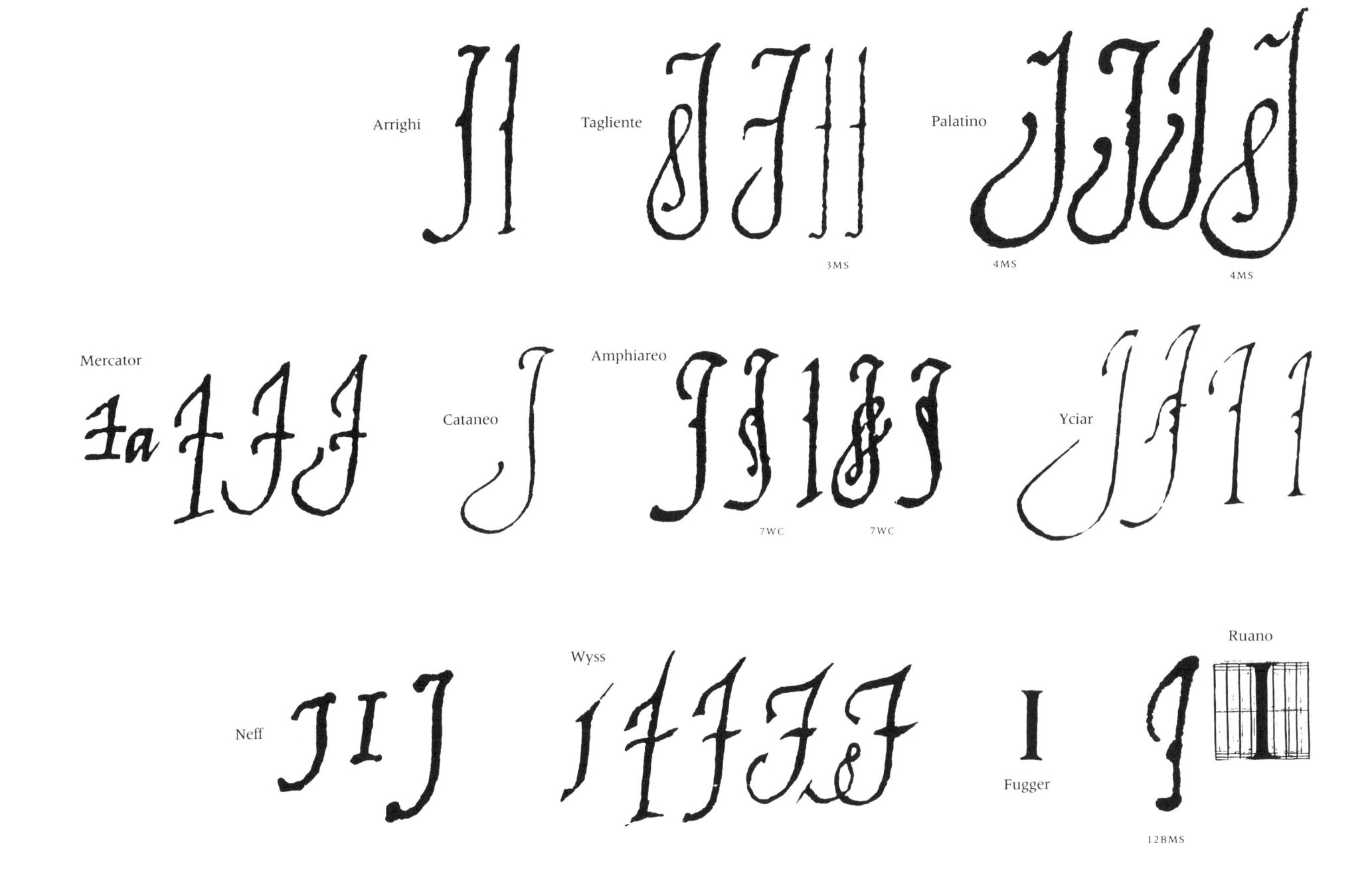

7WC

7WC

Neff

Wyss

Fugger

Ruano

12BMS

147

Cresci 13AMS

Moro

Augustino

Perret

de la Rue

17MS

Lucas

Neudörffer

Brun

Hondius

Beauchesne

22WC

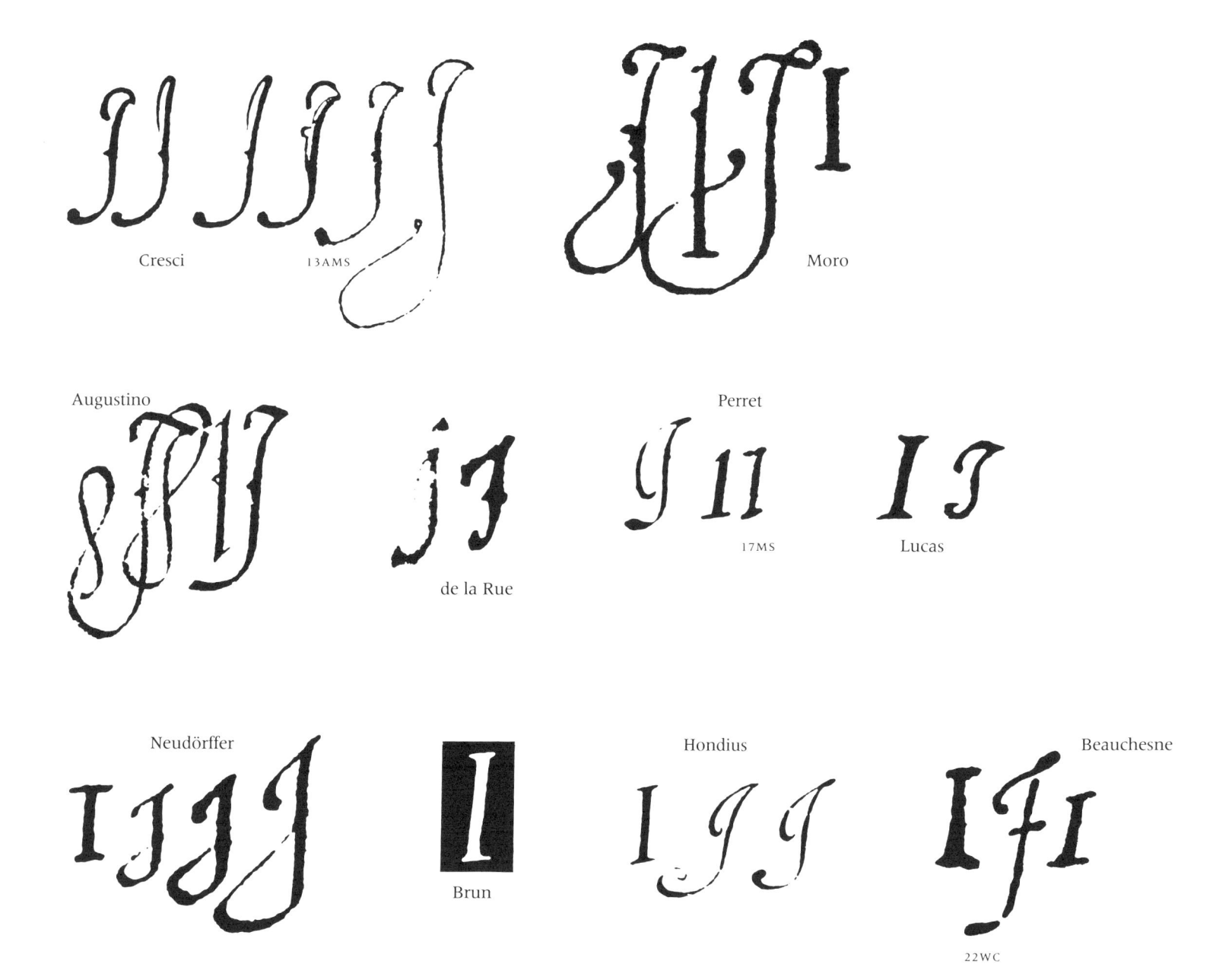

Arrighi   Palatino

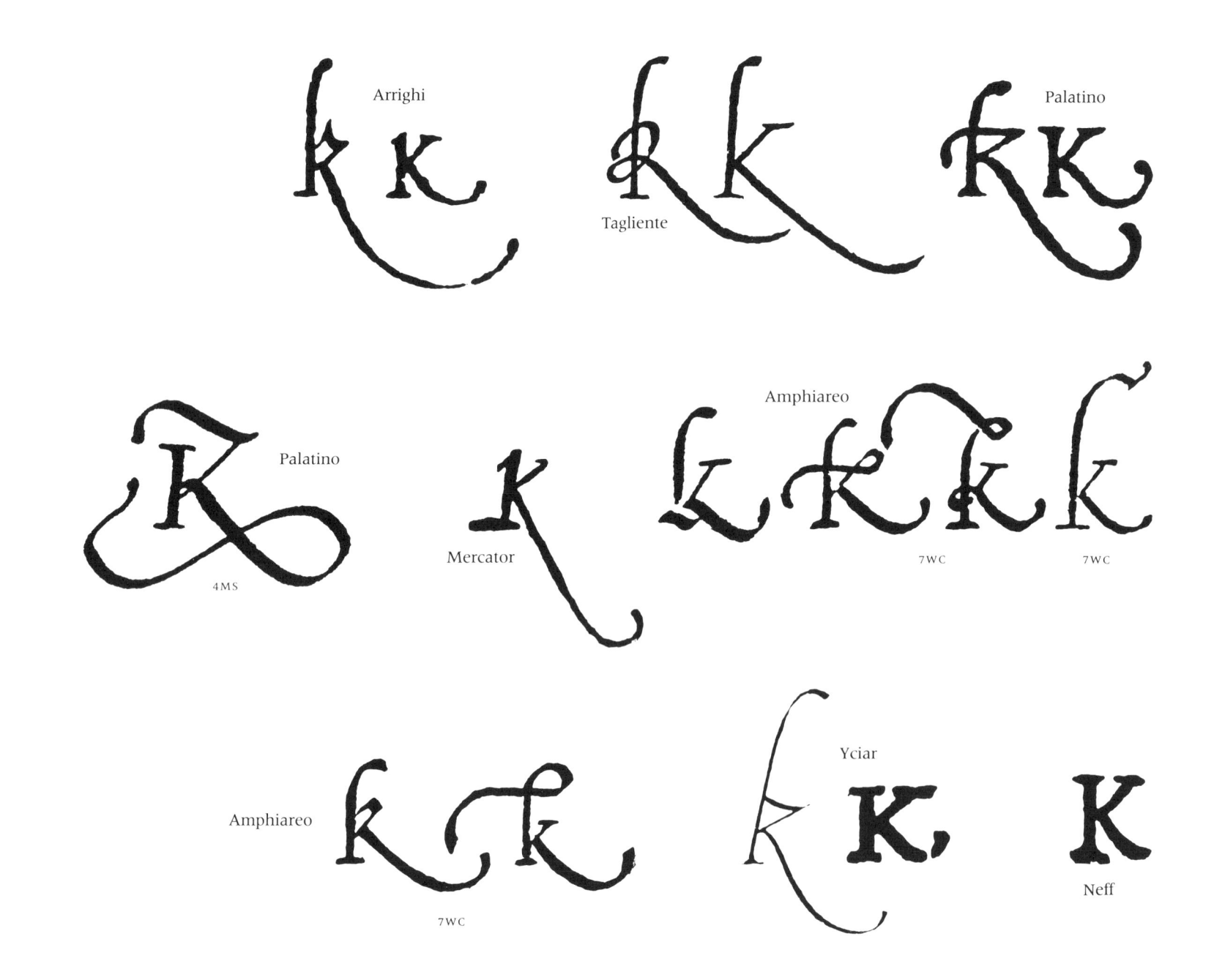

Tagliente

Palatino   Amphiareo

Mercator

7WC   7WC

Amphiareo   Yciar

7WC   Neff

Neff — Wyss — Ruano

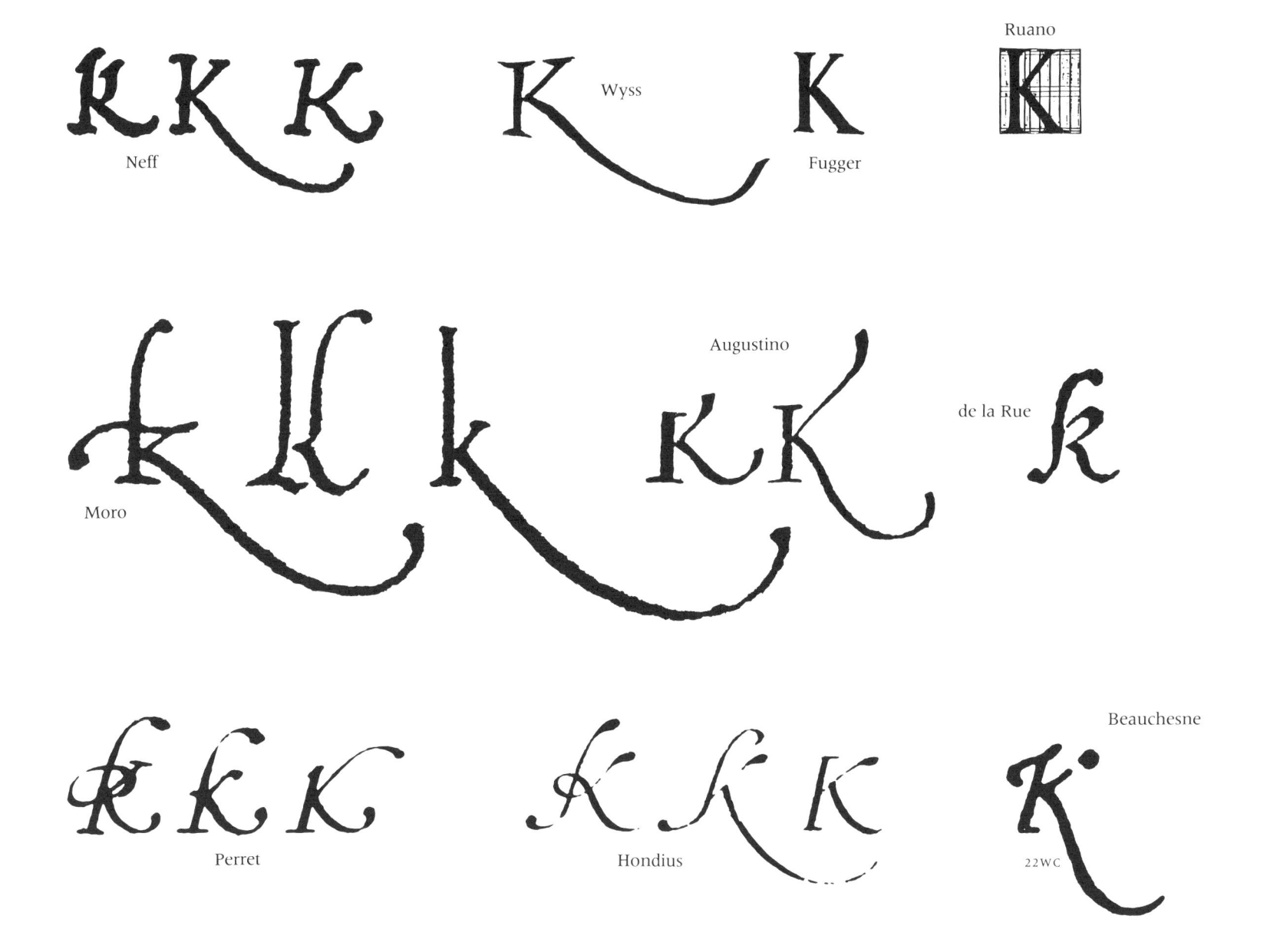

Moro — Augustino — de la Rue

Perret — Hondius — Beauchesne — 22WC

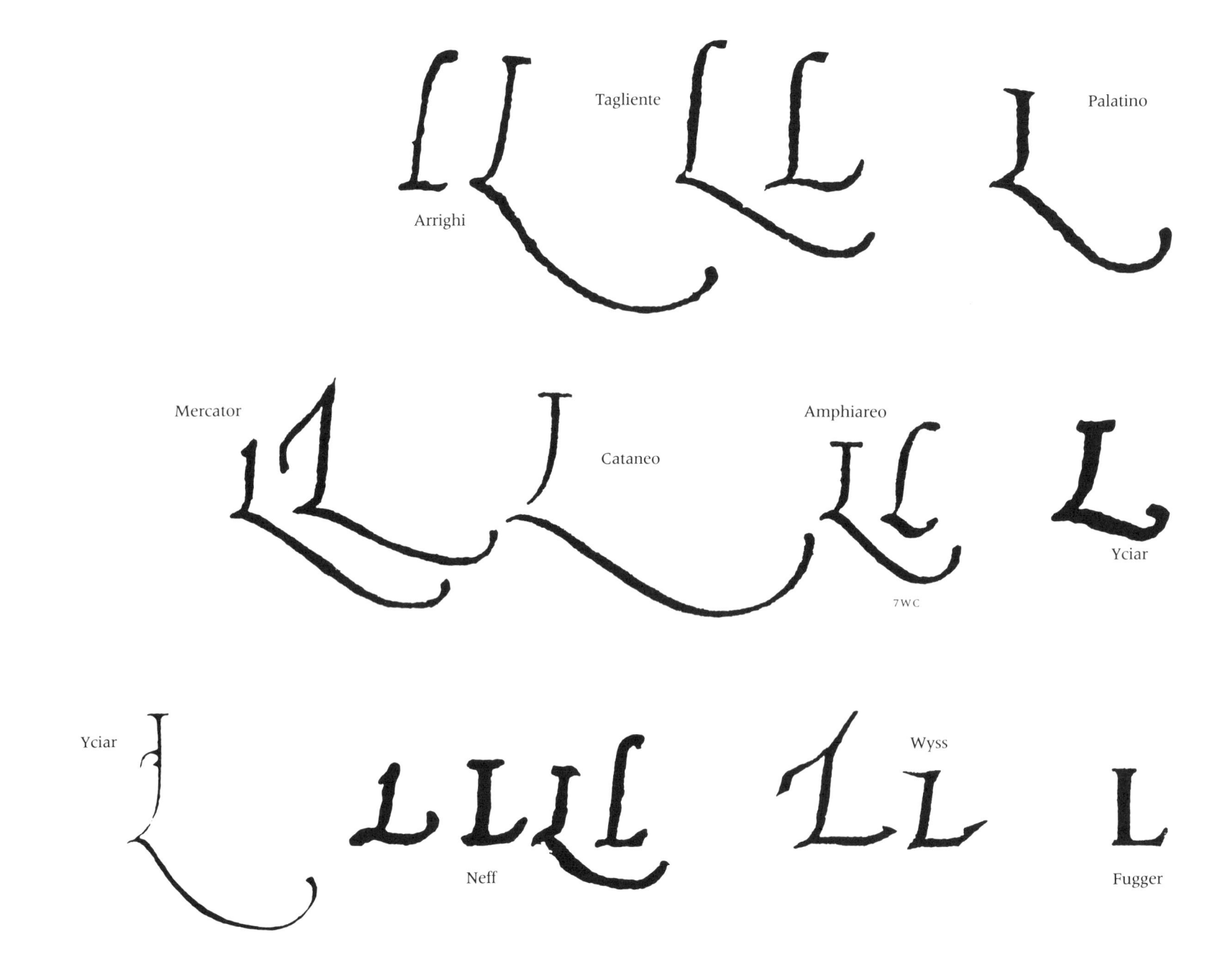

Arrighi · Tagliente · Palatino

Mercator · Cataneo · Amphiareo · Yciar

Yciar · Neff · Wyss · Fugger

Ruano Cresci 13BMS Moro

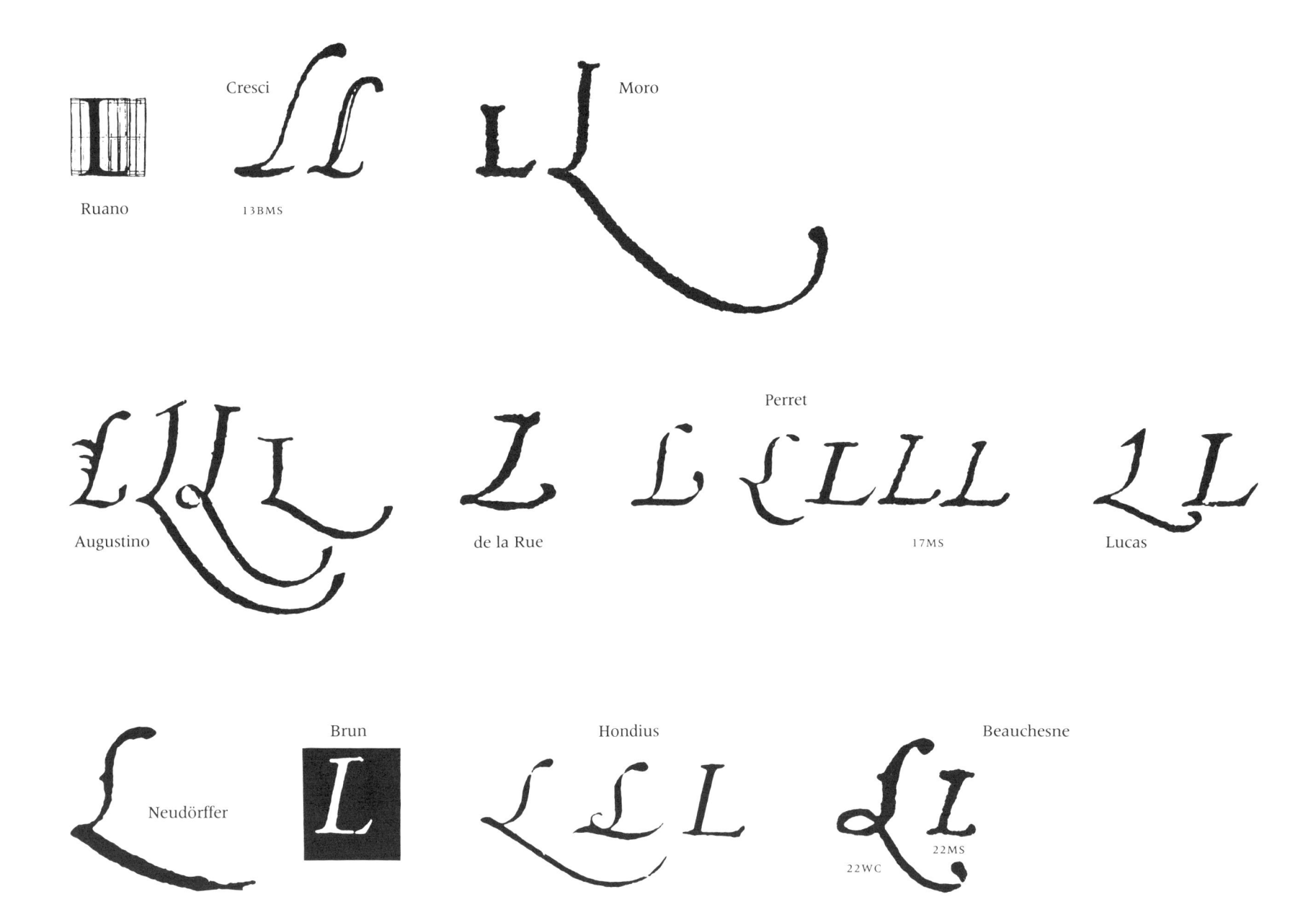

Augustino de la Rue Perret 17MS Lucas

Neudörffer Brun Hondius Beauchesne 22WC 22MS

152

Arrighi Tagliente Palatino

Cataneo

Mercator Amphiareo

4MS 7WC 7WC Yciar

Yciar Wyss

Neff Fugger

Ruano   Cresci   Moro   Augustino

13BMS

de la Rue   Perret   Neudörffer

17MS   Lucas

Brun   Beauchesne

Hondius   22WC

154

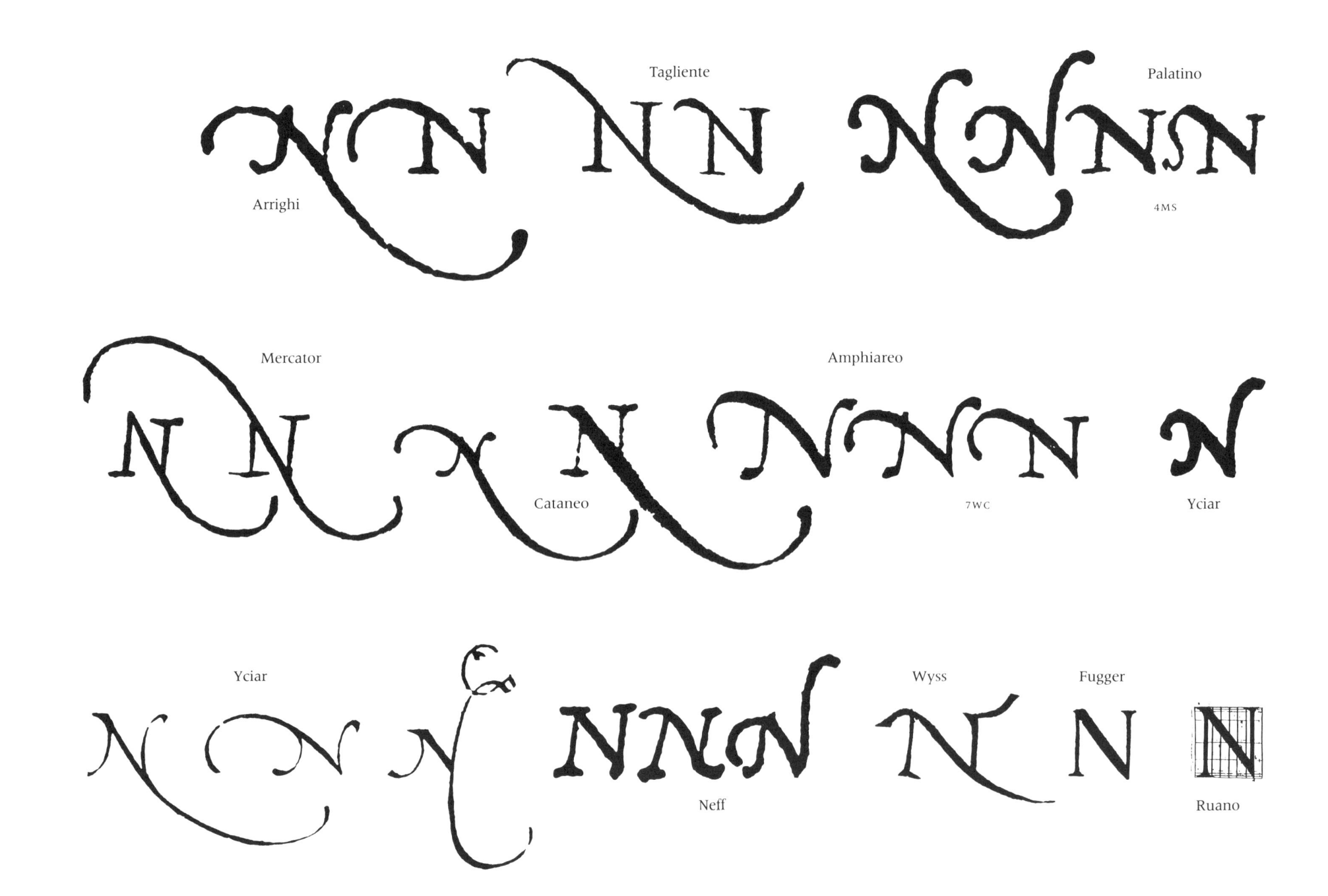

Tagliente · Palatino

Arrighi · 4MS

Mercator · Amphiareo

Cataneo · 7WC · Yciar

Yciar · Wyss · Fugger

Neff · Ruano

Cresci   Augustino

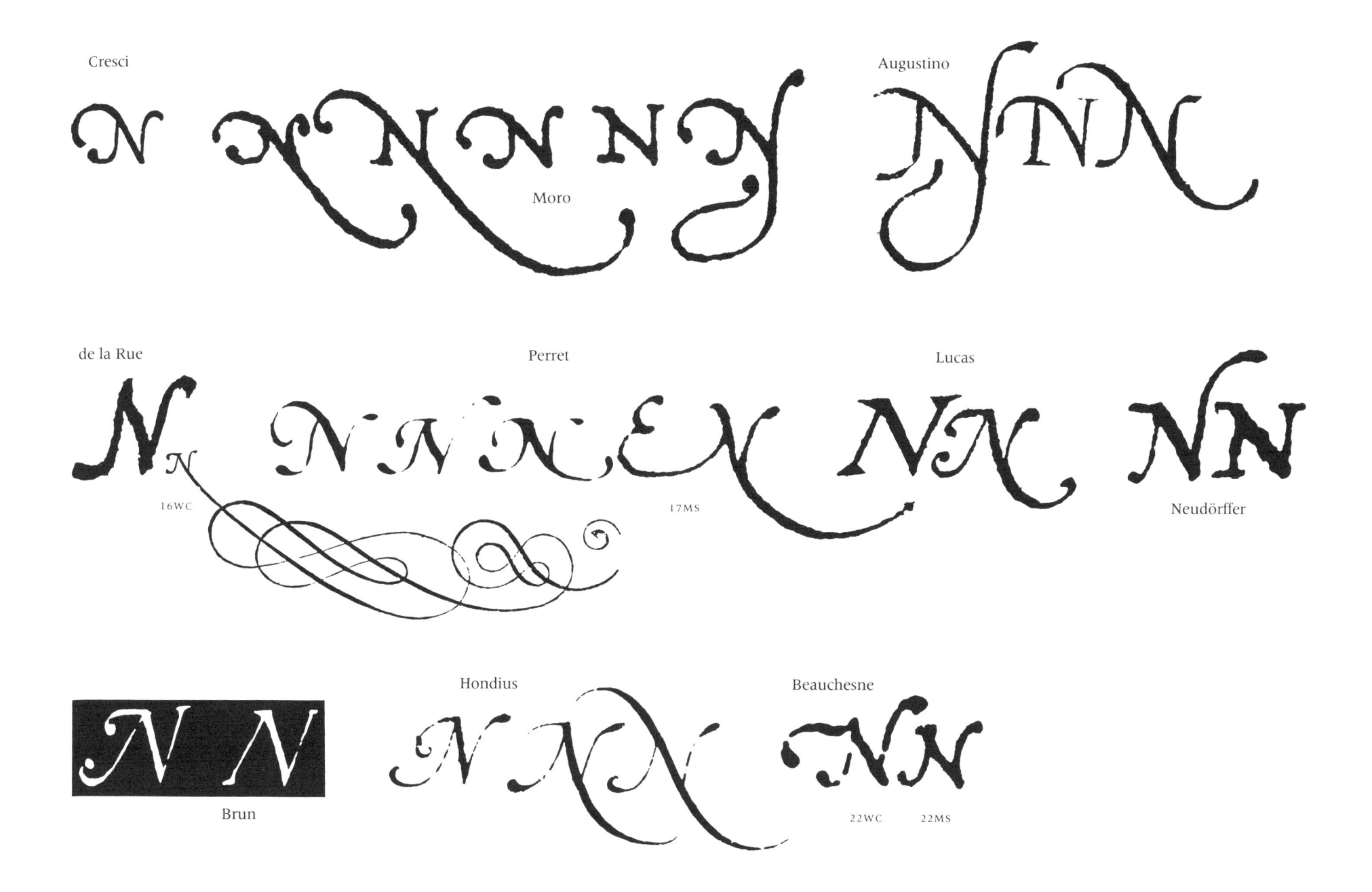

Moro

de la Rue   Perret   Lucas

16WC   17MS   Neudörffer

Hondius   Beauchesne

Brun   22WC   22MS

155

Arrighi   Palatino

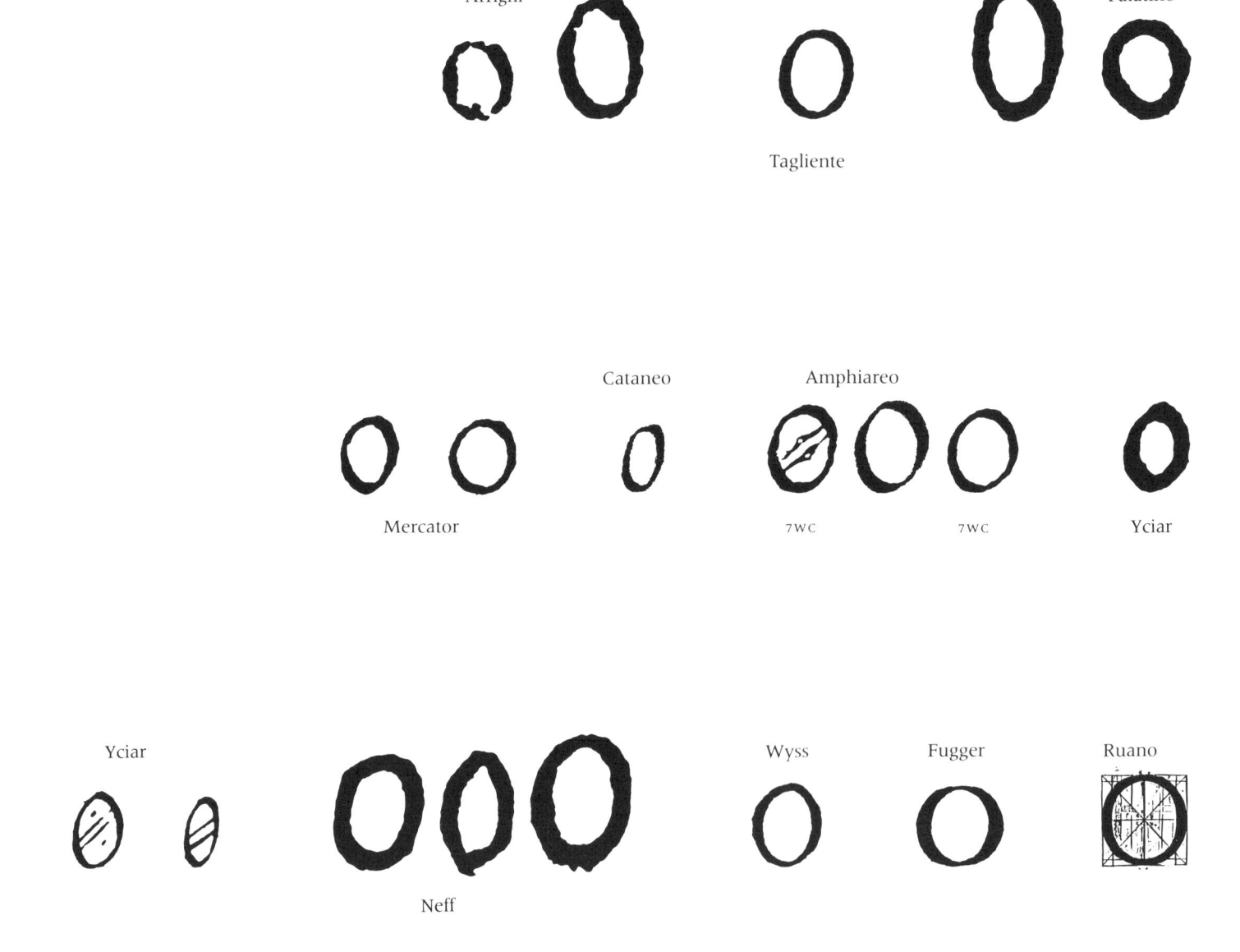

Tagliente

Cataneo   Amphiareo

Mercator   7WC   7WC   Yciar

Yciar   Wyss   Fugger   Ruano

Neff

Moro Augustino

Cresci

Perret

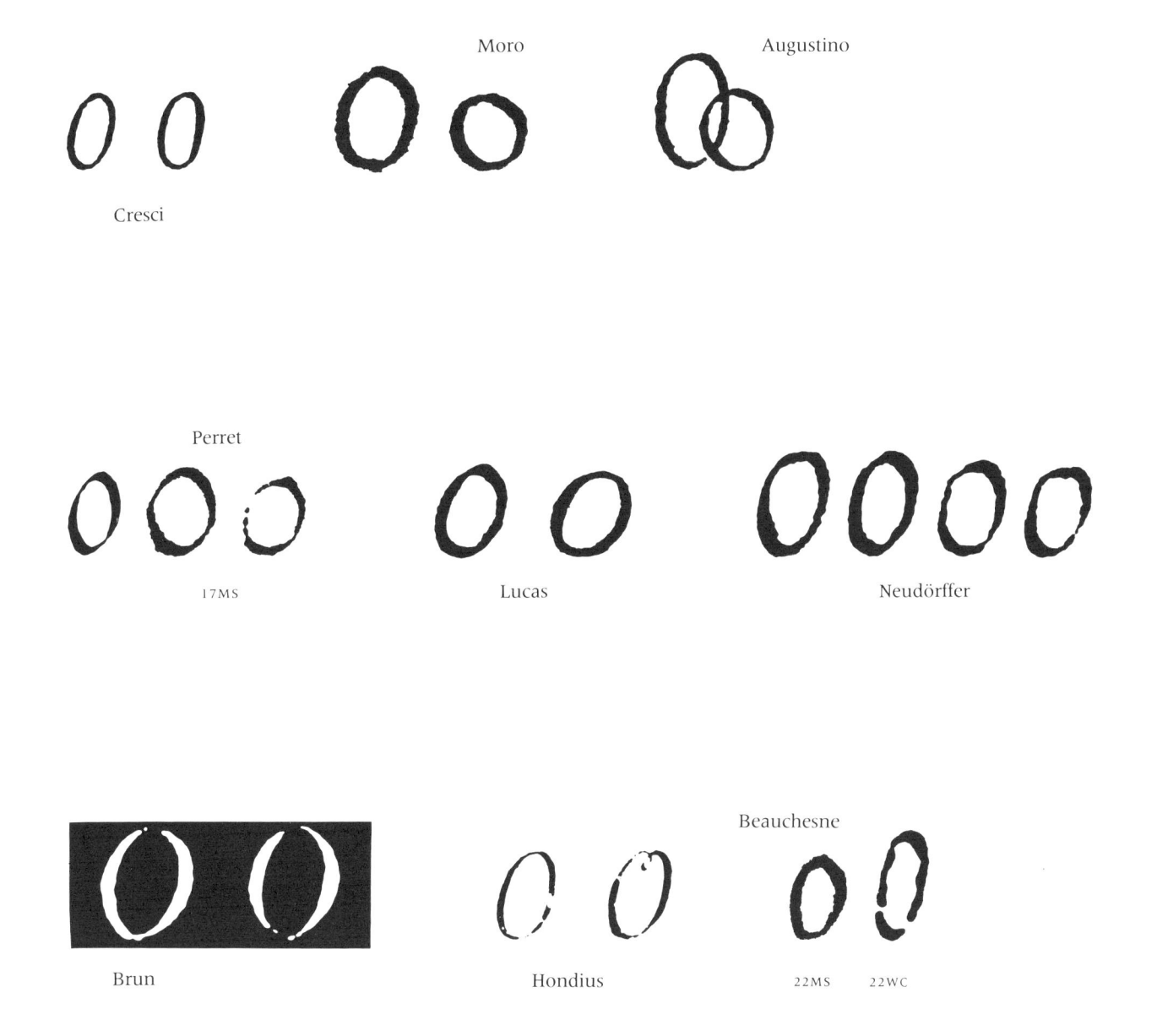

17MS Lucas Neudörffer

Beauchesne

Brun Hondius 22MS 22WC

Tagliente

Arrighi

2MS 3MS 3MS

Palatino

Mercator

Amphiareo

Cataneo

7WC 7WC

Yciar

Neff

Wyss

Ruano

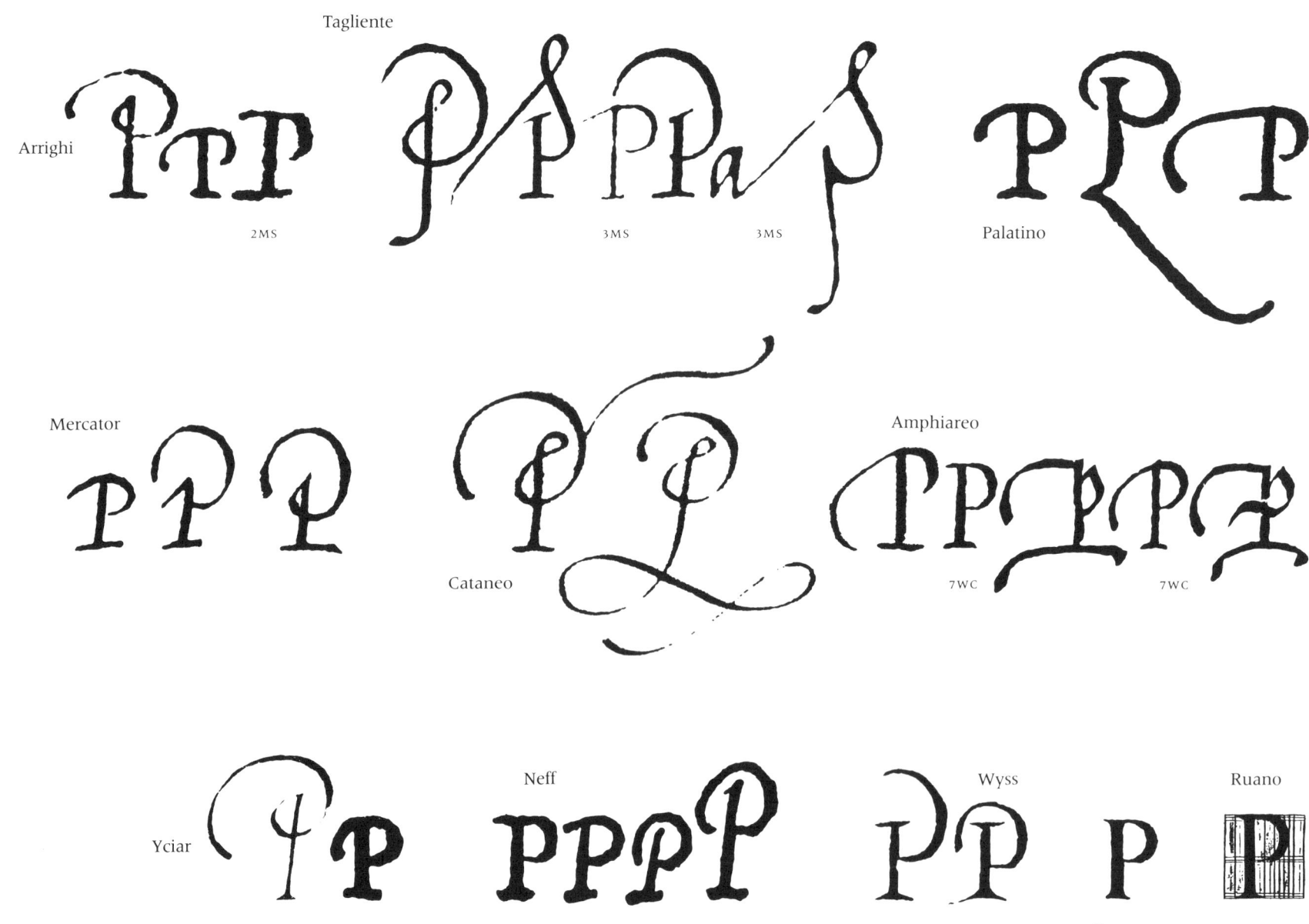

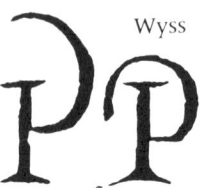

Fugger

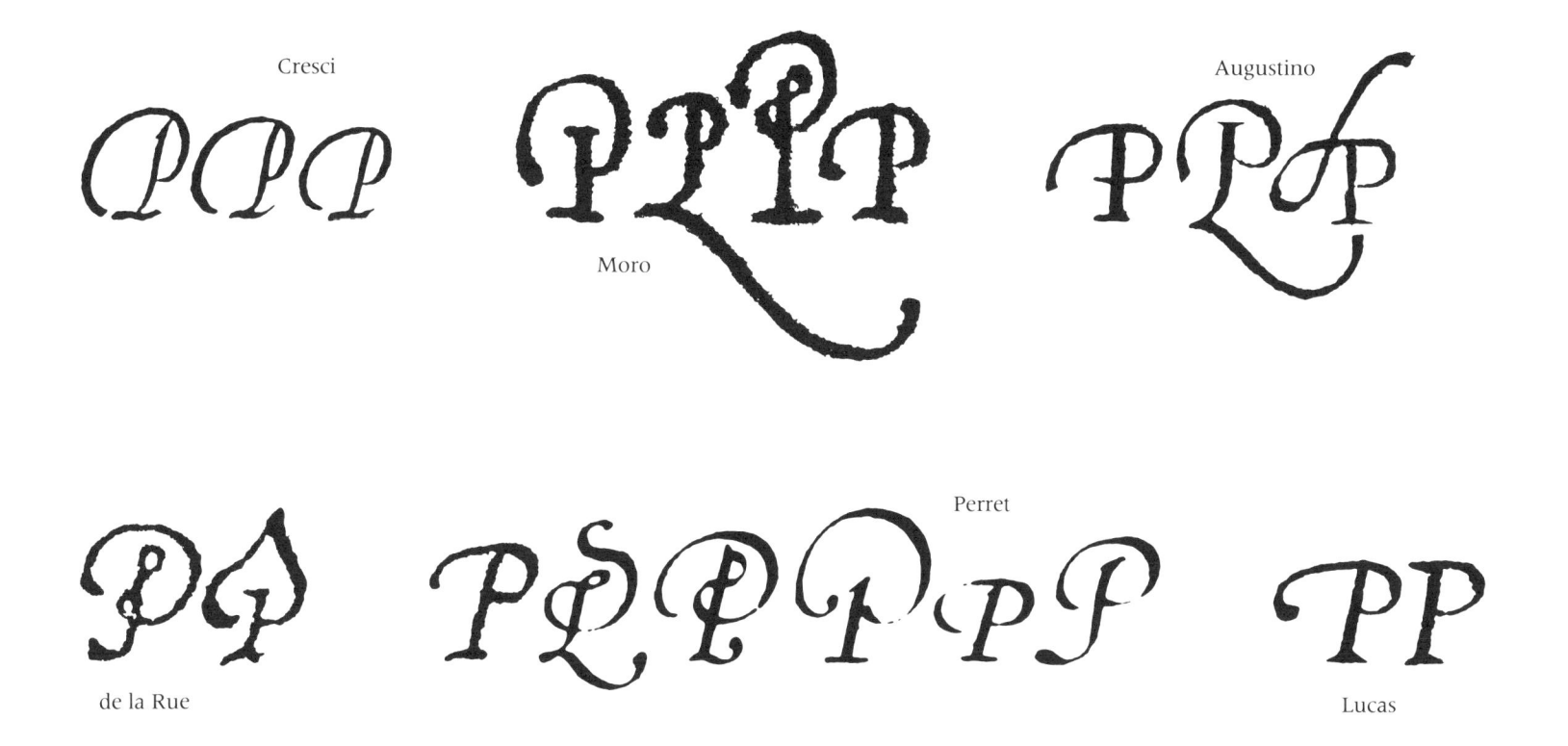

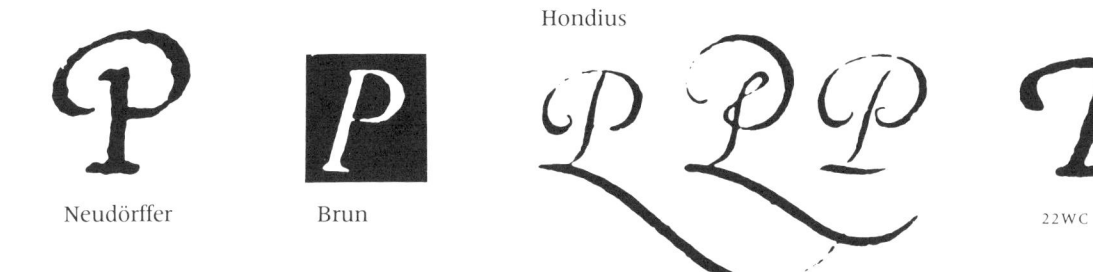

Cresci — Augustino

Moro

de la Rue — Perret — Lucas

Neudörffer — Brun — Hondius — Beauchesne

22WC

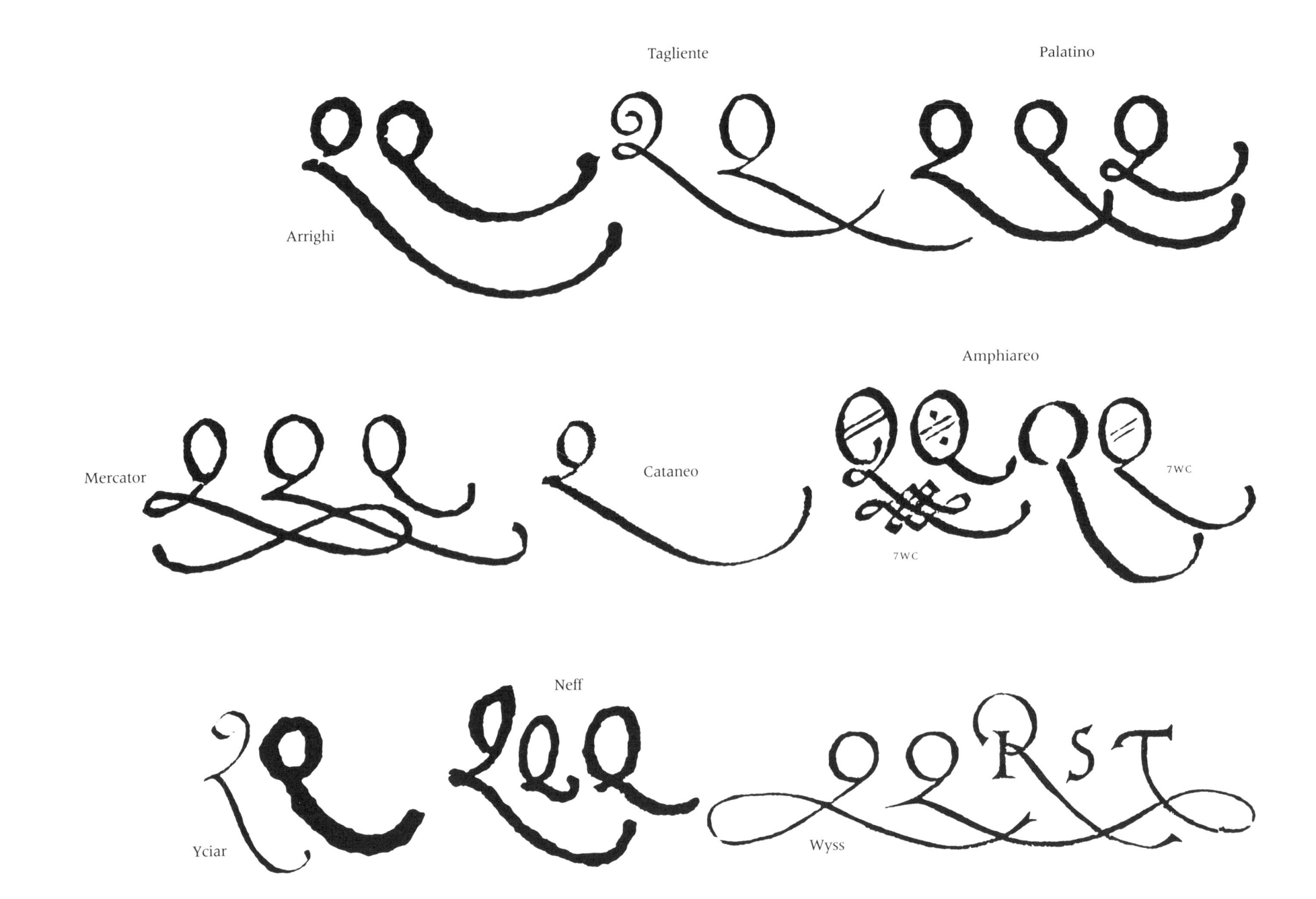

Tagliente Palatino

Arrighi

Mercator Cataneo Amphiareo

7WC

7WC

Neff

Yciar Wyss

161

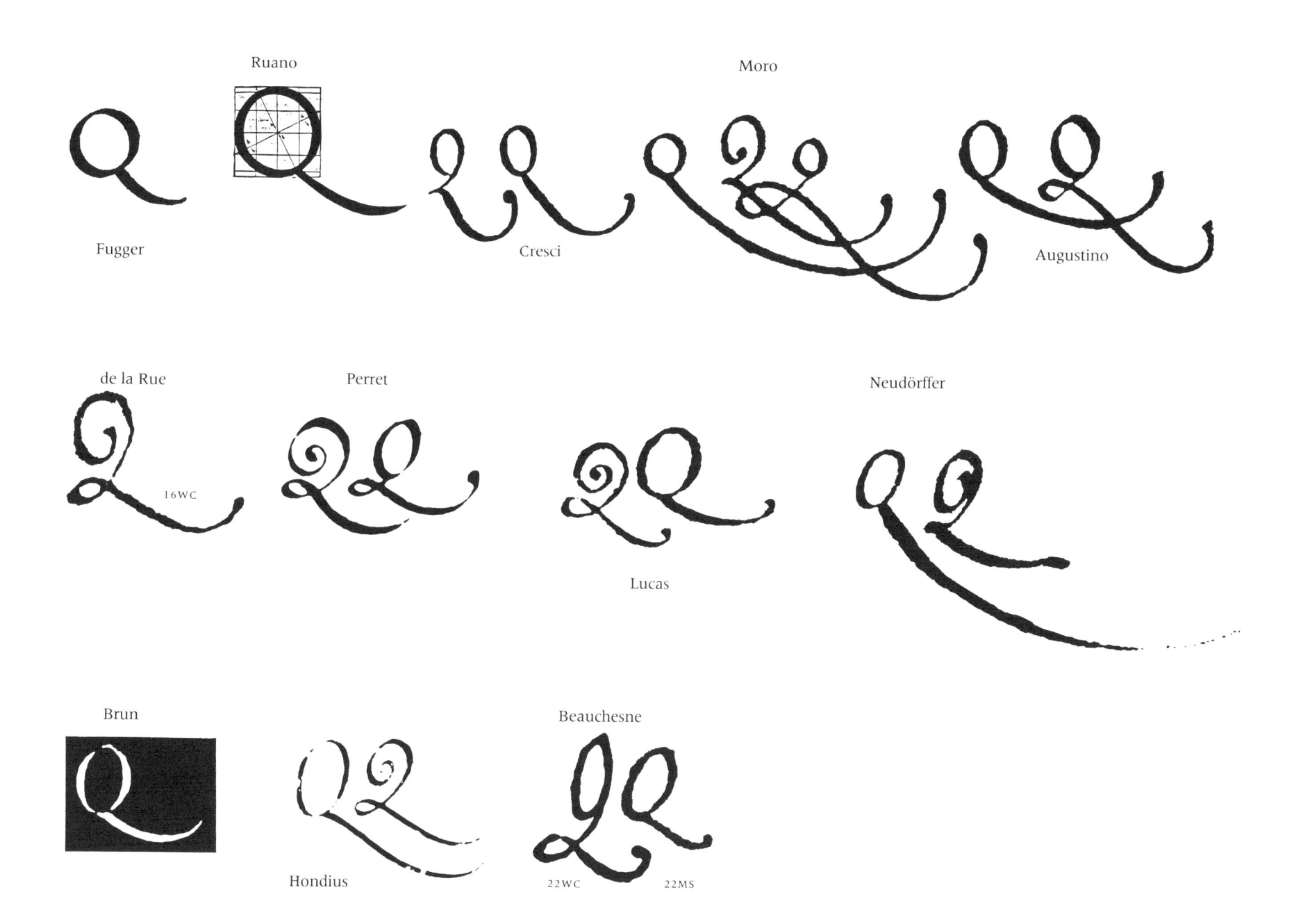

Ruano Moro

Fugger Cresci Augustino

de la Rue Perret Neudörffer

Lucas

Brun Beauchesne

Hondius

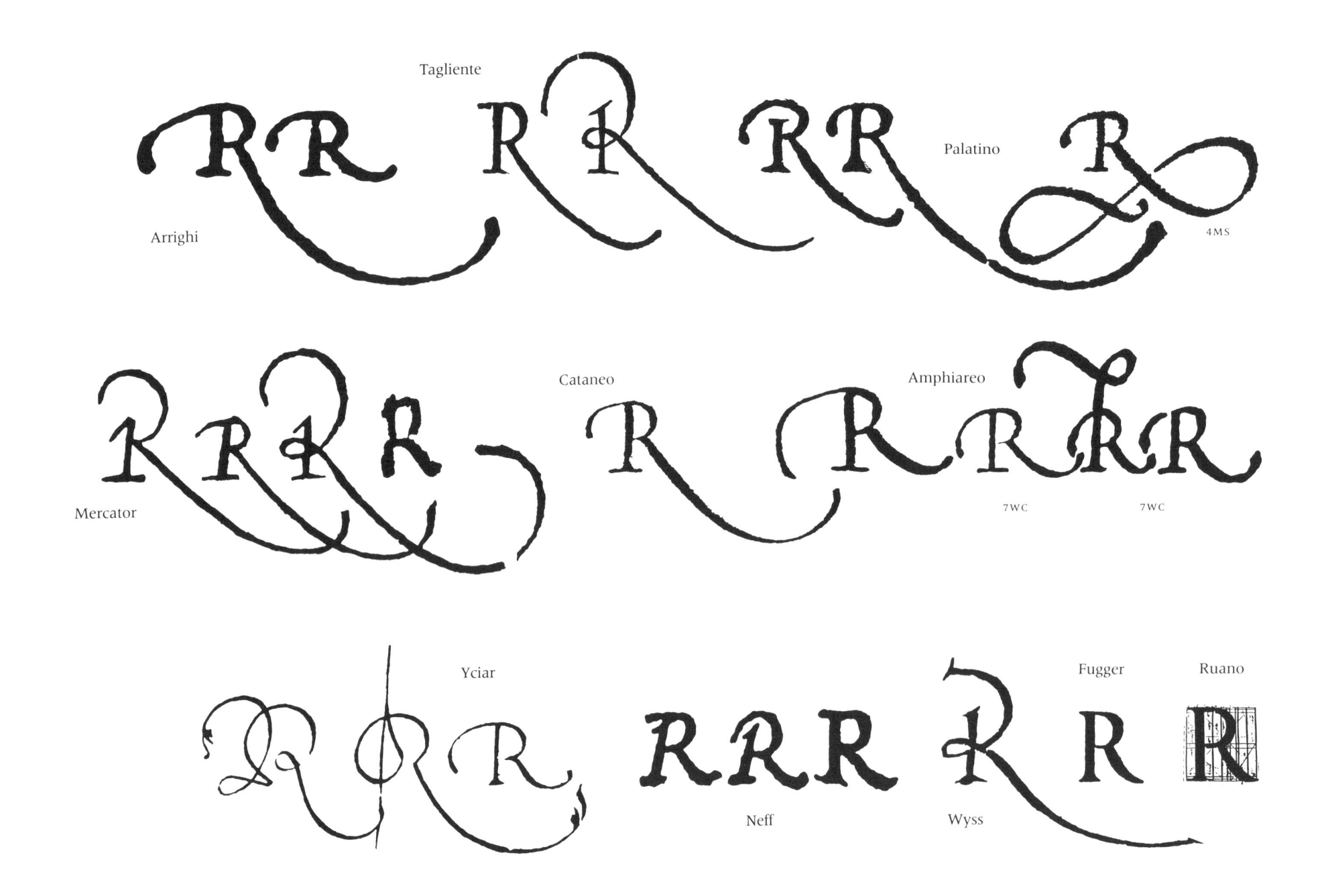

Arrighi · Tagliente · Palatino · 4MS

Mercator · Cataneo · Amphiareo · 7WC · 7WC

Yciar · Neff · Fugger · Wyss · Ruano

Cresci

Moro

Augustino

Perret

Lucas

Neudörffer

Brun

Hondius

Beauchesne

22WC

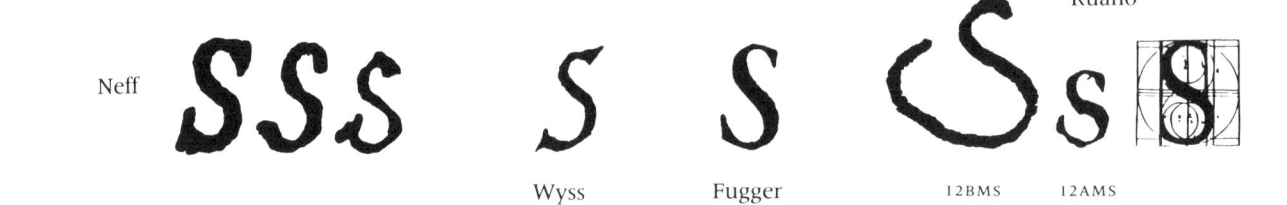

Arrighi $\mathcal{S}s$ Tagliente sss 3MS   Palatino $Ssss$ 4MS

Mercator ssS 5MS   Cataneo ss Amphiareo Ss 7WC   Yciar Ss

Neff Sss Wyss S Fugger S Ruano Ss 12BMS   12AMS

Cresci

ſſss   ſss   ſss

13AMS   13BMS   Moro   Augustino

Lucas   Neudörffer

S   ſſss   ss   ss

de la Rue   17MS   Perret

Brun   Beauchesne

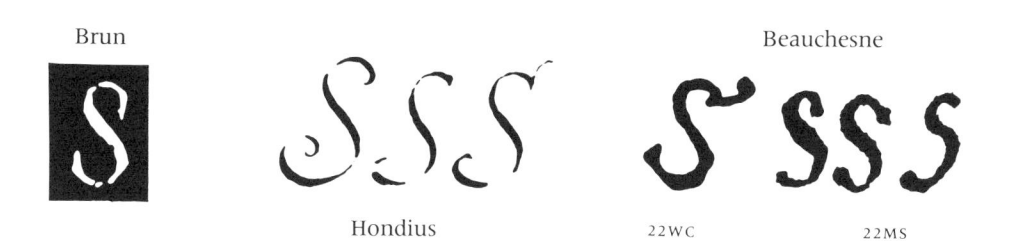

S   sss   s ss s

Hondius   22WC   22MS

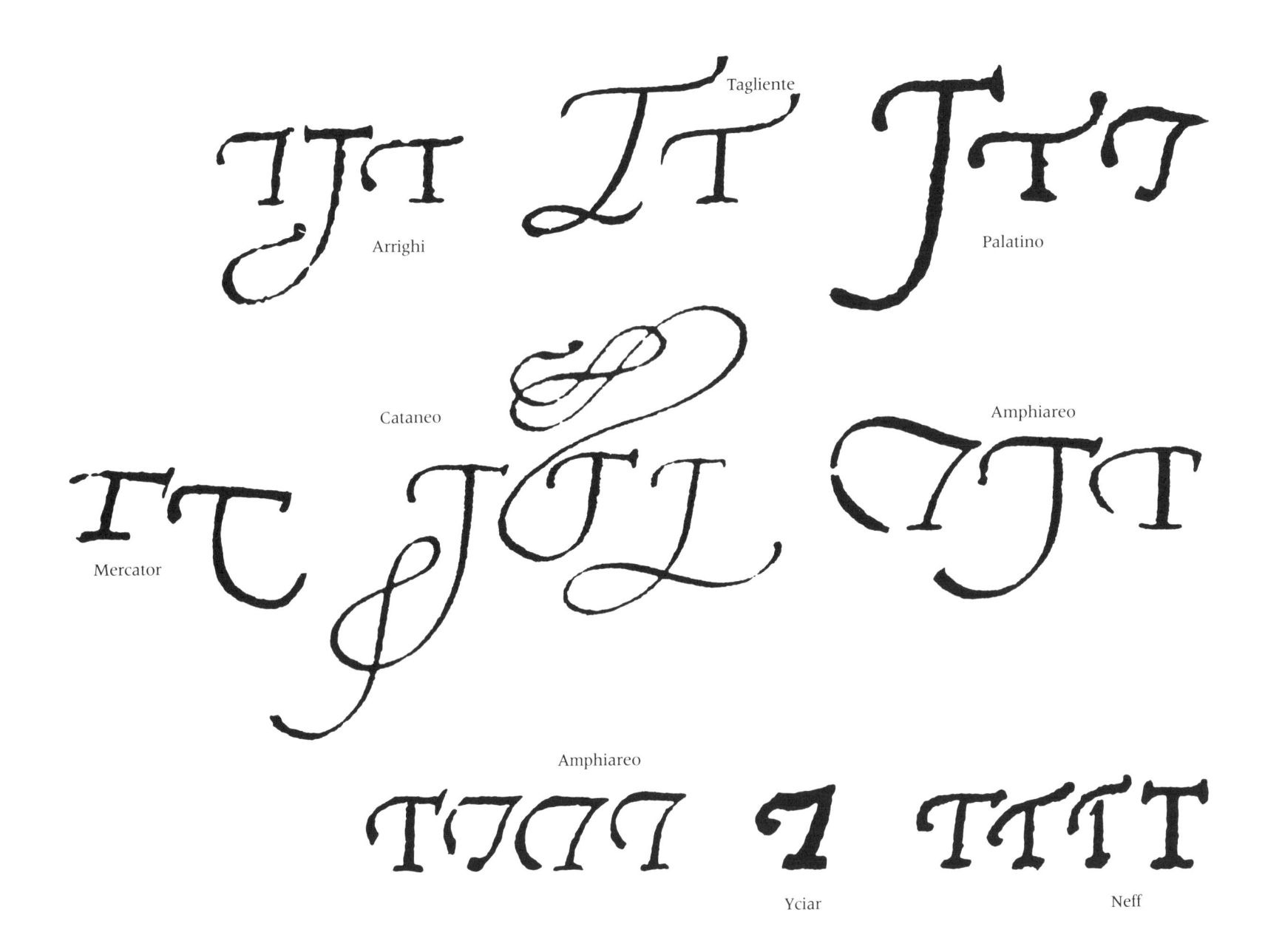

Tagliente

Arrighi

Palatino

Cataneo

Amphiareo

Mercator

Amphiareo

Yciar

Neff

Wyss — Fugger — Ruano — Cresci

Moro — Augustino — Perret — Lucas

Neudörffer — Brun — Hondius — Beauchesne

22MS 22WC

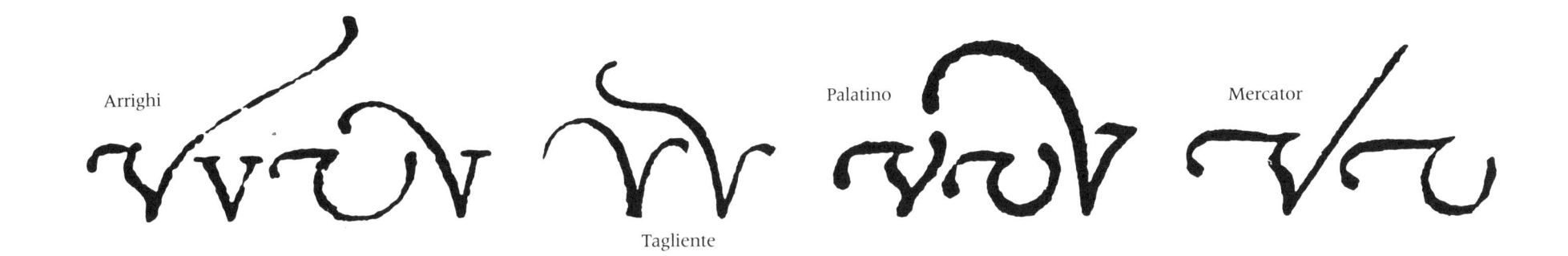

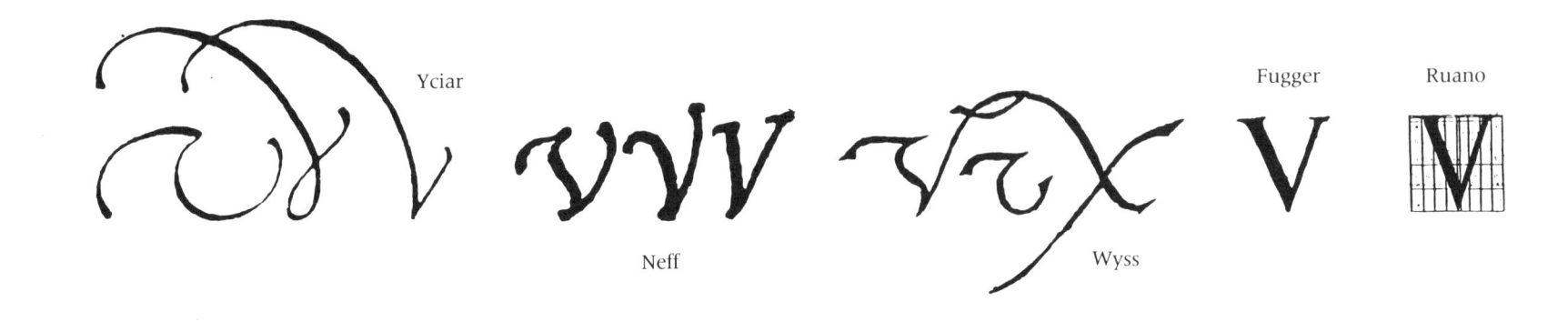

Arrighi · Palatino · Mercator

Tagliente

Cataneo · Amphiareo · Yciar

7MS · 7WC · 7WC

Yciar · Fugger · Ruano

Neff · Wyss

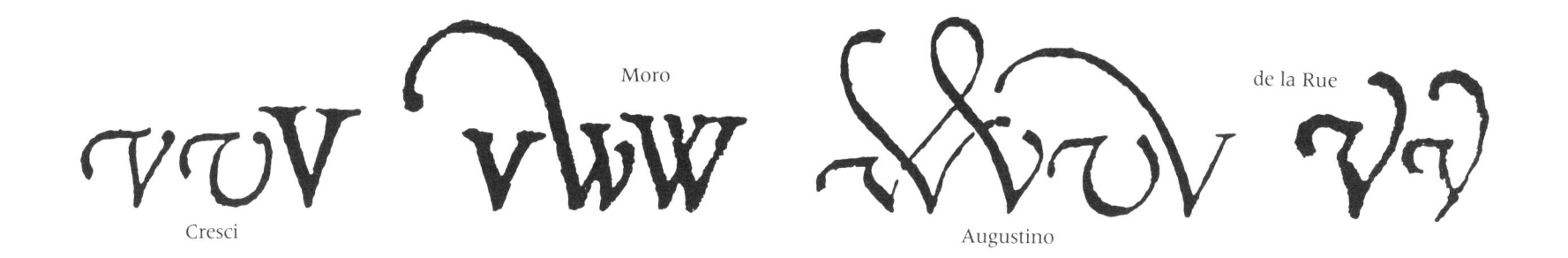

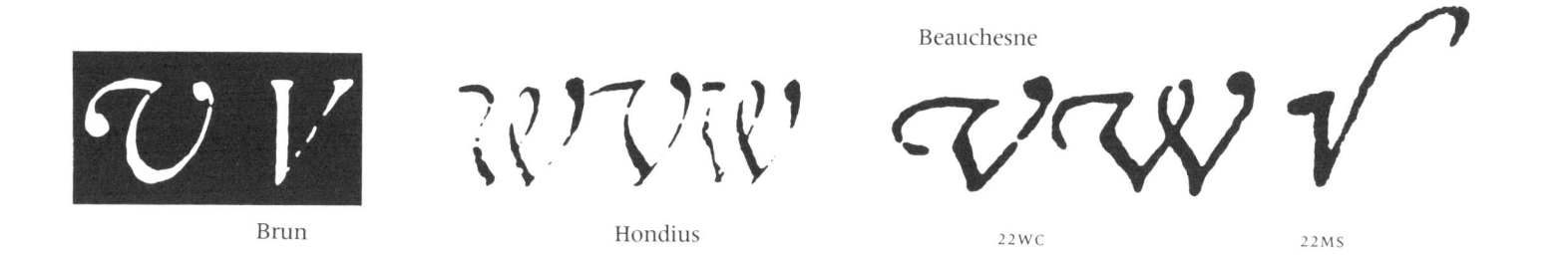

Cresci Moro Augustino de la Rue

Perret 17MS Lucas Neudörffer

Brun Hondius Beauchesne 22WC 22MS

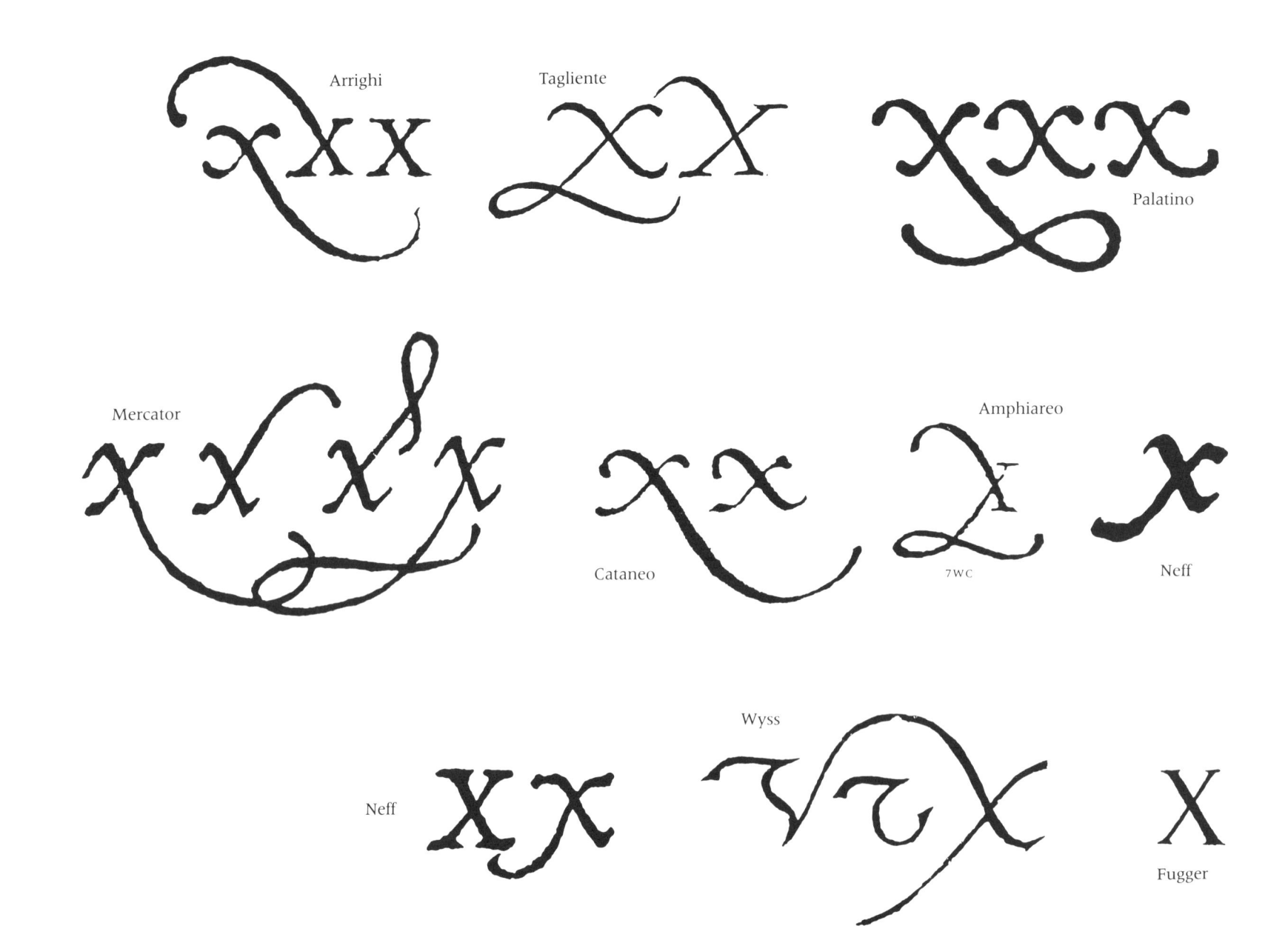

Arrighi　Tagliente

Palatino

Mercator　Amphiareo

Cataneo　7WC　Neff

Wyss

Neff　Fugger

171

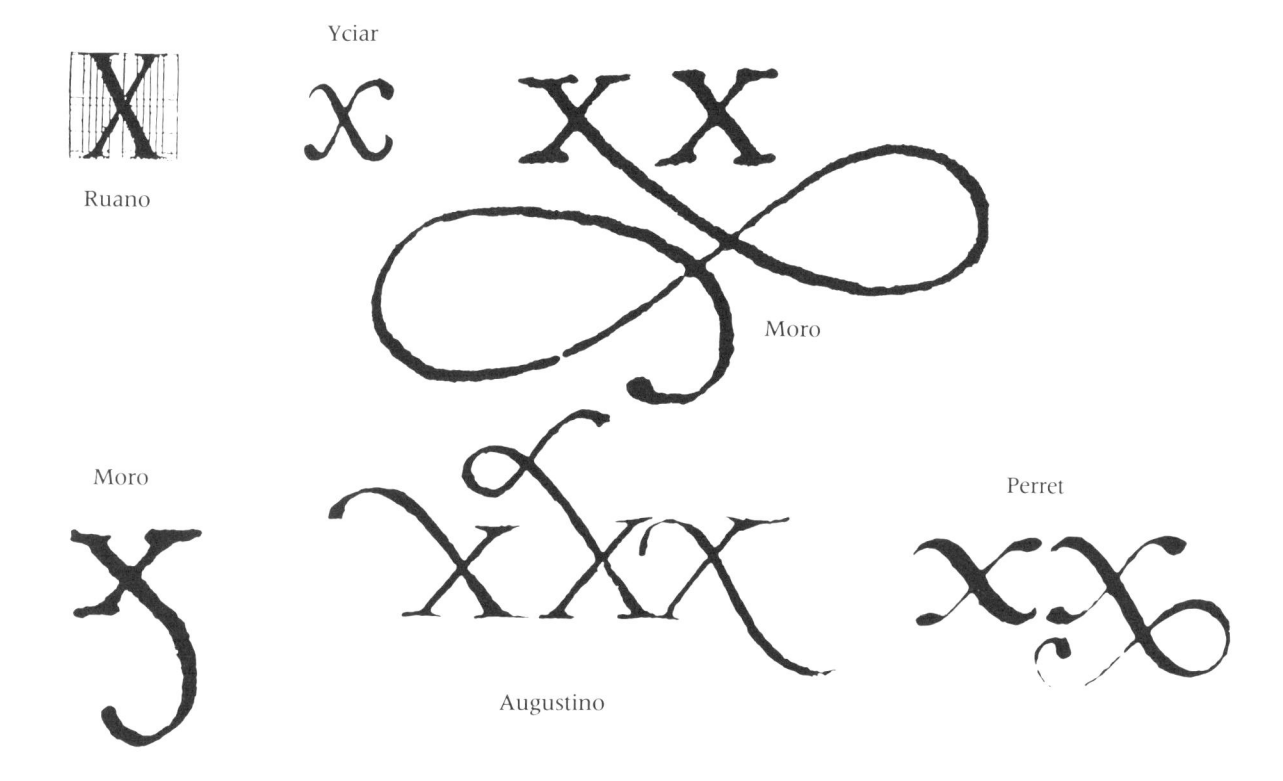

Ruano · Yciar · Moro

Moro · Augustino · Perret

Lucas · Brun · Hondius · Beauchesne

22WC

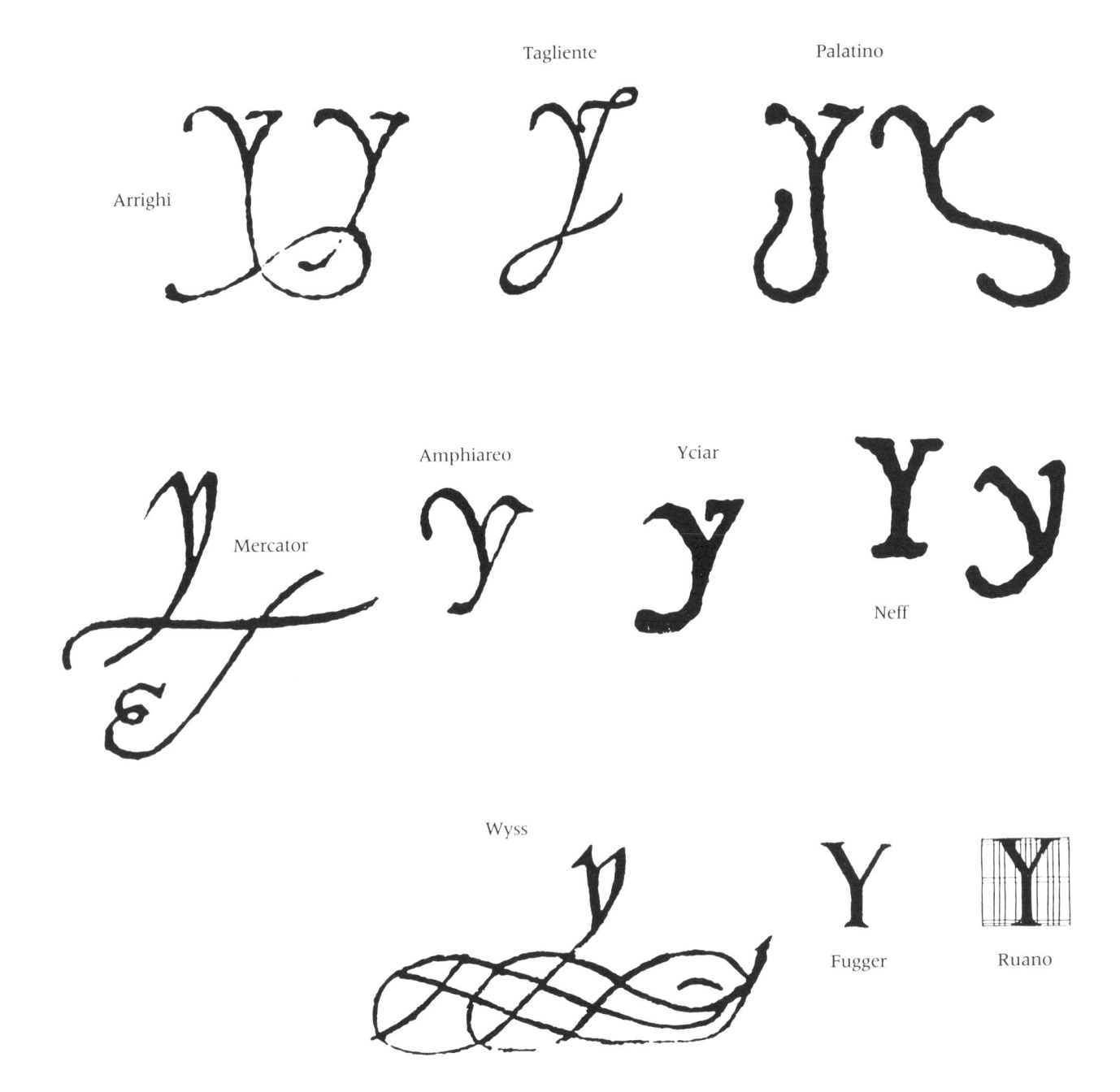

Arrighi Tagliente Palatino

Mercator Amphiareo Yciar Neff

Wyss Fugger Ruano

Augustino

Moro

Perret Lucas Hondius

Brun

Hondius Beauchesne

22WC

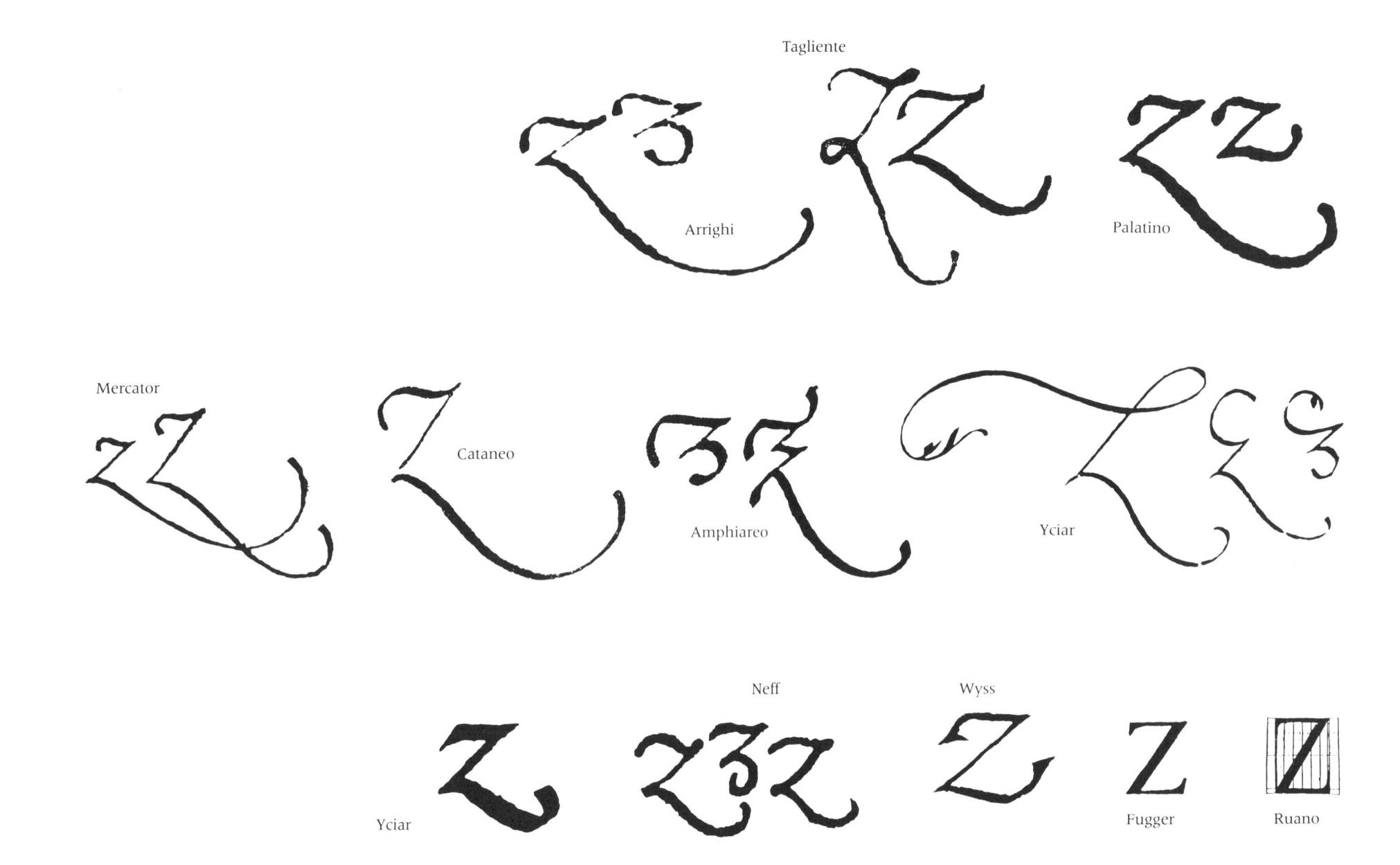

Tagliente

Arrighi Palatino

Mercator Cataneo Amphiareo Yciar

Neff Wyss

Yciar Fugger Ruano

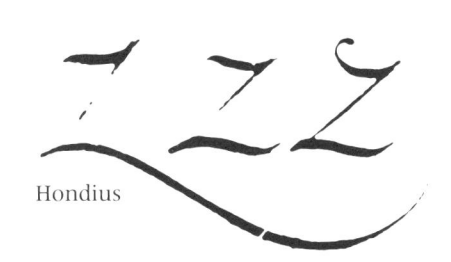

Cresci — Moro — Augustino

de la Rue — 16WC — Perret — Beauchesne

Brun — Hondius — Beauchesne — 22WC

176

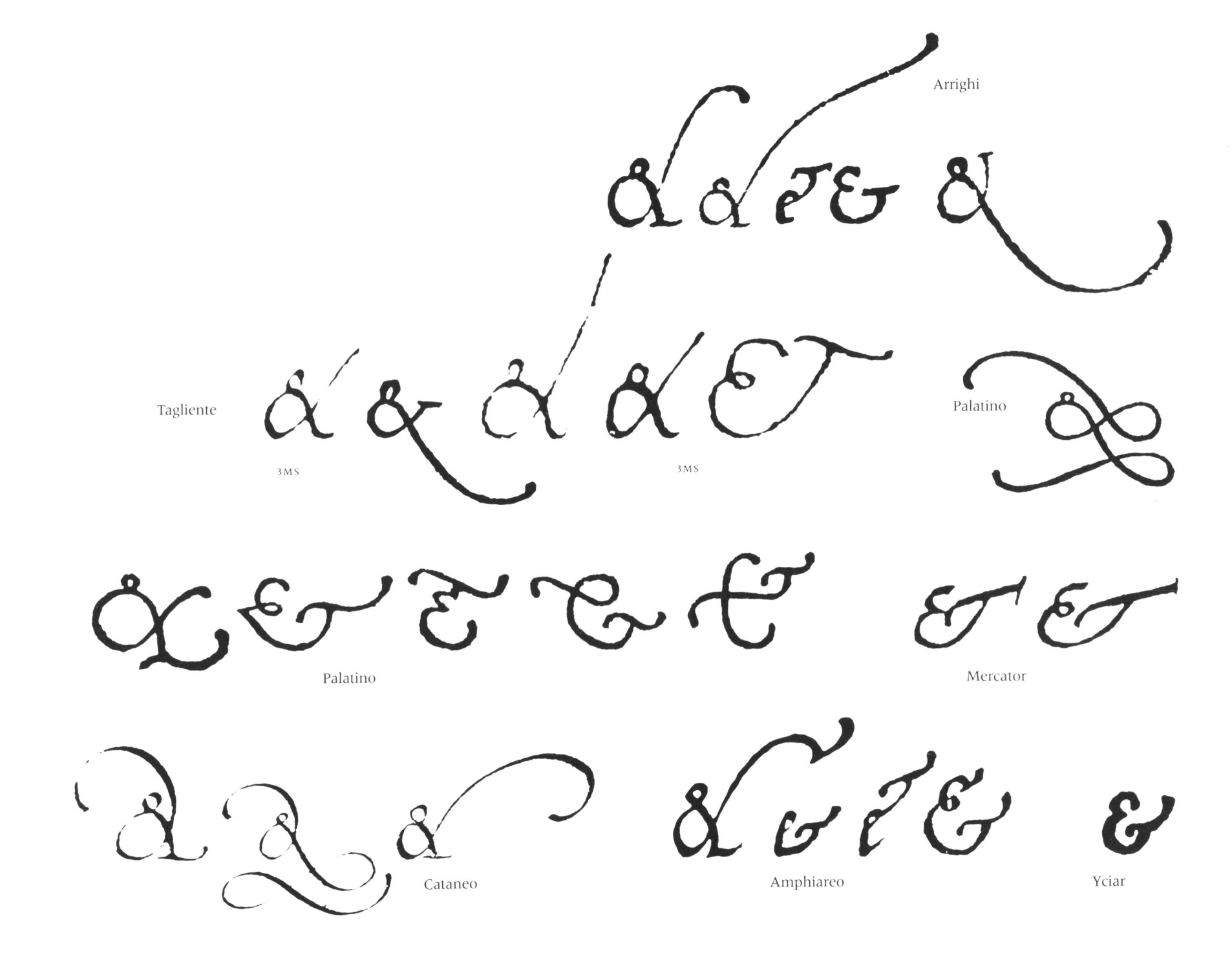

Arrighi

Tagliente
3MS
3MS
Palatino

Palatino
Mercator

Cataneo
Amphiareo
Yciar

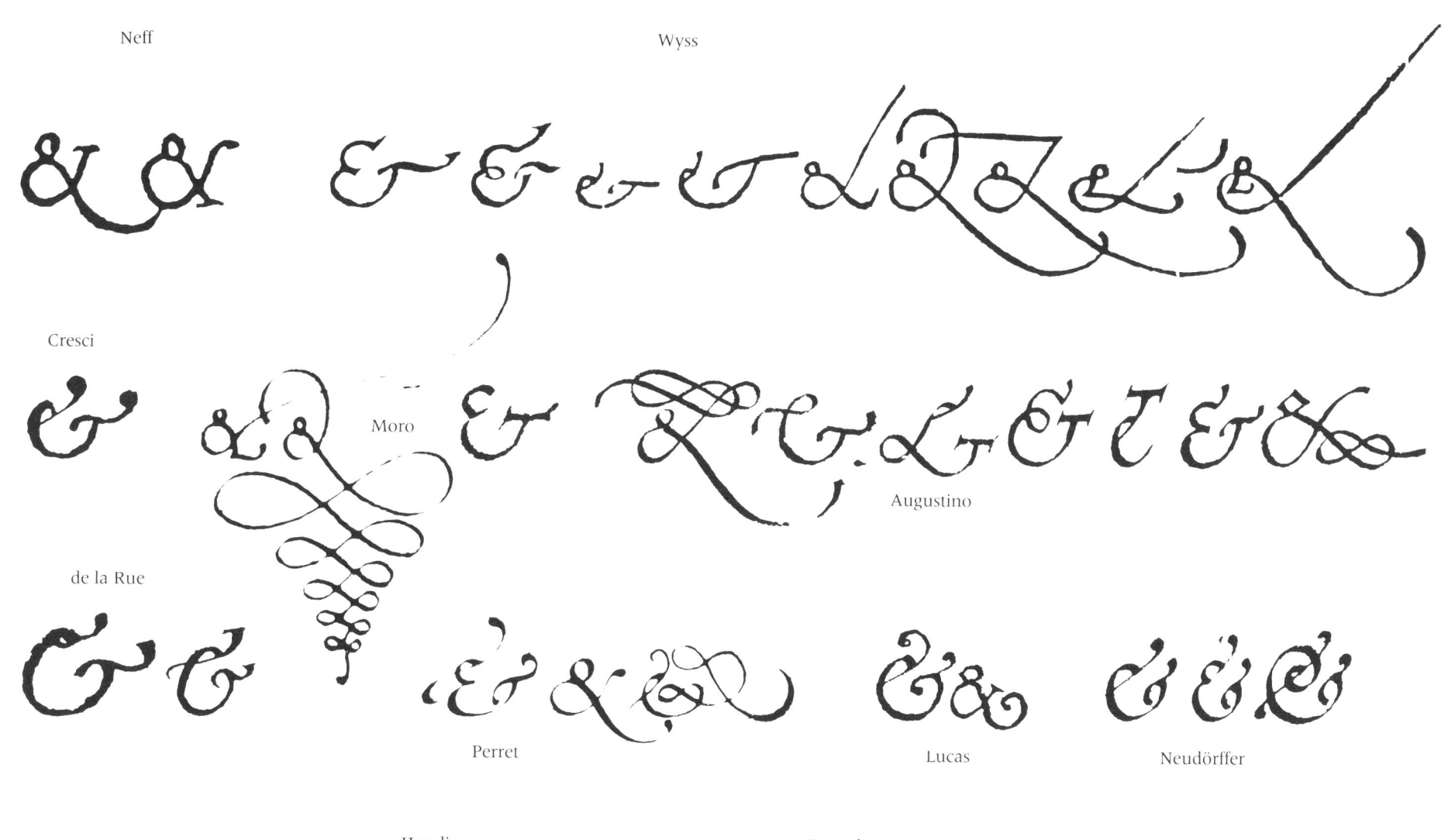

177

Neff   Wyss

Cresci

Moro

            Augustino

de la Rue

        Perret   Lucas   Neudörffer

        Hondius   Beauchesne

Brun

22WC

SELECTED BIBLIOGRAPHY

Sigismondi Fanti

Fanti, Sigismondo. *Triompho di Fortuna,* Vinegia 1527.Sel.2.57. Cambridge University Library.

———. *Theorica et Pratica,* Venice 1514. Typ.W 525.14.383. Cambridge: The Houghton Library.

Osley, A. S. *Scribes and Sources,* 46–55. London: Faber & Faber; Boston: David R. Godine, 1980.

———. *Luminario,* 5–13. Nieuwkoop: Miland Publishers, 1972.

Ryder, John. *Lines of the Alphabet in the Sixteenth Century,* 42. London: The Stellar Press and The Bodley Head, 1968.

Ludovico Vincentino degli Arrighi

Arrighi, Ludovico Vincentino degli. *A Book of Hours,* Italy 1515. MS.Douce 156. Attributed by James Wardrop. Cambridge: Fitzwilliam Museum.

———. Manuscript written for Geoffrey Chamber to give to Henry VIII, 1520. Royal MS.12.C.VIII. Attributed by A. Fairbank. London: British Museum.

———. *Missale Romanum,* 1520. 78.D.17. Signed and dated. Berlin: Kupferstichkabinett.

———. *Benefactors of the Hospital of San Giovanni in Laterino,* 1517. MS.1010. Attributed by James Wardrop. Venice: Archivio di Stato.

———. "A Contemplation of Arrighi." *The Bulletin for the Society of Italic Handwriting* 22: 14–18.

Barker, Nicolas. *Introduction to Catalogue Five Ludovico degli Arrighi Vicentino.* London: Paul Breman, 1970.

Benson, John Howard. *The First Writing Book: An English Translation & Facsimile Text of Arrighi's "Operina", the First Manual of the Chancery Hand.* New Haven and London: Yale University, 1954.

Fairbank, Alfred. "Arrighi and Papal Briefs." *The Book Collector* (Autumn 1970): 328–32.

———. "The Arrighi Style of Bookhand." *The Bulletin for the Society of Italic Handwriting* 26 (Spring 1961): 10–11.

Hofer, Philip. "Variant Issues of the First Edition of Ludovico Arrighi Vicentino's 'Operina'". *Calligraphy and Paleography* 106 (1965).

Morison, Stanley. "The Earliest Known Work of Arrighi." *Fleuron* 7 (1930): 167–8.

———. "The Italic Types of Antonio Blado and Ludovico Arrighi." *Monotype Recorder* 26 (1927).

Morison, Stanley, and F. Warde. *The Calligraphic Models of Ludovico Arrighi, Surnamed Vicentino.* Paris: Pegasus Press, 1926.

Ogg, Oscar. *Three Classics of Italian Calligraphy,* 3–62. New York: Dover Publications, Inc., 1953.

Osley, A. S. *Scribes and Sources,* 70–80. London: Faber & Faber; Boston: David R. Godine, 1980.

———. *Luminario,* 27–39. Nieuwkoop: Miland Publishers, 1972.

———. "Arrighi and his Types." *The Journal of the Society for Italic Handwriting* 40 (Autumn 1964): 8–18. The Appendix of this article includes a list of Arrighi manuscripts and books.

Pratesi, A. "Ludovico Arrighi." *Dizionario Biografico degli Italiani,* Vol. 4, Rome: 1962.

Thompson, Frank Allan. "Arrighi's Writing Books." *The Journal for the Society of Italic Handwriting* 53 (Winter 1967): 20–30.

———. "A Contemplation of Arrighi." *The Bulletin for the Society of Italic Handwriting* 22: 14–18.

Giovannantonio Tagliente

Morison, Stanley, and Esther Potter. *Splendour of Ornament: Specimens Selected from the "Essempio di recammi" by Giovanni Antonio Tagliente.* London: Lion and Unicorn Press, 1968.

Ogg, Oscar. *Three Classics of Italian Calligraphy,* 69–113. New York: Dover Publications, Inc., 1953.

Osley, A. S. *Luminario,* 15–26. Nieuwkoop: Miland Publishers, 1972.

Steinmann, Martin. "A Pupil of Tagliente." *The Journal of the Society for Italic Handwriting* 89 (Winter 1976): 10–14.

Tagliente, Giovannantonio. *La vera arte de lo Excellente scrivere.* Nieuwkoop: Miland Publishers, 1971. A facsimile of the shorter 1524 version.

———. *Opera di Giovannantonio Tagliente.* Chicago: Newberry Library, 1952. A facsimile of Tagliente's 1524 smaller version of his writing book with an introduction by James M. Wells.

Tschichold, Jan. *Schatzkammer der Schreibkunst,* 8. Basel: Verlag Birkhäuser, 1945.

Wardrop, James. "A Note on Giovannantonio Tagliente." *Signature* New Series 8 (1949).

Giovanbattista Palatino

Fairbank, Alfred. "Giovanbattista Palatino." *The Journal of the Society for Italic Handwriting* 48 (Autumn 1966): 11–13.

Marzoli, Carla. *Calligraphy 1535–1885,* 37–39. Milan: La Bibliofila, 1962.

Ogg, Oscar. *Three Classics of Italian Calligraphy,* 123–248. New York: Dover Publications, Inc., 1953.

Osley, A. S. *Luminario,* 49–63. Nieuwkoop: Miland Publishers, 1972.

———. *Palatino on Cryptography.* Wormley: The Glade Press, 1970.

———. *Scribes and Sources,* 82–96. London: Faber & Faber; Boston: David R. Godine, 1980.

Palatino, Giovanbattista. *Poem in Octava Rima,* c. 1540. ADD. MS.25454. London: British Library.

———. MS.5280. Berlin: Kunstgewerbemuseum.

Wardrop, James. "Civis Romanus Sum: Giovanbattista Palatino and His Circle of Friends." *Signature* New Series 14 (1952): 3–40.

Gerard Mercator

Denuce, Jan, and Stanley Morison, eds. *The Treatise of Gerard Mercator.* Verona: Editiones Officinae Bodoni, 1930.

Mercator, Gerard. *1577 Duisberg Letter.* New York: The Morgan Library.

———. *Letter from Mercator to William Camden.* Cotton Julius CV. London: British Library.

———. *Letter to Cardinal Perrenot,* 1514. Cart. Lat. al Obispo de Arra S.2297. Madrid: Biblioteca del Palacio.

———. *Letter to Wilhelm IV,* 31 July 1587. Staatsarchiv, Marburg.

———. *Mercator, a Monograph on the Lettering of Maps in the 16th Century Netherlands with a Facsimile and Translation of Ghim's "Vita Mercatoris."* Translated by A. S. Osley. London: Faber & Faber.

Ortelius, Abraham. *Album Amicorum Abraham Ortelius.* Amsterdam van Gendt, 1969. A facsimile edition of Abraham Ortelius, *Album Amicorum,* 1596.

Osley, A. S. "The Italic Hand of Arnold Mercator." *The Journal of the Society for Italic Handwriting* 98 (Spring 1979): 17–22.

———. "Calligraphy—an Aid to Cartography?" *Imago Mundi* 24 (1970): 63–75.

Ryder, John. *Lines of the Alphabet in the Sixteenth Century,* 50. London: The Stellar Press and The Bodley Head, 1968.

Tschichold, Jan. *Schatzkammer der Schreibkunst,* 2–3. Basel: Verlag Birkhäuser, 1945.

Bennardino Cataneo

Calligraphy—The Golden Age & Its Modern Revival, 19. Portland: Portland Art Museum, 1958.

Fairbank, Alfred, and Berthold Wolpe. *Renaissance Handwriting,* 72. London: Faber & Faber, 1960.

Harvard, Stephen. *An Italic Copybook: The Cataneo Manuscript.* Cambridge, New York, and Chicago: The Houghton Library and The Newberry Library, 1981.

Illuminated & Calligraphic Manuscripts, 124. Cambridge: Harvard College Library, 1955.

Ricci, Seymour. *Census of Medieval and Renaissance Manuscripts in the United States and Canada,* Vol. 2: 2g. New York: H. W. Wilson Co., 1935–40.

Two Thousand Years of Calligraphy, 83. Baltimore: The Baltimore Museum of Art, The Peabody Institute Library, The Walters Art Gallery, 1965.

Wardrop, James. *Six Italian MSS. in the Department of Graphic Arts* 2 (Spring 1953): 7; 223–224.

Vespasiano Amphiareo

Amphiareo, Vespasiano. *Das Schreibbuch des Vespasiano Amphiareo.* ed. Jan Tschichold. Stuttgart-Bad Constatt: Dr. Cantz'sche Druckerei, 1975. A facsimile of Amphiareo's *Opera di Frate* 1554.

Marzoli, Carla. *Calligraphy 1535–1885,* 42–43. Milan: La Bibliofila, 1962.

Osley, A. S. *Scribes and Sources,* 98–111. London: Faber & Faber; Boston: David R. Godine, 1980.

———. *Luminario,* 49–63. Nieuwkoop: Miland Publishers, 1972.

Pratesi, A. "Vespasiano Amphiareo." *Dizionario Biografico degli Italiani,* Vol. 13. Rome: 1962.

Tschichold, Jan. *Schatzkammer der Schreibkunst,* 20–23. Basel: Verlag Birkhäuser, 1945.

Wardrop, James. "Notes on Six Italian Manuscripts in the Department of Graphic Arts of Harvard College Library." *Harvard Library Bulletin* 7 (1953).

Juan de Yciar

Alonso Garcia, Daniel. *Joannes de Yciar, calígrafo dirangués del siglo XVI.* Bilbao: 1953.

Cotarelo y Mori, Emilio. *Diccionario Biographico y Bibliographico de Caligrafos Españoles,* 350–353. Madrid: Tipografia de la "Revista de arch., Bibl. y Museos," 1913–1916.

Echegaray, Carmelo de. *Caligrafos Vascos-Juan de Iciar.* Bilbao: 1914.

Jessen, Peter. *Meister der Schreibkunst aus drei Jahrunderten,* 87 and 123. Stuttgart: Julius Hoffman Verlag, 1923.

Thomas, Henry. "Juan de Vingles (Jean de Vingle), a Sixteenth-Century Illustrator." *The Library* 18, no. 2 (1937).

Tschichold, Jan. *Schatzkammer der Schreibkunst,* 9–13. Basel: Verlag Birkhäuser, 1945.

Yciar, Juan de. *A Facsimile of the 1550 Edition of "Arte Subtilissima".* trans. Evelyn Schuckburgh. London: Oxford University Press, 1960.

Caspar Neff

Doede, Werner. *Bibliographie Deutscher Schreibmeisterbücher von Neudörffer bis 1800,* 43–45. Hamburg: E. Hauswedell & Co., 1958.

Jessen, Peter. *Meister der Schreibkunst aus drei Jahrunderten,* fig. 1, 14–17, 27, 83b. Stuttgart: Julius Hoffman Verlag, 1923.

Osley, A. S. "Caspar Neff of Cologne." *The Journal of the Society for Italic Handwriting* 93 (Winter 1977): 8–15.

———. *Scribes and Sources,* 215. London: Faber & Faber; Boston: David R. Godine, 1980.

Tschichold, Jan. *Schatzkammer der Schreibkunst,* 42–52. Basel: Verlag Birkhäuser, 1945.

Urban Wyss

Doede, Werner. *Bibliographie Deutscher Schreibmeisterbücher von Neudörffer bis 1800,* 44–45. Hamburg: E. Hauswedell & Co., 1958.

Ryder, John. *Lines of the Alphabet in the Sixteenth Century,* 74. London: The Stellar Press and The Bodley Head, 1968.

Tschichold, Jan. *Schatzkammer der Schreibkunst,* 34–39 and 56–57. Basel: Verlag Birkhäuser, 1945.

Wyss, Urban. *Das Schreibbuch des Urban Wyss.* ed. H. Krenzle. Basel: Henning Opermann, 1927. A facsimile of the Libellus valde doctus.

Wolffgang Fugger

Fugger, Wolffgang. *Wolffgang Fugger's Handwriting Manual Entitled "A Practical and Well-grounded Formulary for Divers Fair Hands".* A translation of the 1553 edition by Frederick Plaat. London: Oxford University Press, 1960.

———. *Wolffgang Fuggers Schreibbüchlein: vollständige Faksimile-Ausgabe des 1553 in Nürnberg erschienen Werkes.* Introduction by Fritz Funke. Leipzig: Institut für Buchgestaltung an der Hochschule für Grafik und Buchkunst by Otto Harrassowitz, 1958.

Ryder, John. *Lines of the Alphabet in the Sixteenth Century,* 46. London: The Stellar Press and The Bodley Head, 1968.

Tschichold, Jan. *Schatzkammer der Schreibkunst,* 54–55. Basel: Verlag Birkhäuser, 1945.

Ferdinando Ruano

Cotarelo y Mori, Emilio. *Diccionario Biographico y Bibliographico de Caligrafos Españoles,* 224. Madrid: Tipografia de la "Revista de arch., Bibl. y Museos," 1913–1916.

Osley, A. S. *Luminario,* 49–63. Nieuwkoop: Miland Publishers, 1972.

Ruano, Ferdinando. *De rebus antiquis memorabilibus,* 1543. Cod.Vat.Lat. 3790. Rome: Vatican Library.

———. *Epistolae,* 1551. Cod.Vat.Lat. 3841. Rome: Vatican Library.

———. *Maffeo Vegio,* 1543. Vat.Lat. 3750. Rome: Vatican Library.

———. *Expositio Rationis Dominicae,* 1554. Vat.Lat.317. Rome: Vatican Library.

———. *Holograph receipt to Federico Ranaldi,* 1556. Arch.Bibl.Vat.II. Rome: Vatican Library.

———. *Letter from Antonio Draga to Pope Pius IV,* December 1560. Arch.Vat.Div.Cam.203, f.63. Rome: Vatican Library.

———. *Marc Antonio Flammio.* Harley 3541. Attributed to Ruano. London: British Library.

Ryder, John. *Lines of the Alphabet in the Sixteenth Century,* 62. London: The Stellar Press and the Bodley Head, 1968.

Wardrop, James. "Vatican Scriptors: Documents for Ruano and Cresci." *Signature* 5 (1948).

Giovanni Francesco Cresci

Cresci, Giovanni Francesco. *Account of Gianfrancesco Cresci with Cales, the stationer,* 1556. Arch.Bibl.Vat.II. f.345(n.s.9). Rome: Vatican Library.

———. *Motus proprius of Paul IV,* 1556. Arch.Vat.Div.Cam.178,ff.151v, 152. Rome: Vatican Library.

———. *Giovanni Francesco Cresci, "Il Perfetto Scrittore".* Nieuwkoop: Miland Publishers, 1972. A facsimile of the 1570 edition.

———. *Cresci: "Essemplare di piu sorti lettere",* 1578. London: Nattali & Maurice, 1968. A facsimile edition.

———. *A Renaissance Alphabet: "Il Perfetto Scrittore, Parte Seconda".* Introduction by Donald M. Anderson. Milwaukee & London: The University of Wisconsin Press, 1971.

Jessen, Peter. *Meister der Schreibkunst aus drei Jahrunderten,* fig. 88, 8. Stuttgart: Julius Hoffman Verlag, 1923.

Marzoli, Carla. *Calligraphy 1535–1885,* 44–45. Milan: La Bibliofila, 1962.

Meynell, Sir Francis. "Cresci." *The Bulletin for the Society of Italic Handwriting* 1 (Autumn 1954): 9–13.

Osley, A. S. *Luminario,* 69–83. Nieuwkoop: Miland Publishers, 1972.

Tschichold, Jan. *Schatzkammer der Schreibkunst,* 58–64. Basel: Verlag Birkhäuser, 1949.

Wardrop, James. "Vatican Scriptors: Documents for Ruano & Cresci." *Signature* 5 (1948).

Francesco Moro
Conretto da Monte Regale. *Un Novo et Facil Modo d'imparar' a scrivere*, Venice, 1576. London: Victoria and Albert Musuem. The Preface mentions a "Prete Moro da Padova."

Moro, Francesco. "Hunting, Hawking, Shooting." In *Schwerdt Catalogue* 2. (1928): 347 and 165.

———. Sotheby's Schwerdt Collection. *Sale Catalogue*, lot 2237 (11–12 March 1946): pl.83, f.12.

Moro, Francesco. *James Wardrop Collection*, Vol. London. fol. 3r. A notation written by James Wardrop in the margin: "There are instructions by this accomplished calligrapher in the Sala de Gilanti at Padua seen by me. Sept. 1948. James Wardrop."

Augustino da Siena
Augustino da Siena. *Augustino da Siena, The 1568 Edition of his Writing-Book in Facsimile.* ed. Alfred Fairbank. London: Merrion Press, 1968; Boston: David R. Godine, 1975.

Osley, A. S. *Luminario*, 85–92. Nieuwkoop: Miland Publishers, 1972.

———. *Scribes and Sources*, 98–111. London: Faber & Faber; Boston: David R. Godine, 1980.

Potter, Esther. *Augustino's Birds: A Calligraphic Frieze.* London: Merrion Press, 1976.

Jacques de la Rue
Brunet, Jacques-Charles, *Manuel du Libraire et de l'Amateurs de Livres*, 852 and 1132. Paris: G. P. Maisonneuve & Larose, n.d.

Catalog of French Books, 1470–1600. London: Oxford University Press, 1966.

French Sixteenth-Century Books. Cambridge, Massachusetts: Harvard University Press, 1970.

Jessen, Peter. *Meister der Schreibkunst aus drei Jahrunderten*, fig. 160b. Stuttgart: Julius Hoffman Verlag, 1923.

Osley, A. S. *Scribes and Sources*, 216–227. London: Faber & Faber; Boston: David R. Godine, 1980.

Ryder, John. *Lines of the Alphabet in the Sixteenth Century*, 64. London: The Stellar Press and The Bodley Head, 1968.

Clément Perret
Marzoli, Carla. *Calligraphy 1535–1885*, 66. Milan: La Bibliofila, 1962.

Ortelius, Abraham. *Album Amicorum Abraham Ortelius.* Amsterdam: van Gendt, 1969. A facsimile edition of Abraham Ortelius, *Album Amicorum*, 1596.

Osley, A. S. *Scribes and Sources*, 212–225. London: Faber & Faber; Boston: David R. Godine, 1980.

Perret, Clément. *Clément Perret, "Exercitatio Alphabetica".* Nieuwkoop: Miland Publishers, 1972.

Francesco Lucas
Cotarelo y Mori, Emilio. *Diccionario Biographico y Bibliographico de Caligrafos Españoles*, 426–430. Madrid: Tipografia de la "Revista de arch., Bibl. y Museos," 1913–1916.

Jessen, Peter. *Meister der Schreibkunst aus drei Jahrunderten*, fig. 129. Stuttgart: Julius Hoffman Verlag, 1923.

Osley, A. S. *Scribes and Sources*, 160–170. London: Faber & Faber; Boston: David R. Godine, 1980.

Tschichold, Jan. *Schatzkammer der Schreibkunst*, 13–19. Basel: Verlag Birkhäuser, 1945.

Johann Neudörffer the Younger
Doede, Werner. *Schön schreiben, eine Kunst: Johann Neudörffer und seine schule.* Munchen: Prestel Verlag, 1957.

———. *Bibliographie deutscher Schreibmeisterbucher von Neudörffer bis 1800.* Hamburg: 1958.

Jessen, Peter. *Meister der Schreibkunst: aus drei Jahrunderten*, fig. 96–97 and 74–75. Stuttgart: Julius Hoffman Verlag, 1923.

Neudörffer, Johann the Elder. *Johann Neudörffer d. Ä., der grosse Schreibmeister der deutschen Renaissance.* Introduction by Albert Kapr. Leipzig: Otto Harrassowitz, 1956.

Neudörffer. Johann the Younger. *Kurtze Ordnung*, 1567. 5253. Berlin: Berlin Library.

———. 5258. Berlin: Berlin Library.

———. 5257. Berlin: Berlin Library.

Jodocus Hondius
Hondius, Jodocus. *Jodocus Hondius, Theatrum Artis Scribendi.* Nieuwkoop: Miland Publishers, 1969. A facsimile of the 1594 edition.

———. *Achievement of Royal Arms*, 1614. 47187.fz add. London: British Library. A drawing.

———. *Map of the World by Jodocus Hondius 1611*. New York: The Hispanic Society of America, 1907. A facsimile edition edited by E. Stevenson and J. Fischer, S.J.

Osley, A. S. *Scribes and Sources*, 204–211. London: Faber & Faber; Boston: David R. Godine, 1980.

Andres Brun
Brun, Andres. *Andres Brun, Calligrapher of Saragossa, Some Account of His Life and Work.* ed. Henry Thomas and Stanley Morison. Paris: Pegasus Press, 1929.

Cotarelo y Mori, Emilio. *Diccionario Biographico y Bibliographico de Caligrafos Españoles*, 162–164. Madrid: Tipografia de la "Revista de arch., Bibl. y Museos." 1913–1916.

Osley, A. S. *Scribes and Sources*, 178–183. London: Faber & Faber; Boston: David R. Godine, 1980.

Ryder, John. *Lines of the Alphabet in the Sixteenth Century*, 24. London: The Stellar Press and The Bodley Head, 1968.

Jean de Beauchesne
Beauchesne, Jean de. *A New book of copies*, 1574. Don.e.379. Oxford: The Bodleian Library.

———. *Poem to Queen Elizabeth by George de la Motthe*, 1586. MS.Fr.e.1. Oxford: The Bodleian Library.

———. *Heroica Eulogia Guiliel . . .*, c 1570. San Merino: The Huntington Library.

———. *La Tresor d'escriture*, Lyon 1580. Wing ZW 539.B383. Chicago: The Newberry Library.

———. *A Newe Booke of Copies*, 1574. London: Lion and Unicorn Press, 1959. A facsimile edition with an introduction by Berthold Wolpe.

Osley, A. S. *Scribes and Sources*, 226–240. London: Faber & Faber; Boston: David R. Godine, 1980.

Ryder, John. *Lines of the Alphabet in the Sixteenth Century*, 22. London: The Stellar Press and The Bodley Head, 1968.

Tschichold, Jan. *Schatzkammer der Schreibkunst*, 65–67. Basel: Verlag Birkhäuser, 1949.

GENERAL BIBLIOGRAPHY

"An Anthology of Italic." *The Journal of the Society for Italic Handwriting* 92. (Autumn 1977): 14–21.

Anderson, Donald M. *The Art of Written Forms: The Theory and Practice of Calligraphy.* New York: Holt, Rinehart & Winston, 1969.

Astle, Thomas. *The Origin and Progress of Writing.* 2d ed. London: 1803.

Bank, Arnold. "Calligraphy and Its Influence in the Time of Plantin. *Gedenkboek der Plantin-Dagen, 1555–1955.* Antwerp: De Nederlandsche Boekhandel, 1956.

Barker, Nicolas. *Catalogue five Ludovico degli Arrighi Vicentino*, introduction. London: Paul Breman, Ltd., 1970.

Bonacini, Claudio. *Bibliografia delle arti scrittorie e della calligrafia.* Florence: Sansoni Antiquarto, 1953.

Brunet, Jacques-Charles. *Manuel Du Libraire et de L'Amateurs de Livres.* Paris: G. P. Maisonneuve & Larose, n.d.

Calligraphy and Palaeography: Essays presented to Alfred Fairbank on his 70th Birthday. ed. A. S. Osley. London: 1965.

Carter, John. *ABC for Book-Collectors.* London: Hart-Daris, 1961.

Catalog of French Books 1470–1600. Oxford: Oxford University Press, 1966.

Cotarelo y Mori, Emilio. *Diccionario Biográfico y Bibliográfico de Caligrafos Españoles.* Madrid: Tipografia de la "Revista de arch., Bibl. y Museos," 1913–1916.

Delitsch, Hermann. *Geschichte der abendländischen Schreibschriftformen.* Leipzig: Karl W. Hiersemann, 1928.

Dictionary Catalog of the History of Printing from the John M. Wing Foundation in The Newberry Library. 6 vols. Boston: G. K. Hall & Co., 1961.

de la Mare, Dr. Alvinia. *The Handwriting of Italian Humanists.* Oxford: Oxford University Press, 1973.

Doede, Werner. *Bibliographie Deutscher Schreibmeisterbücher von Neudörffer bis 1800.* Hamburg: E. Hauswedell & Co., 1958.

———. *Schön schreiben, eine Kunst: Johann Neudörffer und seine Schule.* Munich: Prestel Verlag, 1957.

Degering, Hermann. *Die Schrift, Atlas der Schriftformen des Abendlandes vom Altertum bis zum Ausgang des 18. Jahrhunderts.* Berlin: Verlag Ernst Wasmuth, 1929.

Eggage, Geoffrey. "The Evolution of the Chancery Hand." *The Bulletin for the Society of Italic Handwriting* 4 (Autumn 1955): 4–5.

Fairbank, Alfred. "Bartolomeo Fonzio." *The Journal of the Society for Italic Handwriting* 91 (Summer 1977): 8–12.

———. *A Book of Scripts.* rev. ed. London: Penguin Books, n.d.

———. *A Handwriting Manual.* rev. ed. London: Faber & Faber, 1975.

———. "Description and Photography of Public Records Office S.P.1-14, f.15." *The Bulletin for the Society of Italic Handwriting* 4 (Autumn 1955): 12–13.

———. "A Medici Letter." *The Bulletin for the Society of Italic Handwriting* 9 (Winter 1956–57): 14–15.

———. "A Letter to Henry VIII." *The Bulletin for the Society of Italic Handwriting* 10 (Spring 1957): 13–15.

———. "Description and Photograph of Cotton MS. at British Museum." *The Bulletin for the Society of Italic Handwriting* 11 (Summer 1957): 13–14.

———. "Ascenders in Writing Models." *The Bulletin for the Society of Italic Handwriting* 17 (Winter 1958–59): 10–11.

———. "Bartholomew Dodington," *The Bulletin for the Society of Italic Handwriting* 19 (Summer 1959): 12.

———. "The Supplements." *The Bulletin for the Society of Italic Handwriting* 27 (Summer 1961): 11 and Supplements I–IV.

———. "A Letter to Wolsey about Alum." *The Bulletin for the Society of Italic Handwriting* 30 (Spring 1962): 15–17.

———. "Some Renaissance Manuscripts." *The Journal of the Society for Italic Handwriting* 15 (Summer 1958): 12–15.

Fairbank, Alfred, and Berthold Wolpe. *Renaissance Handwriting.* London: Faber & Faber, 1960.

French Sixteenth-Century Books. Cambridge, Massachusetts: Harvard University Press, 1970.

Heal, Ambrose. *The English Writing-Masters and Their Copy Books 1570–1800.* Cambridge: Cambridge University Press, 1931.

Highet, G. A. *Classical Tradition: Greek and Roman Influences on Western Literature.* London: Oxford U. Press, 1949.

Horn, Bartholomaeus. *Kurtze Unterweissung Artlichs Unnd Andeutlichs Schreibens,* 1598. Wing zw 547.H782. A Manuscript book in the John M. Wing Foundation of The Newberry Library.

Jackson, Donald. *The Story of Writing.* New York: Taplinger Publishing Co., 1981.

Jessen, Peter. *Meister der Schreibkunst aus drei Jahrunderten.* Stuttgart: Julius Hoffman Verlag, 1923.

Johnson, A. F. "A Catalogue of Italian Writing Books of the Sixteenth Century." *Signature* 10 (1950).

Johnston, Edward. *Writing & Illuminating & Lettering.* London: Sir Isaac Pitman & Sons, Ltd., 1906.

Lowe, E. A. Handwriting, *The Legacy of the Middle Ages.* Oxford: Oxford University Press, 1926.

Luminario: Book III. Translation of text by A. F. Johnson. Cambridge, Massachusetts: Harvard College Library and Newberry Library, 1947.

Marzoli, Carla C. *Calligraphy 1535–1885: A Collection of seventy-two writing books and specimens from the Italian, French, Low Countries and Spanish Schools.* Milan: La Bibliofila, 1962.

Meynell, Sir Francis. "According to Cocker" *The Bulletin for the Society of Italic Handwriting* 6 (Spring 1956): 5–12.

Miller, George. "Medieval Capitals." *The Bulletin of the Society for Italic Handwriting* 8 (Autumn 1956): 6.

Moreau, Brigette. *Inventaire Chronologique Des Epitions Parisiennes Du XVI Siecle.* Paris: Imprimerie Municipale, 1972.

Morison, Stanley. "The Art of Printing." *Proceedings of the British Academy XXIII* (1938): 12, 23 and facsimiles 25 and 26.

———. "Early Printed Manuals of Calligraphy, Italian and American, in the Newberry Library." *Newberry Library Bulletin* 2nd series 1 (July 1948): 12–24.

———. *Eustachio Celebrino da Udene, Calligrapher, Engraver and Writer for the Venetian Printing Press.* Paris: Pegasus Press, 1927.

———. *Latin Script since the Renaissance.* Cambridge: 1938.

———. *Letter Forms: Typographical & Scriptorial.* New York: The Typophiles, 1968.

Nash, Ray. *Calligraphy & Printing in the sixteenth century. Dialogue attributed to C. Plantin.* Cambridge, Massachusetts: Harvard University Press, 1940.

Nesbitt, Alexander. *The History and Technique of Lettering.* New York: Dover Publications, Inc., 1957.

Ogg, Oscar. *Three Classics of Italian Calligraphy.* New York: Dover Publications, Inc., 1953.

Osley, A. S. "Canons of Renaissance Handwriting." *Visible Language* 13,1 (1979): 70–94.

———. "Instruments of Writing: A Note." *The Journal of the Society for Italic Handwriting* 94 (Spring 1978): 6–7.

———. *Luminario: An Introduction to the Italian Writing-Books of the Sixteenth and Seventeenth Centuries.* Nieuwkoop: Miland Publishers, 1972.

———. *Scribes and Sources.* London: Faber & Faber; Boston: David R. Godine, 1980.

Pacioli, Fra Luca de. *De Divina Proportione.* Translated in part by Stanley Morison. Cambridge: Cambridge University Press, 1933.

Pratesi, A. "Vespasiano Amphiareo." *Dizionario Biografico degli Italiani.* Vol. 3. Rome: Instituto della Enciclopedia Italiana, 1960–1962.

Ricci, Seymouir de. *Census of Medieval and Renaissance Manuscripts in the United States and Canada.* 2 vols. New York: The H. W. Wilson Company, 1935.

Ryder, John. *Lines of the Alphabet in the Sixteenth Century.* London: The Stellar Press and The Bodley Head, 1968.

Short Title Catalog of Book printing in Italy & books in Italian Printed Abroad 1501–1600. Boston: G. K. Hall & Co., 1970.

Standard, Paul. *Calligraphy's Flowering, Decay, and Restoration.* Chicago: The Sylvan Press, 1947.

Steinberg, S. H. "Medieval Writing-Masters." *The Library* 4th series XXII (1941).

Strange, E. F. "The Writing Books of the Sixteenth Century." *Transactions of the Bibliographical Society* Vol. 10 (London, 1896): 44–69.

Tschichold, Jan. *Formenwandlungen der & Zeichen.* Frankfurt am Main: D. Stempel A.G., 1954.

———. *Schatzkammer der Schreibkunst.* Basel: Verlag Birkhäuser, 1945.

Two Thousand Years of Calligraphy. Baltimore: Walters Art Gallery, 1965. A comprehensive catalog of a three-part exhibition organized by The Baltimore Museum of Art, Peabody Institute Library, and The Walters Art Gallery, June 6–July 18, 1965.

Ugo da Carpi, *"Thesauro de Scrittori, 1535."* Introduction by Esther Potter. London: Natalli & Maurice, 1968. A facsimile edition.

Ullman, B. L. *The Origin and Development of Humanistic Script.* Rome: Edizioni di Storia e Letteratura, 1960.

Wardrop, James. *The Script of Humanism.* Oxford: Oxford University Press, 1963.

———. "Six Italian Manuscripts in the Department of Graphic Arts of Harvard College Library." *Harvard Library Bulletin* VII,7 (1953): 221–224.

Wartena, S. "The Amsterdam Exhibition." *The Journal for the Society of Italic Handwriting* 66 (Spring 1971): 12–13.

Wells, James M. "The Bureau Academique d'Ecriture: A Footnote to the History of French Calligraphy." PBSA,LI.3 (Third Quarter, 1957): 203–213.

———. "The Wing Foundation: An Account of the Graphic Arts Collections of the Newberry Library by Its Curator." *Print* VII,6. (March 1953): 13–20.

"The Work of Stanley Morison." *Newberry Library Bulletin* V,5. (August 1960): 159–172.

Wolpe, Berthold. "A Quartet of Italics." *The Journal of the Society for Italic Handwriting* 96 (Autumn 1978): 6–13.

The book design is the work of Howard T. Glasser. The small creatures that decorate section headings are enlarged from the plates of *Exercitatio alphabetica nova utillissima* by Clèment Perret. The Meridien type is the design of Adrian Frutiger and was set by DEKR Corporation, Woburn, Massachusetts. The board paste-up was done by Howard T. Glasser, Kay Atkins, Kathy Parker, and Carol Ann Millner in Assonet, Massachusetts and Newport, Rhode Island. The book has been printed by Meriden-Stinehour Press, Meriden, Connecticut on Mohawk Vellum paper. It has been bound by Horowitz/Rae, Fairfield, New Jersey.